YOU DON'T REPRESENT US

ANSWERING OCCUPY WALL STREET

I0447498

BY

SHARIF RAHMAN & AMY NORWOOD

If the rich is getting richer and the poor is getting poorer all the time, wouldn't the graph of the two when trended, move on the opposite direction and given enough time, one will go to infinity and the other, goes to zero?

If this wouldn't happen, then clearly some of the time, they will have to go in the same direction. How much of the time exactly? We found that it is most of the time actually. Therefore the statement that the rich is getting richer and the poor is getting poorer is pure fallacy, driven by those who have little understanding of the statistics they are presenting.

Such are the disconnection between economists and the general public, that extreme organizations such as Occupy Wall Street, to rise and create havoc, on false premises, false understanding of the economic health of the country.

Don't believe the economists because they are economists, read what we have to say! We trust you will be impressed and you will be able to understand how the economy rewards its participants.

YOU DON'T REPRESENT US

ANSWERING OCCUPY WALL STREET

BY: SHARIF RAHMAN & AMY NORWOOD

ALSO FROM THE AUTHORS:

THE 259 TRILLION VS 5 TRILLION TRILOGY

BOOK 1

THE CONUNDRUM OF ASSETS & MONEY

Kindle Edition – Oct 2011   **Printed Version – Nov 2011**

BOOK 2

PAPER MONEY AND THE BANKING SYSTEM IN ACTION

Kindle Edition – Dec 2012   **Printed Version – Jan 2011**

BOOK 3

WEALTH OF THE UNITED STATES

Plus Major Questions Since The Financial Crisis

(Slated for release in July 2012)

TABLE OF CONTENTS

DEDICATION ix

ACKNOWLEDGMENTS x

FOREWORD 1

QUICK FACTS 7

PART 1: STATISTICAL PERPLEXITY OF USING "TOP-1%" AND "BOTTOM-99%" IMAGINARY LINES 11

ILLOGICALITY OF RICH GETTING RICHER AND POOR GETTING POORER 12

THE TOP 1% IS A DYNAMIC PLACE (SO IS THE BOTTOM 99%) 22

CLASSES WITHIN CLASS 36

WHY CURRENT COMPARISON METHODS ARE VERY ERRONEOUS 40

BEST WAY TO COMPARE INCOME 91

PART 2: HIDDEN STATISTICS   95

    BIGGEST CONTRIBUTOR TO TAXES   97

        Tax Share Burden   95

        How Much Tax Do Each Of The Classes Pays   107

        Tax Rate Of Each Income Group   112

        Percentage of All Population That Pay Income Taxes   122

        Summary of Tax Statistics   130

    WHY THE BOTTOM MOST CLASS INCOME EARNERS IN THE IRS DATA MAY BE RICHER THAN WE THINK   136

PART 3: CONUNDRUM THAT ISN'T   141

    RICH ARE GETTING RICHER, WHILE THE POOR ARE GETTING POORER FALLACY   142

    THE BOTTOM 99% IS CONTROLLING MORE WEALTH TODAY THAN EVER BEFORE   164

    ANSWERING THE ACCUSATION OF HIGH CEO PAY   184

        Case Study #1   194

        Case Study #2   201

        Case Study #3   205

        Case Study #4   210

        Conclusions   214

        Why CEO Deserves a High Pay   216

PART 4: CAPITALISM IS MORE EQUITABLE THAN THE OLYMPICS 219

    SOCIETY'S 80:20 RULE 220

    THE RISK TAKERS 227

PART 5: HISTORY REPEATS ITSELF 237

    OCCUPY AMERICA NOW 238

    OWS AND NAZI—WHAT THEY HAVE IN COMMON? 245

    CAN WE TAKE THE WEALTH OF THE TOP 1%? 253

    OCCUPY WALL STREET IS NOT THE LEGITIMATE REPRESENTATIVE OF THE BOTTOM 99% 268

    THE BOTTOM CLAIMS OF NO SAY IN THE GOVERNMENT 272

OTHER ILLOGICAL DEMANDS 275

QUICK REVIEW 287

END THOUGHTS 293

AUTHORS' BIOGRAPHIES 297

DEDICATION

We would like to dedicate this book to every one of you that believe in justice, freedom and honor.

There is no honor in taking away someone else's, by force.

There is no freedom when someone is forced to let go of his or her possessions.

There is no justice when the innocent is accused wrongly.

ACKNOWLEDGMENTS

We would like to credit the followings for the use of their materials, which were made public. We have taken pains on checking the licenses for the images/artwork/clipart/vectors use in this book and used only commercial free arts. We thank them for their efforts and generosity.

Thanks a million to All-Silhouettes.com for making many of the silhouettes used in our illustrations and also other artists and sites that gave their arts freely (fuzzimo.com, vectorlady.com). Clipart and images from Microsoft ClipArt (trademark of Microsoft Corp) are used with permission and images from Wikimedia Commons are appropriately credited when used.

The use of their work does not mean they endorse our book in any way.

All illustrations compositions are of our own works.

Many data used in our analysis, charts and graphs came from the United States government (Federal Reserve, FDIC, Treasury, Labor Department, etc.). We are very impressed with the data collection and archiving efforts made by the US Gov. including the Fed. There is no stinginess on their part to which, only benefits to all is the outcome. We thank them and all those who made their contribution. Historical inflation data and wealth/investment calculator is from MeasuringWorth.com and are used with permission.

Other quotes from various internet articles and books were used to illustrate a point or disagreement on certain issues and were not intended as an endorsement from those authors nor to infringe on their copyright.

FOREWORD

Dear Readers,

We watched in amazement when a few 'organized' groups of people tried to occupy' many public places, breaking many laws, and show selective regards to the properties and assets of the public for a stupendous shock and awe effect. They claimed that they are the marginalized and the oppressed of this capitalist world. Clearly, their actions are overboard, no doubt doing that in order to gain media coverage and hypes for their movement.

The purpose of this book is to expose the many economic studies out there that showed the rich are getting richer, and no doubt again, at the expense of the poor. When we wrote our **259 TRILLION VS 5 TRILLION** book series, we had discovered and confirmed without any misgiving, where the 'disappearing' middle class went. This book is a continuation of that writing and study, and it is exceptionally more in-depth with plenty of data and illustrations to back our claims.

It is certainly not our aim to discredit certain groups or to claim righteousness over others. We are not here to bully, mislead or scare the public, like many other hyped studies out there. Neither are we here to side with the elite group. Our goal is simple. We want the public to read the truth by presenting all facts in a professional manner. In this book, we published all our important data and explained how we arrived at our conclusions, unlike many economists' papers out there. In our three books series, **259 TRILLION VS. 5 TRILLION**, we wrote how something that looks so logical, makes a lot of common sense and is very popular, is unfortunately not necessarily is the truth. Similarly in this case, it sounds logical that the rich is getting richer while the poor is not. The phrase makes a whole lot of sense and is simple to understand. It is very popular indeed to blame the rich for whatever ails the poor, but is it really the truth? Can the rich become richer, while the poor become poorer? We, just like everyone else, assumed and thought that is the case, until we crunched the numbers and arrived at a different conclusion. It is impossible for the rich to become richer, while the poor becomes poorer. There is no such thing. It is all a lie, due to misrepresented data done by those who hardly understand their own data, let alone interpreting them correctly!

These misleading but overly hyped studies fueled the frustrations of the public further in order to advance the agendas of certain groups. These groups are riding on top of these simple minded, self-professed 'marginalized' groups such as the Occupy Wall Street, trying to create disturbances and revolutions akin to the Arab Spring. The Arab Spring has different root causes, different backers and certainly, the outcome was different than the current aim of these so-called 'marginalized' groups of people here in the United States as well as in other troubled European countries. As an example, the Arab Spring occurred due to limitations (curbs) on freedom of expression, brutal dictatorship (that hides behind fictitious enemies, patriotism and religion) which all came to a head by their worsening economic situation. In contrast to America, the land of the free, it is poles apart. All levels of society felt the effect of America's declining fortune due to the Financial Crisis, not just these 'marginalized' groups. To make matters worse, those groups that claimed that they were 'marginalized', accused other members of the society of taking advantage on them, taking away what were theirs and many other improbable accusations. The truth is however, we found out, and again, far from what they actually said.

In the upcoming third book of our **259 TRILLION VS. 5 TRILLION** book series, we explained that when the economic pie grows larger, nobody is taking from the other, class warfare style. We will prove it mathematically as well. All the hostilities are caused by misrepresentation of data by those who have no clear understanding of what they were analyzing and presenting.

Whether you think you are in the Bottom 99% or the Top 1% or if you think there are no groups, please have a go at this book; you will not be disappointed. We specifically wrote this book to clear the air, so that you can sleep well at night. You will believe that what you have now or what you do not have are the result of your own actions and not somebody else's.

We want these 'marginalized' groups to find their place in our democracy properly, by using all of the available democratic institutions in voicing their issues, but not by inciting violent protests and blatant public wealth destruction. The more wealth is destroyed, the less there will be available for helping the deserving people in the economy. If the rich is stealing yours, sue them. Bring it up. Everyone must respect the rule of law, except the laws and decrees from an Arab dictator. We have nothing against anyone voicing their opinions and showing their anger. But do not break the law and destroy public properties. And most important of all, be honest in yourself. Why go camping for days to ask for money if you can work? Go and do some work. If nobody can give you a job, just do your own job. Thousands of people on the streets do not mean they are the majority.

In this book, you will find unusual but remarkable explanations never before mentioned by any economist. We studied various sources of data extensively and we also crosschecked our data with other databases, and as a result, we are confident that our data is as accurate as it can be. One of our secret that we want to share with everyone is that, we crosschecked published studies multiple times from multiple angles. The results are astonishing. We can reveal the real truth, the real explanations as to why something is the way it is and with the extensive analysis conducted, there won't be any other explanation or possibility left to argue. This is the crux of our many presentations and findings, and we certainly are very proud with our methodologies for finding the truth. Of course, such in depth and thorough analyses from many different angles are very time consuming, taking a large chunk of our own free time. But the truth must be told, and so, here we are.

Thank you.

Don't Give Up!

Sharif Rahman & Amy Norwood Maine

QUICK FACTS

For every ONE dollar that is created at the top, SEVEN dollars are created at the bottom

The Bottom 99% increased their yearly incomes by 3.2 trillion dollars from 1990 to 2009. The rich? Just a tad less than a hundred billion.

Your economic problems are not caused by the rich. Stop blaming the wrong group!!

The rich cannot get richer unless the poor also got richer. So how about the famous statement of, "The rich is getting richer and the poor is getting poorer"? It is mathematically a false statement and impossible to occur in real life!

CEO pay are not increasing through the roof, in fact in many instances, they are shrinking in per revenue basis!

RICH

POOR

YEAR 4   YEAR 5   YEAR 6

2

Who are the rich? We found that they, once upon a time, were sitting at the Bottom 99%, or even bottom 1%. The rich are actually, made up of the previous poor who made it in life. Majority of the Top 1% came from the bottom, so they enriched the bottom actually. So why wasn't their wealth calculated within the bottom 99%?

CAPITALISM MORE ~~EQU~~ITABLE ~~THA~~N THE ~~OLY~~MPICS

Current comparison methods are erroneous. The rich was said to capture 93% of all income growth from 2009 to 2010. Well, what if the bottom 99% never loses theirs to begin with? Nobody mentioned that the rich were simply recouping their loses, not making gains. Therefore, the comparison made is invalid! It is so easy to hide behind "percentage" of this and that. How about the real numbers in dollars

Income Bracket	Taxes Paid In 1986	Taxes Paid In 2009	Change in Tax Paid
Top 1%	$ 92,559	$ 230,496	149%
2-5%	$ 15,122	$ 34,400	127%
6-10%	$ 8,711	$ 14,821	70%
11-25%	$ 5,111	$ 7,042	38%
26-50%	$ 2,520	$ 2,622	4%
Bottom 50%	$ 464	$ 283	-39%

The louder they are, the less taxes they pay.

Who is hiding behind the half truths?

The exposed facts revealed that the bottomers are paying less and less

The Bottom 99% controls 83% of all incomes but only shouldering 63% of the tax burden.

The Top 1% controls 17% of all incomes but is supporting 37% of Uncle Sam's income.

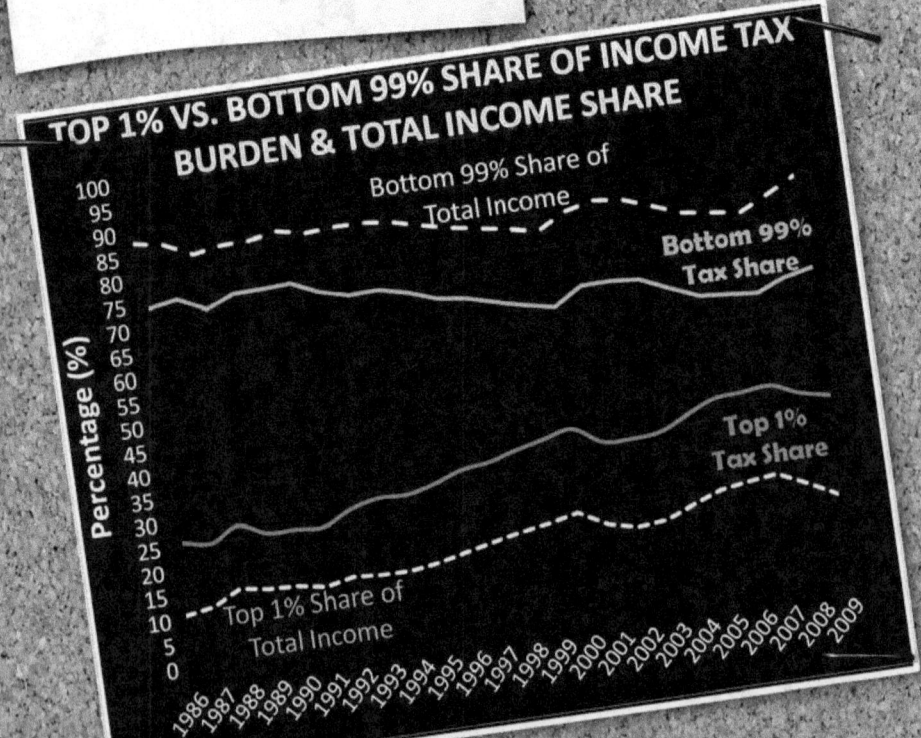

TOP 1% VS. BOTTOM 99% SHARE OF INCOME TAX BURDEN & TOTAL INCOME SHARE

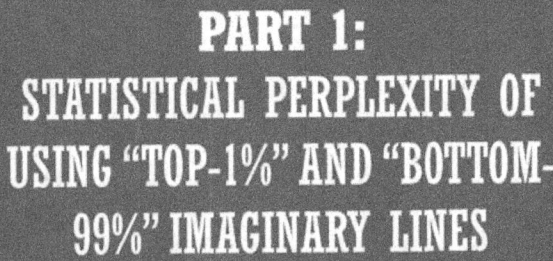

PART 1:
STATISTICAL PERPLEXITY OF USING "TOP-1%" AND "BOTTOM-99%" IMAGINARY LINES

ILLOGICALITY OF RICH GETTING RICHER AND POOR GETTING POORER

Look at the simple graph and you will be left wondering why so many simply accept the fallacy

The Occupy Wall Street (OWS) movement rose due to frustration of the high unemployment, declining incomes and the purported imbalance in the distribution of the so-called economic pie. As usual, in order to gain traction, the many claims made against the puny 1% are generally not in the proper context, as it should. Many are simply hyping and sensationalizing their data and reports, misleading the public. We understood clearly the frustration of this movement; however, the underlying root cause is most definitely not brought about by the 1% of the population taking in more than their fair share. If you help to make the pie bigger, it is all yours to take (explained in **Book** 3). However, if you do not, it is not yours to take (mathematical details are explained fully in Book 3 of the series). In short, when the rich grows their income, it is not coming from the bottom 99% portion, but comes from their own work. No stealing is taking place.

Based on justice, fairness, and equality, this movement's drive to forcefully tax and take ever more from the top 1%, for OWS own benefits are so wrong, it is bound to fail.

Do not forget, the poor are not always going to be poor, and the rich, may not stay rich forever.

Now, let us show you a simple graph, of what will happen when the rich are getting richer, while the poor are getting poorer.

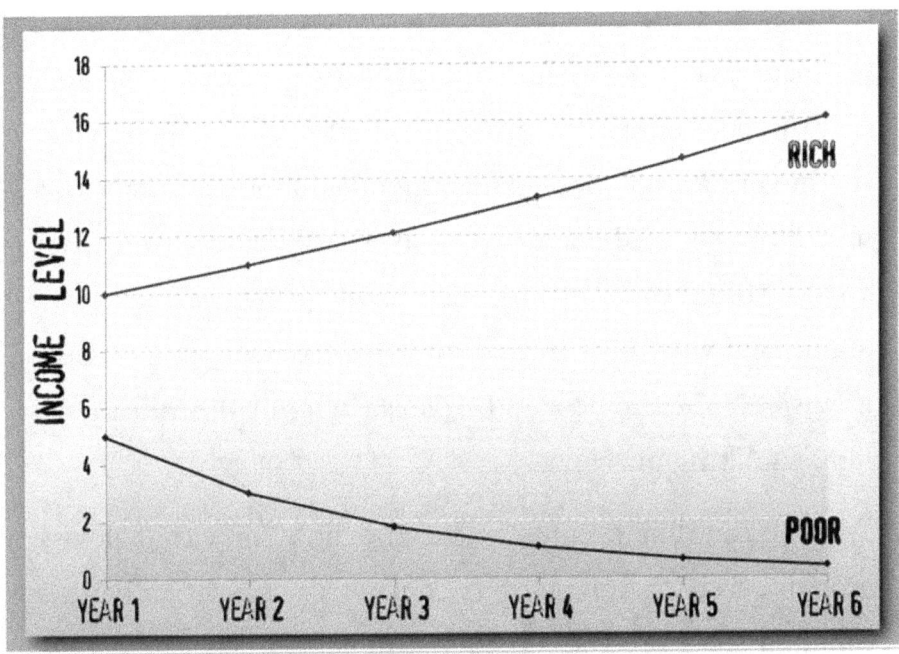

Illustration 1: If the poor is getting poorer, then we would see their income levels going down until it goes to zero and you would see this graph everywhere.

When the rich are getting richer, their income keeps going up. So the graph's trend for the rich is a continuously increasing line. After years and decades, this line will go to very high, towards infinity! For the poor, as you might have suspect, with decreasing income, their graph's trend will be a continuously decreasing line, and after many decades, given enough time, it will go to zero!

Clearly, the reality is far from this. The rich is not getting richer while the poor is getting poorer. Our findings conclude that the rich will only be richer, when the poor get to be richer too. The gap between the rich and the poor cannot be growing, for if it is, then who were the buyers for all those Ipads, mobiles, laptops numbering in the tens of millions or more all these years? And what do we think these people use their purchases for? To make new wealth of course. For that reason, it is simply impossible for the poor to be poorer when they make such moneymaking purchases.

Another big problem with the data of our 'beloved' economists is the presence of "outliers". Statistically, it is common to ignore the top most and bottom most of a set of data, to ensure accurate representation because these parts of the data are the outliers. A study by Osborne,

Christiansen, and Gunter (2001) found that only about 8% of all published papers out there, are checked for outliers by their authors. The presence of outliers can severely distort the findings of a population of data. Normally a valid data set will have about 99% of its data, to reside within three standard deviations from its center. If it is more, the outliers should be discarded, especially if the impact is huge. Now, the presence of these 'outliers' in economists' incomes data had severely distort their conclusions as what we had found.

If we run a statistical distribution analysis on the income and the number of people in each of the income bracket from the IRS data which is used by an award-winning economist cited for his widely reported income gap studies and used by the OWS movement and the likes, the chart might look like the following:

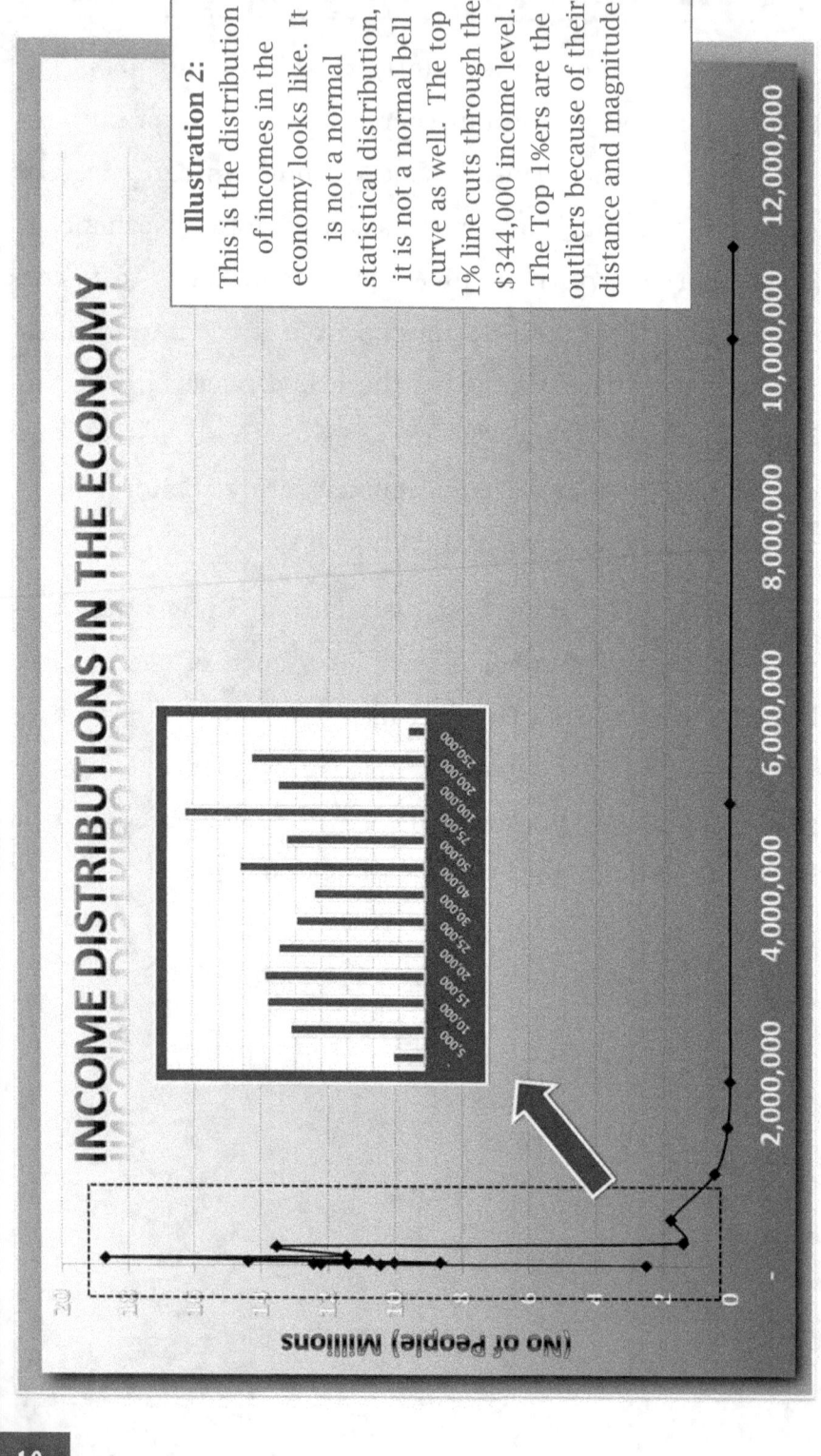

Illustration 2:

This is the distribution of incomes in the economy looks like. It is not a normal statistical distribution, it is not a normal bell curve as well. The top 1% line cuts through the $344,000 income level. The Top 1%ers are the outliers because of their distance and magnitude

As you can see from the graph, the study cited by the OWS using the "award-winner" economist data that uses the IRS income tax data to chart the Top-1% and the Bottom-99% is statistically flawed. The outliers are so far apart, it is like comparing the IQ of the majority of the population to a couple of Einsteins and Da Vincis and then concluding all sorts of things about the public education.

The illustration on the next page is a depiction of the distribution of incomes of the economic participants, in a way that everyone can easily comprehends. The distance between the income earners homes depicted in the illustration is matched up exactly to the actual distribution in real life. In addition, the further away a person is from the main neighborhood, the higher the incomes of the person will be.

99% of all economic participants reside within the same neighborhood, which means they are statistically close enough to each other. However the remainders, the one percenters, are very far out and no longer within the same neighborhood, but far out of town. Some of them are even hundreds of miles away from the 99%ers, and their number is so few. Even the 1% themselves live very far apart from each other.

Illustration 3: Drawings of how the incomes are distributed, distance is representative of the difference between the brackets

CANADA

Just a few of the income earners, are residing in a far away place, hundreds of miles away.

NEIGHBORING CITY

Most of the rest of income earners are residing in a neighboring city, it is just a 20 minute drive.

99% of income earners are residing in the same neighborhood, all within walking and cycling distance

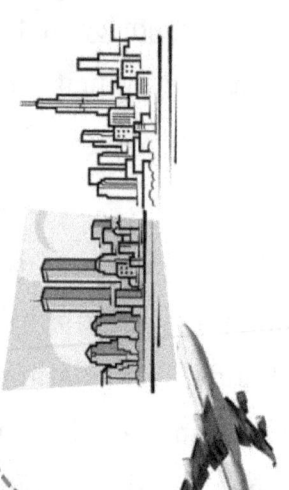

Note to all:

Economists and the OWS preoccupation with the "1% line" is beyond us. It is illogical and does not have any significance in real life situation.

The 1% line cuts through people with income of $344,000 (in 2009), which means the bottommost of the 1%-group will earn just as much as the top most person in the 99%-group (maybe only by a few dollars!). What kind of line is that?

Why is that top most person in the 99% is not "evil" and the bottommost person in the 1% as "evil" (as per OWS), when in fact they earn the same amount of money, give or take a few dollars?

This conundrum is beyond our comprehension and thus, we can only conclude the economist and the OWS have a few screws loose in their heads.

When we talk about the middle class, we are referring to those earning above $35,000 up to $390,000 (or the $30,000 to $500,000 of the IRS brackets due to wide bracket which limit accuracy of data, thus one of the reason why the data used by the OWS supporters is suspicious).

There are only about 0.5% earning above $500,000 and they are what we consider outliers.

Illustration 4: The 1% line is a stupid line....why one percent? Why not two percent? Why not 0.001 percent? Why is there a line in the first place? Today's 1%ers are not the even the same the 1%ers before this, so what use is there for this line?

Illustration 5

There are so many people at the middle class. They are big and strong and are working hard. Why does it when economists talk about the top and the bottom, the very large middle is ignored? If they are included, they are lumped into the bottom, as the Bottom 99%.

The fact is, there are middle-class in the top 1% as well since the 1% line cut through the upper middle class. The birds are well, the outliers and they are in a class of their own.

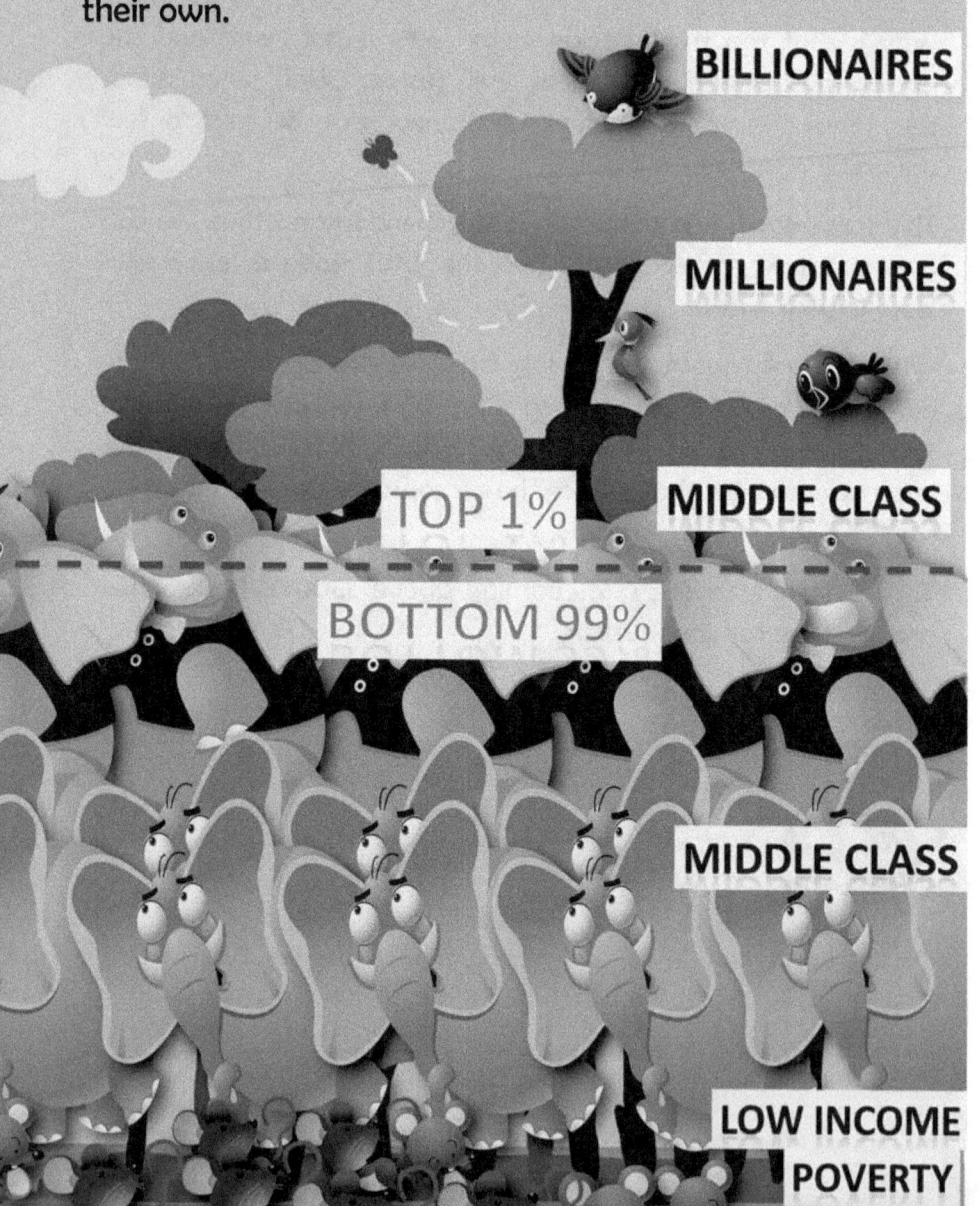

BILLIONAIRES

MILLIONAIRES

TOP 1%   MIDDLE CLASS

BOTTOM 99%

MIDDLE CLASS

LOW INCOME
POVERTY

Statistically speaking, the middle class is the major power in the income equation; they work hard and contribute vastly to the economy. They are not the bottom 99%, they are not even the bottom 50% and yet, they are the one that shoulder a lot in the economy. Combining this big group of people together either with the "evil 1%" group or with the "poor souls that can't even feed themselves" group is truly horrendous. As you can see, the middle-income people are not the birds and are not the mice either. They are in a class of their own and should not be grouped into a smaller group, be it the Top 1% or the Bottom 99%, and then claiming to be representing them.

To put things into perspective, in 2009, the middle class represent a whopping 52.2% of the whole of taxpayers as reported in the IRS data, making them as the authentic absolute majority. The middle class also generated income in excess of 5.6 trillion dollars (74.4% of all incomes), a full two thirds of all incomes in the nation. We found that the middle class, share their aspirations with the Top 1%ers, and together they represent the majority as Americans. When the middle class speaks, all politicians and other power centers in the country listen to them attentively.

THE TOP 1% IS A DYNAMIC PLACE
(SO IS THE BOTTOM 99%)

Think those who are rich, stays rich all the time? And the poor stays poor indefinitely? Well, think again!

This top 1% is a dynamic place; there are many new faces going in and of course, leaving. For example, of the top 400 tax contributors of the nation, less than 25% appear more than once in the top 400 list in a period of a decade, the rest will leave the list. A mere four people remained in the top 400 list for more than 17 years (data from IRS). This means you won't be richer than everyone else will, all the time.

Table 4—Frequency of Appearing in the Top 400 Tax Returns by Adjusted Gross Income, Tax Years 1992-2008 [1]

Number of years in Top 400	Number of primary filers in group [2]	Percent of primary filers represented by each group	Number of returns in total Top 400 population over 17-year period	Percent of returns represented by each group
(1)	(2)	(3)	(4)	(5)
1	2,676	72.88	2,676	39.35
2	439	11.96	878	12.91
3	171	4.66	513	7.54
4	113	3.08	452	6.65
5	65	1.77	325	4.78
6	48	1.31	288	4.24
7	35	0.95	245	3.60
8	24	0.65	192	2.82
9	18	0.49	162	2.38
10	18	0.49	180	2.65
11	13	0.35	143	2.10
12	6	0.16	72	1.06
13	9	0.25	117	1.72
14	13	0.35	1	
15	13	0.35	1	
16	7	0.19	1	
17	4	0.11	1	
Total	3,672	100.00	6,8	

Illustration 6: Only four person out of the Top 400 taxpayers remain in the list for long period of time. The rest went down of course.

(Table from IRS Top 400 Taxpayers)

This dynamic and fluid condition appears to be the same for the bottom 90% (or 99%). However, out of frustration, the 1% is targeted. Perhaps due to their small numbers, they are targeted. We will defend those who are marginalized, we also defends the truth and make it known to everyone. Nevertheless, the more probable reason the top 1% is targeted is simply due to wrong understanding of complex data and of the economic system. Real hard data out there is actually showing that today's malaise is not due to the rich, it is brought on by the actions of— none other than the bottom 99% and also the Top 1% who lack critical education in finance, health and knowledge in general (discussed in detail in Book 3). We presume that one day, many of the very supporters of OWS themselves will become rich and move into the top 1% segment, and of course will then be targeted, perhaps by their very own friends! These top one-percenters, are targeted for what exactly? Not paying enough taxes? Not contributing enough?

Since 1990, the USA economy has enriched thousands of the bottom 99% so they can join the coveted millionaire's income club. As a percentage of total income tax filed, there was an increase of 414% of individuals filing under the 7-figure income bracket. They are all fresh millionaires and therefore must come from the bottom, not outer space. On top of that, there is an increase of 351% of people earning in the 6-figure bracket. The fact is, about 9 million people moved up from the bottom brackets to the upper brackets, mostly to the upper middle and top most brackets. There were also several million new individuals joining the ranks of middle and top bracket each year, bypassing the bottom most bracket altogether.

Thus, the bottom most is not getting poorer; in fact, it is getting less crowded because they are fewer of them. The 1% vs. 99% is not a valid comparison because the rich and poor alike move between each other brackets constantly; and these movements will always skewed the Top 1% data because when the economic participants are all getting richer due to economic growth, they all will move en masse to the top.

We will show exactly how the distortion occurs, when a poor individual made it in life and become rich, jumps up to the top bracket, thereby skewing all related statistics. Once you understand that, we will then take the fight to the OWS own backyard by using the 1% vs. 99% statistics that THEY HID, knowingly or not. Lastly, we will explain why the OWS is wrong in many fronts.

Below are illustrations of some statistics to show the movements within these two groups (the 1% and the 99%). Take a particular note on the movements; you will see just how changeable and dynamic life can be. All individuals can go up the ladder, as well as coming back down. This is all a regular and universal characteristic of our system. The rich will not stay rich forever; the poor will not stay poor forever. When the economy is prospering, everybody would be thriving, but when the economy is regressing, everybody would have to endure that market correction. Regressing economy is normal occurrence, as market has to correct the excesses and waste brought by ALL economic participants, not the Top 1% only. When enough majority (the Top 1% is not the majority) of the economic participants lunge in excessive speculation, then sooner rather than later, it will come back in the form of a correction and will bite everyone, even the bystanders. If you have read book 1 and 2 of the **259 TRILLION VS 5 TRILLION** series, you would have understand that, there is no easy way of making money. Only by creating value adding and useful products and services will anyone be allowed to have a growing and lasting wealth.

THE BOTTOM MOST MOVES UPWARD

From 1990, 50.4% of people out of 113 million total income earners received incomes at the lowest bracket ($1- $19,999) but in 2007, that number fell to 33.3% of a total of 141 million people. That is a massive 33% drop.

So where did all these people go?

56.9% went to the next bracket ($20,000 to less than $100,000), 41.8% went into the upper middle income ($100,000 to $999,999) and the rest (1.3%) went on to earn 7-figures income!

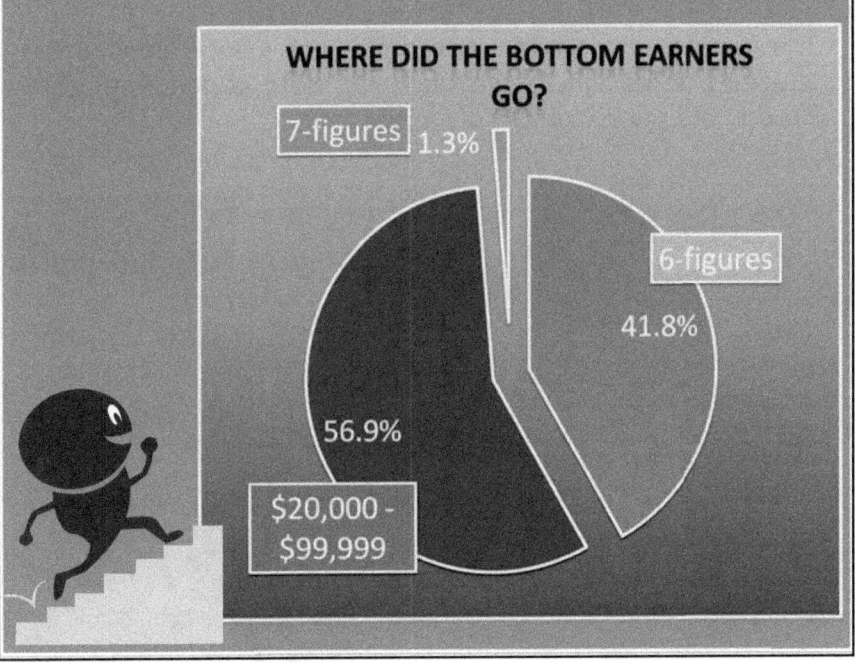

Illustration 7: They are 33% less people earning at the bottom bracket in 2007 compared to 1990. They climbed up the income bracket......

THE BOTTOM MOST MOVES UPWARD

If we use constant dollar of 1990, the trend is similar. Even after an over correction, the lowest bracket ($1- $19,999) registered a drop of 7.3% in 2007. There were 7.3% less people as a whole, earning at the lowest income bracket even after an increase of 25% of the workforce. The next bracket of $20,000 to below $50,000 also registered a drop, reaching 5.9%. Thus, there was 16.7% less people as a whole earning incomes of below $50,000, per annum.

So where did all these people go?

To the upper brackets of above $50,000 of course! (equivalent to around $80,000 in 2009 dollars).

The findings are similar to our findings in our Book 3 of 259Tvs5T series where we analyzed data taken from the Bureau of Labor Statistics of United States.

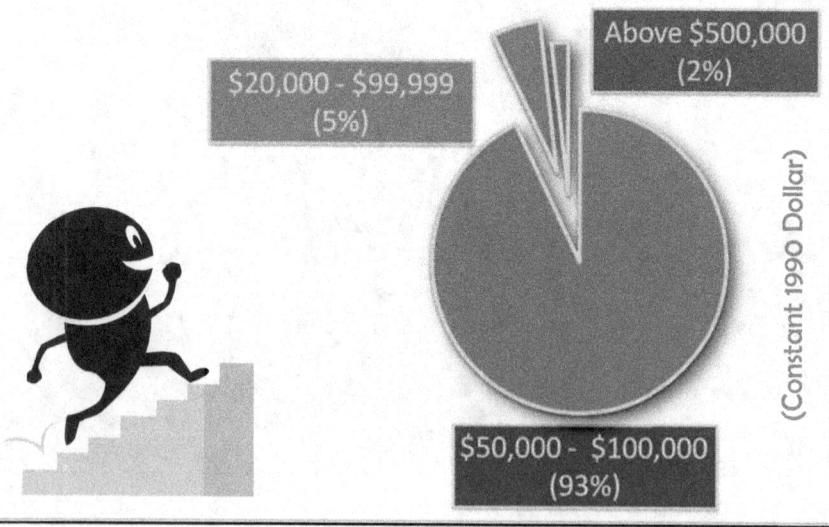

Illustration 8: They were 16.7% less people earning at the bottom bracket in 2007 compared to 1990 in real terms. They climbed up the stairs …

THE TOP MOVES DOWN

The recession of 2008, increased the percentage of people earning at the lowest bracket to 34.9% in 2009. Where did they come from? Of course from the upper brackets (the bottom-most cannot go further down, they are there already).

Thus, many rich people's income went down all the way to the lowest bracket or to no income during the recession. The hardest hit is the 7-figure income earners that declined from 0.22% of total to only 0.17% in 2009. That is a 40% decline, and they were beamed back to their previous 1999 number (% of total people).

Don't forget, as the rich gets poorer, the poor will get poorer too. A total of 3 million people dropped out totally from all brackets, and we don't know where they went.

From the peak year of 2007, a record 155,337 out of 392,220 who used to have incomes of over a million, dropped all the way even to the bottom most bracket, in 2009. Can you imagine 40% of the middle class suddenly become poorer or are out of jobs?

IT IS A DYNAMIC PLACE!

Illustration 9: The 7-figures income earners went tumbling in 2008 and 2009 into the lower income or no income. Their number as percentage of tax filers drop a massive 40% in two years back to 1999 figures.

INCOME BRACKET	% Change (2007 to 2009)	
$1 - Under $20,000	1.03%	(Current Dollar)
$20,000 - Under $50,000	-0.03%	
$50,000 - Under $100,000	-1.16%	
$100,000 - Under $500,000	0.83%	
$500,000 - Under $1,000,000	-22.65%	
Above $1,000,0000	-38.25%	

Illustration 10: Table showing the percentage of change in the number of people in 2009 compared to 2007, the aftermath of the recession. As a whole, the economy loses 3 million income earners, but not from the lower income bracket.

In 1990 dollars, in 2009 compared to 2007, 38% of those with income above $1 mil stumbled down and off their income brackets and 23% of the $500,000 to $999,999 got kicked out of their brackets As a whole, there are less people in every bracket of above $100,000 compared to 2007. Thus, the recession hit the top more than the bottom.

The recession also shelves 2.2% off the total number of income earners.

Graph on the next page shows the changes on the percentage of people residing in the brackets below $20,000, against all other economic participants. Their percentage is decreasing and most moved up to the upper income brackets. During this 20 year period, millions more new workers entered the workforce, and they were fortunate of not entering the lowest income bracket. So, the people in the IRS data are made up of real people with real movements, and most important of all, real improvements. The rich do not stay rich and the poor did not stay poor. They move between the brackets in natural capitalistic order unless they do not pass the "Wealth Management By Capitalism" rules mentioned at the backend of this book.

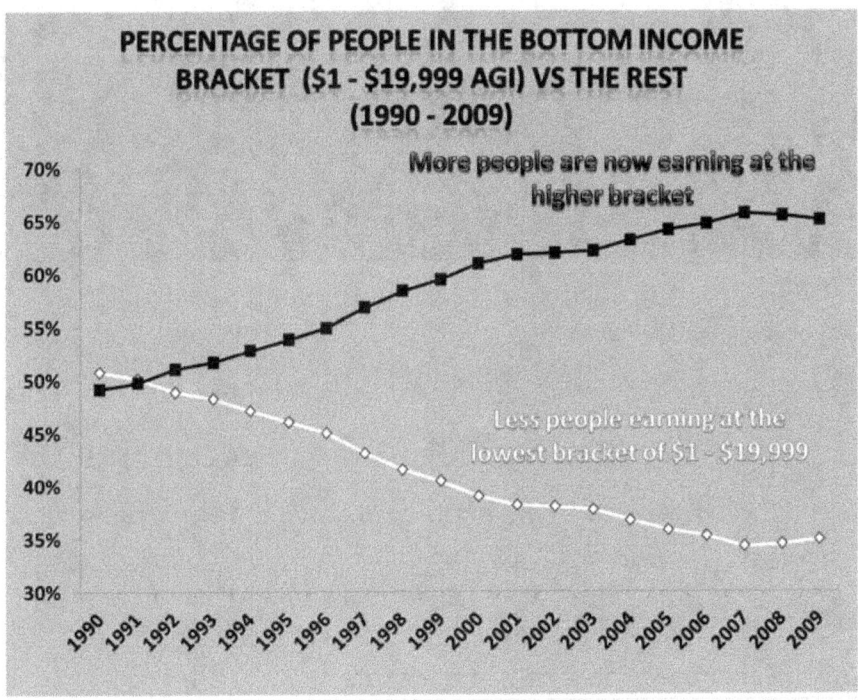

Illustration 11: There are more people earning higher incomes in 2009 compared to 1990 (in current dollars)

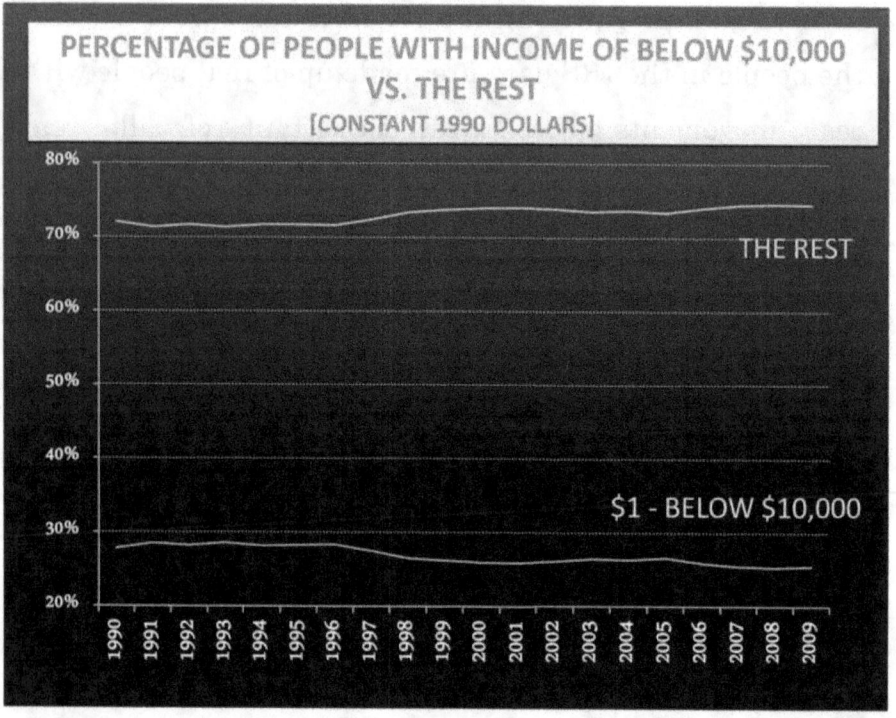

Illustration 12: There are STILL more people earning higher incomes in 2009 compared to 1990 in this inflation adjusted data.

When we adjust for inflation, the effect is still the same. There are less people in the lowest bracket of $10,000 (in 1990 constant dollars). This shows that there are movements of the poor to the top. Remember, people in the income brackets are not static!

What was your own income bracket compared to several years ago?

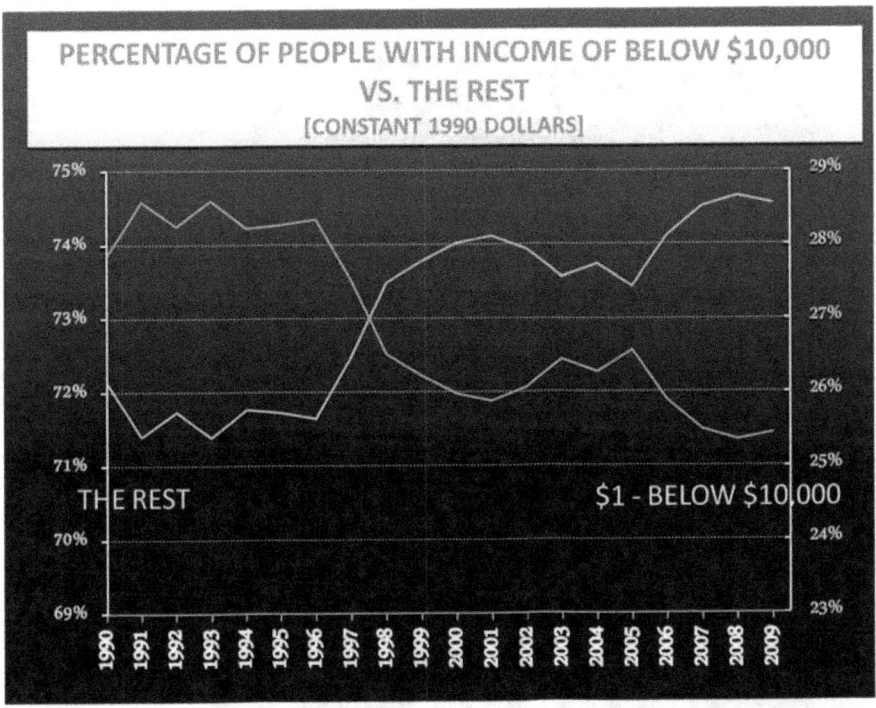

Illustration 13: The percentage of people in the $1 - Under $10,000 bracket decreased from 27.9% to 25.4%. The number did not decrease at a higher rate due to the fact that the amount of people which migrated to upper income are being replaced by new entrants into the economy. More on this migration in the next topic – "WHY CURRENT COMPARISON METHODS ARE VERY ERRONEOUS".

This dynamicity of the top 1% and the bottom 99% is not taken into account whenever the OWS talks about inequality. They forgot that most of the rich were the poor, who had made it in life and were rewarded for their hard work and ingenuity. They also forgot that **most** people receive higher salaries as they progress in life.

LOSSES

Back in 2002, a record 70,000 millionaires lost their status (from a high of 239,000 in the year 2000).

For the world's billionaire, numbering only a scant 1125 individuals in total (2008), their culling was just as terrible. 373 dropped out and lost their billionaire status, with trillions of dollars worth of wealth, extinguished.

One billionaire from India, lost a record 32 billion dollars in just a year, losing 76% of his wealth, but his was not comparable to another famous billionaire from Japan, who lost a heartbreaking 77 billion dollars in two years during the previous slump.

29 Indian billionaires lost their coveted billionaire status leaving only 24 survivors in 2009.

One noted billionaire even committed suicide due to stress...

Not dynamic enough?

Think again!

Illustration 14: The rich could go down as well. In fact, it is easier to lose money than to make it!

The higher you go to the top, it looks like it get even more dynamic! The changes affecting millionaires and billionaires are constant and severe. Imagine 36% of the middle class drops out and falls into the low income and poor bracket, that's what routinely hitting the Top 1%ers. Check out in later part of this book, how the fortunes of billionaires change on daily basis, which can be so stressful and may cause regular people to have heart attacks.

It is a false assumption to make that the rich is always getting richer while the poor is not. It is such a terrible supposition. We will continue to show throughout this fine book, how dynamic the top brackets are, as well as the bottom brackets. One may not stay rich all the time or forever, much so a poor person may not stay poor forever. For this reason, the claim of OWS that the rich is getting richer while the poor is getting poorer, is bogus!

CLASSES WITHIN CLASS

Inequality fills the Bottom 99% own class. We offer clues just how terrible it is

Do the OWS even know that within their own Bottom 99% grouping, there exist similar income gaps? These gaps are similar in nature to the gaps between the Top 1% and the Bottom 99%. What it mean is that the gaps between the Top 1% and the Bottom 99% actually occurs inside their respective group themselves, so the 'top 1% of the Bottom 99%', is raking in more incomes than the 'bottom 99% of the Bottom 99%'. Within the Top 1%, there exist similar trends as well.

The 'bottom 99% of the Top 1%', is as 'poor' as the Bottom 99% in the general economy. We post two graphs below, you can figure it out yourself, which one is the bottom 99% income gaps, within its own class, and which one is the income gaps within the Top 1% itself.

Income level within the group itself, showing the bottommost and topmost.

Is this the Top 1% or is it the Bottom 99% group?

INCOME SPREAD WITHIN TOP 1% AND BOTTOM 99%

Income level within the group itself, showing the bottommost and topmost.

Is this the Top 1% or is it the Bottom 99% group?

Didn't we tell you that the 1% line is a stupid line to measure income disparity?

Illustration 15: Which is which?

Have fun finding it out, but the point is, once the Top 1% is destroyed, there is already a gaping huge income gaps within the leftover Bottom 99% present at the moment. Perhaps the OWS has no idea about this, but we hope they do, because it is just a never-ending thing, because it is a natural order of things in the economy. Unless they want equal amount for everyone in the name of fairness, then that is communism. We are sure they do not know what the outcomes of those communists' countries are. They were destroyed from within due to terrible economic performance.

Why is everyone so fixated on the "1% line"? Economists and their friends gave it such a nice and catchy name, but our data showed data these "lines" are so moveable, it will bound to confuse anyone. Real people are referred to arbitrarily this way. Then they grouped them together for convenience. It is a practice that's bordering stupidity, with many unintended consequences. We think it is madness to group some people as the "Top 1%" whilst some other people, the "Bottom 99%". Have a look at the following illustration we made specifically to describe just one of the idiotic results of the imaginary 'lines' they created.

TOP 1%

EVIL

DEVIL

GREEDY

$343,927

$ 250,000—$ 500,000

1% LINE

$343,926

1,776,459

How can a one dollar difference make two people being labeled differently, one as part of the bottom 99% and therefore not evil (and not to be occupied) and the other as the top 1%, the evil reincarnate and the epitome of greed?

This 1% LINE cut through the $250k to $500k income bracket where 1.8 million people reside. Thereby cutting through people with nearly equal amount of income...but putting them in different brackets of being "occupied" or not.

POOR SOD

VICTIM

BOTTOM 99%

$0 **GOOD**

Illustration 16: The stupid 1% line

WHY CURRENT COMPARISON METHODS ARE VERY ERRONEOUS

We cannot compare the classes using the simple 'Top 1%' to the 'Bottom 99%'. Find out why it is erroneous to do so.

Has anyone ever question why the OWS and the rest of their supporters, the government, the economists and virtually everyone out there, always use the term, Top 1% and Bottom 99%? OWS includes those relatively rich individuals earning $100,000 or more, into their group. This will simply skew their data terribly, it is simply improper. These rich individuals do not appoint OWS to represent them. OWS tries to delude the whole population by claiming to represent them, while the truth of the matter is, they only represent themselves (some young people and those who do not want to work hard and do not want to pay their dues). Previous generations worked very hard without much complaining, sharing their fate together, enriching America and ended up making it as the richest country on the planet. Kudos to them! We will talk more about this misrepresentation by OWS throughout this book.

Has anyone question whether comparing data over time, in percentage terms will tend to mislead miserably? We had discussed this in Book 2 of the series and we cautioned everyone not to simply compare two economic periods, many decades apart (when we talked about inflation). It is a similar situation here. Using percentage top and bottom over a long period of time will be erroneous for the same reasons mentioned in Book 2 of the 259 Trillion Vs. 5 Trillion series. However, for this comparison we will focus on the fluidity and movements between "the poor and the rich" (the Top 1% and the Bottom 99%) and other type of income brackets — which we have shown to occur in the previous topic.

Why is that so?

Let's analyze in depth, why the existing predominant method of comparing the Top 1% and the bottom 99%, or any percentage for that matter, is inaccurate.

Here, we will use a known number of samples of students and workers to show how the data can easily be misunderstood. We will then prove how this phenomenon occurs in real life by using IRS data (same data is also used by an award-winning economist parroted by the OWS).

In a well-distributed class of 20 students, each student obtained a specific score, from the lowest, to the top most. The lowest student obtained a score of five and the next lowest obtained a 10, and the other students will each obtain their own score in a fixed increment of five, between them.

NAME	MARK (INITIAL)	GROUP
Student A	100	TOP 20%
Student B	95	
Student C	90	
Student D	85	
Student E	80	
Student F	75	
Student G	70	
Student H	65	
Student I	60	
Student J	55	
Student K	50	
Student L	45	
Student M	40	
Student N	35	
Student O	30	
Student P	25	
Student Q	20	
Student R	15	
Student S	10	BOTTOM 20%
Student T	5	

KEY RATIOS	Before Addition
Ave Top 20% / Ave Bottom 20%	7.40
Ave Top 20% / Ave Bottom 80%	2.18

Illustration 17: Tables showing a sample of 20 students marks and the associated key ratios

What will happen if we increase the top 20% students' scores by 40% each, and we do the same for the bottom 20% as well?

The result will shock you, despite our additions being fair and just, to the Top as well as the Bottom group!

NAME	MARK (INITIAL)	Change	MARK (AFTER)
Student A	100	add 40%	140
Student B	95	add 40%	133
Student C	90	add 40%	126
Student D	85	add 40%	119
Student E	80		80
Student F	75		75
Student G	70		70
Student H	65		65
Student I	60		60
Student J	55		55
Student K	50		50
Student L	45		45
Student M	40		40
Student N	35		35
Student O	30		30
Student P	25		25
Student Q	20	add 40%	28
Student R	15	add 40%	21
Student S	10	add 40%	14
Student T	5	add 40%	7

You will notice that one peculiar thing will happen. One of the students in the bottom 20%, will have a score higher than the lowest scoring student in the middle bracket.

Illustration 18: Table showing changes to the sample of 20 students marks when the students at the top and bottom brackets get an increase of 40% each

43

NAME	MARK (INITIAL)	Change	MARK (AFTER)	NAME	MARK (INITIAL)	MARK (AFTER)	GROUP
Student A	100	add 40%	140	Student A	100	140	TOP 20%
Student B	95	add 40%	133	Student B	95	133	
Student C	90	add 40%	126	Student C	90	126	
Student D	85	add 40%	119	Student D	85	119	
Student E	80		80	Student E	80	80	
Student F	75		75	Student F	75	75	
Student G	70		70	Student G	70	70	
Student H	65		65	Student H	65	65	
Student I	60		60	Student I	60	60	
Student J	55		55	Student J	55	55	
Student K	50		50	Student K	50	50	
Student L	45		45	Student L	45	45	
Student M	40		40	Student M	40	40	
Student N	35		35	Student N	35	35	
Student O	30		30	Student O	30	30	
Student P	25		25	Student Q	20	28	
Student Q	20	add 40%	28	Student P	25	25	
Student R	15	add 40%	21	Student R	15	21	
Student S	10	add 40%	14	Student S	10	14	BOTTOM
Student T	5	add 40%	7	Student T	5	7	20%

Illustration 19: Tables above show that one student from the bottom bracket would move up to the next, knocking down the person originally residing at that spot. Also look at the key ratios in the next illustration.

As you can see in the illustrations, the up-going student from the bottom 20% will displace the lowest scoring student in the middle bracket. Thereby effectively moves up from the bottom group to the middle group.

What will happen to the key ratios?

KEY RATIOS	Before Addition	After Addition	% Change
Ave Top 20% / Ave Bottom 20%	7.40	7.73	4%
Ave Top 20% / Ave Bottom 80%	2.18	2.96	36%

Illustration 20: Table show the key ratios before and after the increases

They indicated that the smarts are getting smarter, higher than anyone else is. The smart (Top 20%) over the 'dumb' (Bottom 20%) ratio increased from 7.40 to 7.73. This is illogical, because we knew beforehand that we did add both the top and the bottom, by equal proportion. However, the key ratio 'misled' us, by showing the smarts are getting far smarter, by an extra 4%.

If compared to the rest of the Bottom 80%, the change is even more astonishing. The Top 20% students are getting smarter by 36% more, than the Bottom 80%. Many economists and other analyst will say that the top 20% will capture an extra 36% more score that was added —which we know for fact, is not true.

The key ratios were too focused on the "Bottom 20%", "Top 20%" or the other group "Bottom 80%". The top and bottom people always switch places; they are not static. There is no study out there that captures this movement; therefore, their conclusions are bound to be wrong.

	Marks (Initial)	Share of Total	Marks (After)	Share of Total	% Change of Share
Top 20%	370	35.2%	518	42.5%	21%
Bottom 20%	50	4.8%	67	5.5%	16%
Bottom 80%	680	64.8%	700	57.5%	-11%
TOTAL	1050	100%	1218	100%	0%

	Additional Marks Obtained	% Of Additional Marks Captured	Marks Ave (Initial)	Marks Ave (After)	% Change
Top 20%	148	88%	92.5	129.5	40%
Bottom 20%	17	10%	12.5	16.75	34%
Bottom 80%	20	12%	42.5	43.75	2.9%
TOTAL	168	100%	52.5	60.9	100%

Illustration 21: Interesting key data showing that the smarts are capturing 88% of all additional scores, while the rest of the groups 'languish behind'.

In fact, if we "analyze" the data as per what the OWS supporters do, we will arrive to a wrong conclusion as well. We knew very well that we accorded each of the Top 20% and the Bottom 20%, marks of equal proportion and their key ratio, changed for the worse. The Top 20% is shown to capture 88% of all new scores, however the top and bottom 20%, did not change in proportion at all. After a tedious calculation, we were able to show that the top 20% actually received the 40%

additional scores, but the bottom 20%, only a 34% increase. Where the 6% go? If we calculate the bottom 80% instead, the increase is even worse, only 2.9%. [We will show you where the 6% go at the end of this chapter.]

This is what's happening to many studies out there. We knew for a fact that the smarts got increases of equal proportion, and the gap between the top 20% and bottom 20% did not budge at all. Thus, if you do not know the story, then you will believe that the top 20% is unfairly given higher marks by the teacher leaving the bottom behind. Luckily, we actually knew, (in this case) that equal number of people from the top and the bottom, are given equal proportional increase in their scores.

Now, we can make thing even more interesting. Let's add a few fresh students, all making low scores, because either they have never attended school, or they really and actually are dumb.

NAME	MARK (INITIAL)	GROUP
Student A	100	TOP 20%
Student B	95	
Student C	90	
Student D	85	
Student E	80	
Student F	75	
Student G	70	
Student H	65	
Student I	60	
Student J	55	
Student K	50	
Student L	45	
Student M	40	
Student N	35	
Student O	30	
Student P	25	
Student Q	20	
Student R	15	
Student S	10	BOTTOM 20%
Student T	5	

NAME OF NEW STUDENTS	MARK
Student AA	5
Student AB	5
Student AC	5
Student AD	5
Student AE	5
Student AF	10
Student AG	10
Student AH	10
Student AI	10
Student AJ	10

Illustration 22: Table shows the marks for 20 of the original students and the initial key ratios. Now additional ten new fresh students entered the class, they have no pre-schooling (hence the low marks), but they are hardworking and eager!

KEY RATIOS	Initial (20 Students)
Ave Top 20% / Ave Bottom 20%	7.40
Ave Top 20% / Ave Bottom 80%	2.18

A very interesting situation occurred. Study the following illustration carefully.

NAME	MARK (INITIAL)	MARK (AFTER)	GROUP
Student A	100	100	
Student B	95	95	
Student C	90	90	TOP 20%
Student D	85	85	
Student E	80	80	
Student F	75	75	
Student G	70	70	
Student H	65	65	
Student I	60	60	
Student J	55	55	
Student K	50	50	
Student L	45	45	
Student M	40	40	
Student N	35	35	
Student O	30	30	
Student P	25	25	
Student Q	20	20	
Student R	15	15	
Student S	10	10	
Student AF	10	10	
Student AG	10	10	
Student AH	10	10	
Student AI	10	10	
Student AJ	10	10	
Student T	5	5	
Student AA	5	5	
Student AB	5	5	
Student AC	5	5	
Student AD	5	5	BOTTOM
Student AE	5	5	20%

Total number of students are now 30.

Thus, the number of students in the Top 20% increases to six. So is the bottom 20%.

6 students (Previous 4)

6 students (Previous 4)

Illustration 23: With the entry of new students at the bottom, the stupid 'percent' lines moved!

The number of students at the Top 20% increases by two. Somehow, two additional students are now in the top group, and are now considered as getting smarter. How can adding more low scoring students at the bottom results in more 'bright' students? We know darn well that nothing has change for all of the students' scores, except new participants had entered the class. Things have changed, without any of them ever lifting a pen. Now, let's check the key ratios, and prepare to be dumbfounded!

KEY RATIOS	Initial (20 Students)	After Additional Students Added	% Change
Ave Top 20% / Ave Bottom 20%	7.40	17.50	136%
Ave Top 20% / Ave Bottom 80%	2.18	3.50	61%

Illustration 24: The key ratios worsened, showing the top 20% are getting smarter, without doing anything!

The Top 20% (six students) got instantly 'smarter' with the arrival of 10 new students

	Marks (Initial)	Share of Total	Marks (After)	Share of Total	% Share Change
Top 20%	370	35.2%	525	46.7%	32%
Bottom 20%	50	4.8%	30	2.7%	-44%
Bottom 80%	680	64.8%	600	53.3%	-18%
TOTAL	1050	100%	1125	100%	-

	Marks Change	% Increase Share	Marks Ave (Initial)	Marks Ave (After)	%Share of Total
Top 20%	155	207%	92.5	131.25	41.9%
Bottom 20%	- 20	-27%	12.5	7.5	-40.0%
Bottom 80%	- 80	-107%	42.5	37.5	-11.8%
TOTAL	75	-	52.5	56.25	100%

So what does the key ratio tells?

It tells everything except the truth of what had actually happened. There are 10 new students who aren't so bright or just new to school which had entered the pool of students in that class.

Illustration 25: The key detail ratios telling a whole sort of things happening, such as smarts are getting smarter, 'dumb are getting dumber' and other erroneous conclusions. But the truth, is far from what the data is showing.

Well, the key ratios are all showing crazy numbers. We bet those analysts, teachers (and economists of course) will go gaga over the key data. They will expound nonstop of how the smarts are getting smarter while the not so smart, are not. The key ratios totally misled all of us. It could not show us the true picture. Luckily again, we knew exactly what had happened in the class. There are just a few new students entering the class; that is all. Now you will wonder why our economists, the Occupiers and so many more people go crazy over the statistics, while in fact the statistics were all wrong! It just could not show what the actual, true picture on the ground is. If they only look harder, there is an easy solution (we will present it later in this book).

Once again, the danger of using the "top xx percent" line as well as the "bottom xx percent", can trap any unsuspecting group of people towards 'killing' each other.

What happen if very bright students entered the class, from the top? What will happen to the key ratios then? Can you imagine?

We leave that up to your imagination then.

Now, let's move on and make things even more interesting!

We will now try to imagine the salary levels of employees in a corporation.

NAME	PAY (INITIAL)	Designation	GROUP
Worker A	100	CEO	TOP 20%
Worker B	95	VP	
Worker C	90	Manager	
Worker D	85	Manager	
Worker E	75		
Worker F	50		
Worker G	50		
Worker H	50		
Worker I	50		
Worker J	50		
Worker K	50		
Worker L	50		
Worker M	50		
Worker N	50		
Worker O	50		
Worker P	40		
Worker Q	35		
Worker R	5		
Worker S	5		BOTTOM 20%
Worker T	5		

KEY RATIOS	Initial
Ave Top 20% / Ave Bot 20%	7.40
Ave Top 20% / Ave Bot 80%	2.23

Illustration 26: Table shows the pay of each workers (in thousands of dollars) and the key ratio of the top 20% earners and the rest, initially.

On one fateful day, an employee from the bottom-most received a gift from the shareholders (for saving one of their daughter's life). He became the new CEO, with a pay package of 'OWS proportion', that is, 350x of the average worker's pay.

Illustration 27: Table shows the pay of each worker (in thousands of dollars) and that lucky new CEO with OWS's proportion CEO package.

NAME		PAY (INITIAL)	Designation	PAY (AFTER)
Worker	A	100	CEO	100
Worker	B	95	VP	95
Worker	C	90	Manager	90
Worker	D	85	Manager	85
Worker	E	75		75
Worker	F	50		50
Worker	G	50		50
Worker	H	50		50
Worker	I	50		50
Worker	J	50		50
Worker	K	50		50
Worker	L	50		50
Worker	M	50		50
Worker	N	50		50
Worker	O	50		50
Worker	P	40		40
Worker	Q	35		35
Worker	R	5		5
Worker	S	5		5
Worker	T	5		14,547

Now, the guy went on to become the new CEO of the company. From the bottom of the bottoms, he jumped straight to the top, of the tops. What happen to the rest of the workers is shown below.

NAME	PAY (INITIAL)	Designation	PAY (AFTER)		NAME	PAY (INITIAL)	Designation	PAY (AFTER)	GROUP
Worker A	100	CEO	100		Worker T	5	NEW CEO	14,547	TOP 20%
Worker B	95	VP	95		Worker A	100	VP	100	
Worker C	90	Manager	90		Worker B	95	Manager	95	
Worker D	85	Manager	85		Worker C	90	Manager	90	
Worker E	75		75		Worker D	85		85	
Worker F	50		50		Worker E	75		75	
Worker G	50		50		Worker F	50		50	
Worker H	50		50		Worker G	50		50	Displaced
Worker I	50		50		Worker H	50		50	
Worker J	50		50		Worker I	50		50	
Worker K	50		50		Worker J	50		50	
Worker L	50		50		Worker K	50		50	
Worker M	50		50		Worker L	50		50	
Worker N	50		50		Worker M	50		50	
Worker O	50		50		Worker N	50		50	
Worker P	40		40		Worker O	50		50	
Worker Q	35		35		Worker P	40		40	BOTTOM 20%
Worker R	5		5		Worker Q	5		5	
Worker S	5		5		Worker R	5		5	
Worker T	5		14,547		Worker S	5		5	

Illustration 28: Table shows the once POOR person who got a raise and a promotion, will bump two people from their old bracket.

Note that as soon as he reached the top, two people were bumped from their places, one in each bracket. The impacts of his meteoric rise to the key ratios are amazing.

KEY RATIOS	Initial	New CEO	% Change
Ave Top 20% / Ave Bot 20%	7.40	270	3544%
Ave Top 20% / Ave Bot 80%	2.23	83	3628%

Illustration 29: The table below shows the key ratios.

From the initial ratio of 7.4 between the Average Top 20% to the Bottom 20%, the ratio jumps to 270, an increase of 3,544%. Meanwhile, the Average Top 20% to the Bottom 80% also increases, very high for no apparent reason because none in the group actually experienced any increases, except for the bottom most person. It looks like that the key ratios are not telling us the real story here.

Now, look at the additional details of the key ratios in the table below and on the next page.

	Salary (Initial)	Share of Total	Salary (After)	Share of Total	% Change of Share
Top 20%	370	35.7%	14,832	95.4%	167%
Bottom 20%	50	4.8%	55	0.4%	-93%
Bottom 80%	665	64.3%	715	4.6%	-93%
TOTAL	1,035	100%	15,547	100%	-

	Additional Salary Obtained	% Of Additional Salary Captured	Salary Ave (Initial)	Salary Ave (After)	% Change
Top 20%	14,462	99.66%	92.5	3708.0	3908%
Bottom 20%	5	0.03%	12.5	13.8	10%
Bottom 80%	50	0.34%	41.6	44.7	7.5%
TOTAL	14,512	100%	51.75	777.3	-

Illustration 30: Table shows the false change in the key ratios

The Top 20% is shown to capture 99.66% of all additional salary, while we knew for a fact, the guy from bottom-most is the one who received it. No data out there will show or attempt to explain this issue, and they will almost always, mislead you. The Bottom 20% received a massive increase in pay, is shown to receive an increase of only 10%; pathetic they say, and they will go on and claim that the rich, is getting richer. The percentage change of share of salary shows that the Bottom 20% decreases by a massive 93%, and so is for the Bottom 80%. The poor is getting richer in this example because we add more salary to that lucky guy from the bottom most group, but all key indicators showed that the rich are, getting richer. In fact, getting very rich. How terrible is that?

So what if we actually show you the correct key ratios?

Let's see!

	Salary (Initial)	Share of Total	Salary (After)	Share of Total	% Change of Share
Top 20%	370	35.7%	370	2.4%	-93%
Bottom 20%	50	4.8%	14,592	93.7%	1,839%
Bottom 80%	665	64.3%	15,207	97.6%	52%
TOTAL	1,035	100%	15,577	100%	-

	Additional Salary Obtained	% Of Additional Salary Captured	Salary Ave (Initial)	Salary Ave (After)	% Change
Top 20%	0	0%	92.5	92.5	0%
Bottom 20%	14,542	100%	12.5	3,648.0	29,084%
Bottom 80%	14,542	100%	41.6	950.4	2,187%
TOTAL	14,542	-	51.75	778.8	-

As you can see, in actuality, the most bottom person is actually the only winner here when he jump straight to the top!

Illustration 31: Table shows the real calculations of the key ratios, presenting them in the correct way

In the proper version of the key ratios above, the Top 20% is shown to experience no gain whatsoever, because their incomes did not change at all. The Bottom 20% meanwhile, experienced a massive increase within their bracket, as it should. So is the bottom 80%, which includes the Bottom 20% within it. Now, how many economists, media journalists, professors and the OWS that you know of, present their data in this correct way?

None that we know of. Stop thinking the rich is getting richer, and start thinking about the poor that are getting richer!

Now, let us use a real life example of incomes of the population, with data obtained from the IRS, for tax year of 1990 and 2009.

All data presented by economists, politicians, the media and everyone else never correct the impact of new, additional people into the population. In the following series of very interesting data with surprising conclusions, we will attempt to do just that. We will filter out all new additions into the populace and maintain the overall number of people constant, over long period of time. The goal is to follow up on the original taxpayers, over decades, how they will fare within their own original group. Here, we can show very clearly that the poor, is definitely isn't getting poorer.

We picked the interesting year of 1990, which many people claimed as the start of growing income gaps between classes in America. Our data are based on IRS data on taxpayers for 1990, and we crosschecked with the Bureau of Labor Statistic's own data (that data is presented in Book 3).

In 1990:-

	1990	
	Number Of People	Total Income (thousand of dollars)
$1 under $5,000	16,478,272	41,497,039
$5,000 under $10,000	14,952,855	111,951,215
$10,000 under $15,000	13,922,750	173,376,264
$15,000 under $20,000	11,543,228	201,638,041
$20,000 under $25,000	9,572,317	214,321,942
$25,000 under $30,000	7,838,225	215,207,577
$30,000 under $40,000	12,282,786	426,384,692
$40,000 under $50,000	8,837,067	394,730,512
$50,000 under $75,000	10,944,102	657,214,261
$75,000 under $100,000	3,276,142	279,524,997
$100,000 under $200,000	2,036,396	252,138,471
$100,000 under $200,000	293,166	53,429,119
$200,000 under $500,000	644,027	188,004,834
$500,000 under $1,000,000	130,252	87,142,014
$1,000,000 under $1,500,000	29,060	34,978,215
$1,500,000 under $2,000,000	11,581	19,891,323
$2,000,000 under $5,000,000	15,331	45,034,350
$5,000,000 under $10,000,000	3,184	21,463,938
$10,000,000 or more	1,522	33,308,207
	112,812,263	$ 3,451,237,011

Illustration 32: Table shows the number of people and their incomes in 1990

To tally with IRS 2009 summary of historical data (09in01etr.xls) in order to get similar Top and Bottom numbers and incomes, returns with negative incomes are not included, as per the IRS data file and explanations

112.8 million people submitted their tax returns, declaring incomes of 3.45 trillion dollars in 1990. The Top 1% people are those highlighted in yellow and the green cells. We split the people in the $100,000 to $200,000 using IRS historical data of the Top 1% number of returns and their income since the Top 1% in 1990 goes through this bracket. There is a group of people who reported to the IRS to have received zero or negative incomes, therefore they are not included in most calculations, since the IRS also excluded them in their historical data that we use for obtaining the numbers of the Top 1% and its income.

We then compare this 1990 data with the latest and most accurate data available from the IRS, the year 2009. We cannot use data from the year 2011 for example, because the final tax payments are not yet completed due to on-going refunds and many other tax consolidation processes. We saw many economists, many professors even, used those 2011 data, which clearly are from the submitted tax forms, exclusive of refunds data. No doubt, their data will be suspicious.

In 2009, the tax base grew to 137.9 million people.

	2009	
	Number Of People	Total Income (thousand of dollars)
$1 under $5,000	10,447,635	28,968,885
$5,000 under $10,000	12,220,335	95,361,453
$10,000 under $15,000	12,444,512	158,797,392
$15,000 under $20,000	11,400,228	202,165,670
$20,000 under $25,000	10,033,887	228,096,096
$25,000 under $30,000	8,662,392	240,993,189
$30,000 under $40,000	14,371,647	505,807,319
$40,000 under $50,000	10,796,412	488,912,268
$50,000 under $75,000	18,694,893	1,162,579,257
$75,000 under $100,000	11,463,725	1,000,580,260
$100,000 under $200,000	13,522,048	1,825,123,213
$200,000 under $250,000	1,418,580	320,639,058
$250,000 under $500,000	**1,126,087**	**353,207,317**
$250,000 under $500,000	**650,372**	**250,318,253**
$500,000 under $1,000,000	**492,567**	**339,109,307**
$1,000,000 under $1,500,000	108,096	132,558,457
$1,500,000 under $2,000,000	44,273	77,370,065
$2,000,000 under $5,000,000	61,918	185,228,891
$5,000,000 under $10,000,000	14,322	98,352,775
$10,000,000 or more	8,274	241,634,252
	137,982,203	**7,935,803,377**

Illustration 33: Table shows the number of people and their incomes in 2009

The declared incomes were 7.935 trillion dollars, and the top 1% brackets had shifted far to the top, as indicated with the shift of the yellow cells down and the green cell. In 2009, there is an additional bracket created by IRS by splitting up the $200,000 to $500,000 into two, from $200,000 to $250,000 and $250,000 to $500,000. The reason is simple; many more people are now sitting in these brackets. Coincidentally, the 1% line of 2009 goes through this bracket and we split the brackets similarly to 1990 to get the exact number of people in the Top 1% group.

The two selected tax years are not comparable to each other and thus it is difficult to tell how the original taxpayers from 1990 fared, due to the additions of new entrants throughout the 20 years. We decided to remove all of the new additional taxpayers from the 2009 roll, and make them similar in number, to the original 1990. We did this by using a constant reducing factor for all brackets in equal proportion (there is no other method we can use, to do this correction unless the actual individual data is available).

The table in the next illustration shows the number of people in 1990, 2009 and also the corrected 2009 number of people. The proportion of the 2009 people is still the same as in the 'corrected' 2009 proportion.

Illustration 34: Table shows the 2009 data when corrected proportionally to match the data of 1990

The 2009 workers total are now equal in number to 1990

	1990	2009		2009 (CORRECTED)	
	Number Of People	Number Of People	As %	Correcting No. of people to match 1990 numbers	As %
$1 under $5,000	16,478,272	10,447,635	7.57%	8,541,836	7.57%
$5,000 under $10,000	14,952,855	12,220,335	8.86%	9,991,170	8.86%
$10,000 under $15,000	13,922,750	12,444,512	9.02%	10,174,454	9.02%
$15,000 under $20,000	11,543,228	11,400,228	8.26%	9,320,662	8.26%
$20,000 under $25,000	9,572,317	10,033,887	7.27%	8,203,562	7.27%
$25,000 under $30,000	7,838,225	8,662,392	6.28%	7,082,247	6.28%
$30,000 under $40,000	12,282,786	14,371,647	10.42%	11,750,052	10.42%
$40,000 under $50,000	8,837,067	10,796,412	7.82%	8,826,991	7.82%
$50,000 under $75,000	10,944,102	18,694,893	13.55%	15,284,675	13.55%
$75,000 under $100,000	3,276,142	11,463,725	8.31%	9,372,577	8.31%
$100,000 under $200,000	2,036,396	11,820,353	8.57%	9,664,150	8.57%
$100,000 under $200,000	293,166	1,701,695	1.23%	1,391,282	1.23%
$200,000 under $250,000	1,418,580	1,418,580	1.03%	1,159,811	1.03%
$250,000 under $500,000	1,105,500	1,105,500	0.82%	920,673	0.82%
$250,000 under $500,000	650,372	650,372	0.47%	531,735	0.47%
$500,000 under $1,000,000	130,252	492,567	0.36%	402,716	0.36%
$1,000,000 under $1,500,000	29,060	108,096	0.08%	88,378	0.08%
$1,500,000 under $2,000,000	11,581	44,273	0.03%	36,197	0.03%
$2,000,000 under $5,000,000	15,331	61,918	0.04%	50,623	0.04%
$5,000,000 under $10,000,000	3,184	14,322	0.01%	11,709	0.01%
$10,000,000 or more	1,522	8,274	0.01%	6,765	0.01%
	112,812,263	137,982,203		112,812,263	

As you can see from the illustration, the number of people between the two selected years is now the same. We can now check how many of them had moved to other income brackets. Remember, these are the 'same' people in 1990. From now on, we will use the top 1% line of 1990 to indicate the positions where all of the original Top One Percenters (abbreviated as Top 1%ers) of 1990 should reside in 2009.

Below is the actual table that we will be using for comparison, the original 1990 data and the modified or corrected data of 2009.

	1990		2009 (CORRECTED)	
	Number Of People	Total Income (thousand of dollars)	Correcting No. of people to match 1990 numbers	Modified Total Income for each bracket (thousand)
$1 under $5,000	16,478,272	41,497,039	8,541,836	23,684,543
$5,000 under $10,000	14,952,855	111,951,215	9,991,170	77,966,151
$10,000 under $15,000	13,922,750	173,376,264	10,174,454	129,830,462
$15,000 under $20,000	11,543,228	201,638,041	9,320,662	165,287,742
$20,000 under $25,000	9,572,317	214,321,942	8,203,562	186,488,085
$25,000 under $30,000	7,838,225	215,207,577	7,082,247	197,032,562
$30,000 under $40,000	12,282,786	426,384,692	11,750,052	413,540,783
ORIGINAL 1990 TOP 1% LINE ➔	8,837,067	394,730,512	8,826,991	399,727,633
	10,944,102	657,214,261	15,284,675	950,508,066
	3,276,142	279,524,997	9,372,577	818,060,018
$100,000 under $200,000	2,036,396	252,138,471	9,664,150	1,304,407,801
$100,000 under $200,000	293,166	53,429,119	1,391,282	187,786,667
$200,000 under $250,000	285,944	83,473,127	1,159,811	262,149,878
$250,000 under $500,000	226,986	66,262,039	920,673	288,777,218
$250,000 under $500,000	131,096	38,269,667	531,735	204,656,600
$500,000 under $1,000,000	130,252	87,142,014	402,716	277,250,888
$1,000,000 under $1,500,000	29,060	34,978,215	88,378	108,377,886
$1,500,000 under $2,000,000	11,581	19,891,323	36,197	63,256,651
$2,000,000 under $5,000,000	15,331	45,034,350	50,623	151,440,475
$5,000,000 under $10,000,000	3,184	21,463,938	11,709	80,411,813
$10,000,000 or more	1,522	33,308,207	6,765	197,556,686
	112,812,263	3,451,237,011	112,812,263	6,488,198,610

Illustration 35: Table shows the 1990 data and the corrected 2009 data to be used in our comparison

The next illustration will show the net changes of the movement of the original 1990 taxpayers in 2009.

ORIGINAL 1990 TOP 1% LINE	1990 Number Of People	2009 (CORRECTED) Correcting No. of people to match 1990 numbers	In 2009 Number of people moved to higher brackets
$1 under $5,000	16,478,272	8,541,836	-7,994,498
$5,000 under $10,000	14,952,855	9,991,170	-5,029,598
$10,000 under $15,000	13,922,750	10,174,454	-3,817,455
$15,000 under $20,000	11,543,228	9,320,662	-2,285,921
$20,000 under $25,000	9,572,317	8,203,562	-1,424,518
$25,000 under $30,000	7,838,225	7,082,247	-804,118
$30,000 under $40,000	12,282,786	11,750,052	-612,603
$40,000 under $50,000	8,837,067	8,826,991	-70,076
$50,000 under $75,000	10,944,102	15,284,675	+4,236,679
$75,000 under $100,000	3,276,142	9,372,577	+6,032,726
$100,000 under $200,000	2,036,396	9,664,150	+7,528,465
$100,000 under $200,000	293,166	1,391,282	+1,122,258
$200,000 under $250,000	285,944	1,159,811	+507,900
$250,000 under $500,000	226,986	920,673	+897,697
$250,000 under $500,000	131,096	531,735	+544,838
$500,000 under $1,000,000	130,252	402,716	+269,726
$1,000,000 under $1,500,000	29,060	88,378	+58,717
$1,500,000 under $2,000,000	11,581	36,197	+24,370
$2,000,000 under $5,000,000	15,331	50,623	+34,948
$5,000,000 under $10,000,000	3,184	11,709	+8,446
$10,000,000 or more	1,522	6,765	+5,197
	112,812,263	112,812,263	0

Illustration 36: Table shows the 1990 data and the corrected 2009 data to get the changes in the number of migration

The original 113 million taxpayers had improved their lot tremendously, when a massive 21.5 million from the bottom 65%, moved up to higher brackets (these are highlighted in red circle). The net result is that the number of people at the bottom 65% declined by that number of individuals. The largest decliner of all? It is the lowest bracket of course! In 1990, 16.5 million individuals were sitting in the $1 to $5,000 bracket and by 2009, only 8.5 million individuals were left in this group. The other eight million, moved up to higher brackets, even all to way to the top! As you can see, in every bracket at the bottom, all the way to the middle class's bracket, their numbers have declined significantly.

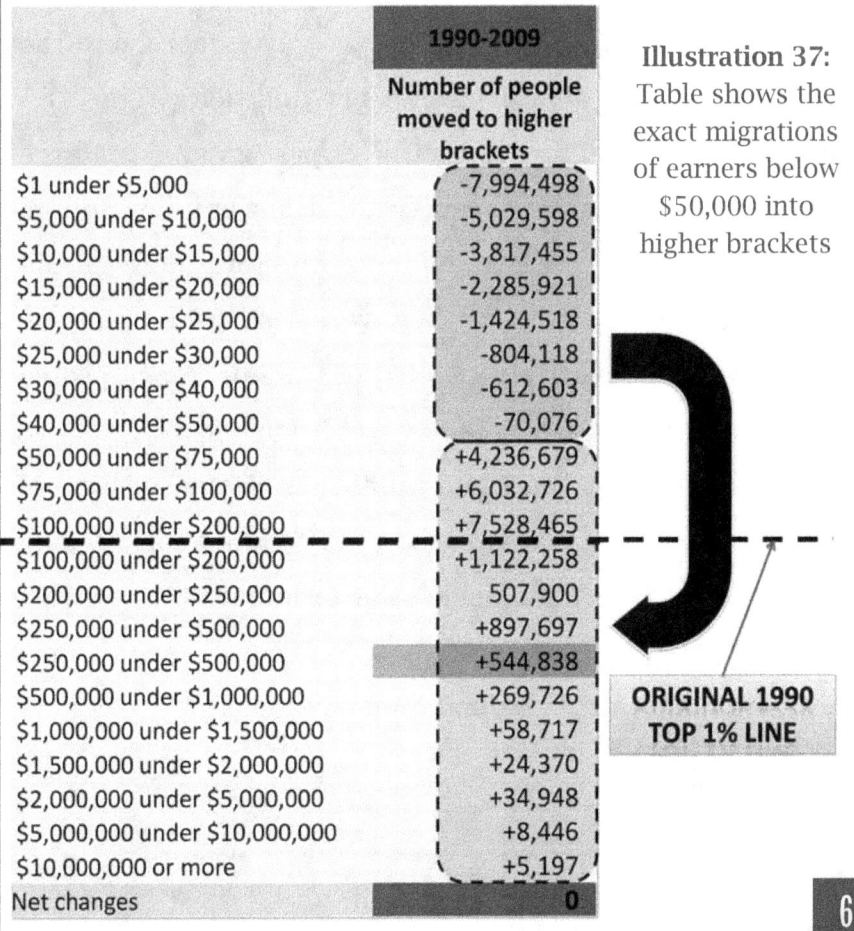

	1990-2009 Number of people moved to higher brackets
$1 under $5,000	-7,994,498
$5,000 under $10,000	-5,029,598
$10,000 under $15,000	-3,817,455
$15,000 under $20,000	-2,285,921
$20,000 under $25,000	-1,424,518
$25,000 under $30,000	-804,118
$30,000 under $40,000	-612,603
$40,000 under $50,000	-70,076
$50,000 under $75,000	+4,236,679
$75,000 under $100,000	+6,032,726
$100,000 under $200,000	+7,528,465
$100,000 under $200,000	+1,122,258
$200,000 under $250,000	507,900
$250,000 under $500,000	+897,697
$250,000 under $500,000	+544,838
$500,000 under $1,000,000	+269,726
$1,000,000 under $1,500,000	+58,717
$1,500,000 under $2,000,000	+24,370
$2,000,000 under $5,000,000	+34,948
$5,000,000 under $10,000,000	+8,446
$10,000,000 or more	+5,197
Net changes	0

Illustration 37: Table shows the exact migrations of earners below $50,000 into higher brackets

ORIGINAL 1990 TOP 1% LINE

The eight million people who moved up, cannot go to the next bracket (of $5,000 to $10,000) because in this bracket, overall, a net of 5 million individuals, left the bracket, moving on up. Therefore the 8 million will move up, to the next, and since the next one is also having a declining number, they will have to move up to the next higher bracket still. The bracket where all of them (all the 21.5 million) can start going in is from the $50,000 to $75,000 bracket, where 4.2 million net entered this bracket. But this is not by far the bracket with the largest net addition, the next one saw even more, and the next, even more at 7.5 million net addition! The 21.5 million entered into all of the upper groups in large numbers, for example the bracket of one million dollars and above, only 60,678 individuals were originally inside back in 1990, but in 2009 they were 192,356 individuals inside. This is exactly a tripling of the number of people residing in the top brackets. Well, don't forget, we are still talking about the same number of people in both of the selected years, no increase at all! What we are seeing is large movements inside the original 113 million individuals. The actual number of people earning one million or more in 2009, including newcomers?

236,883!

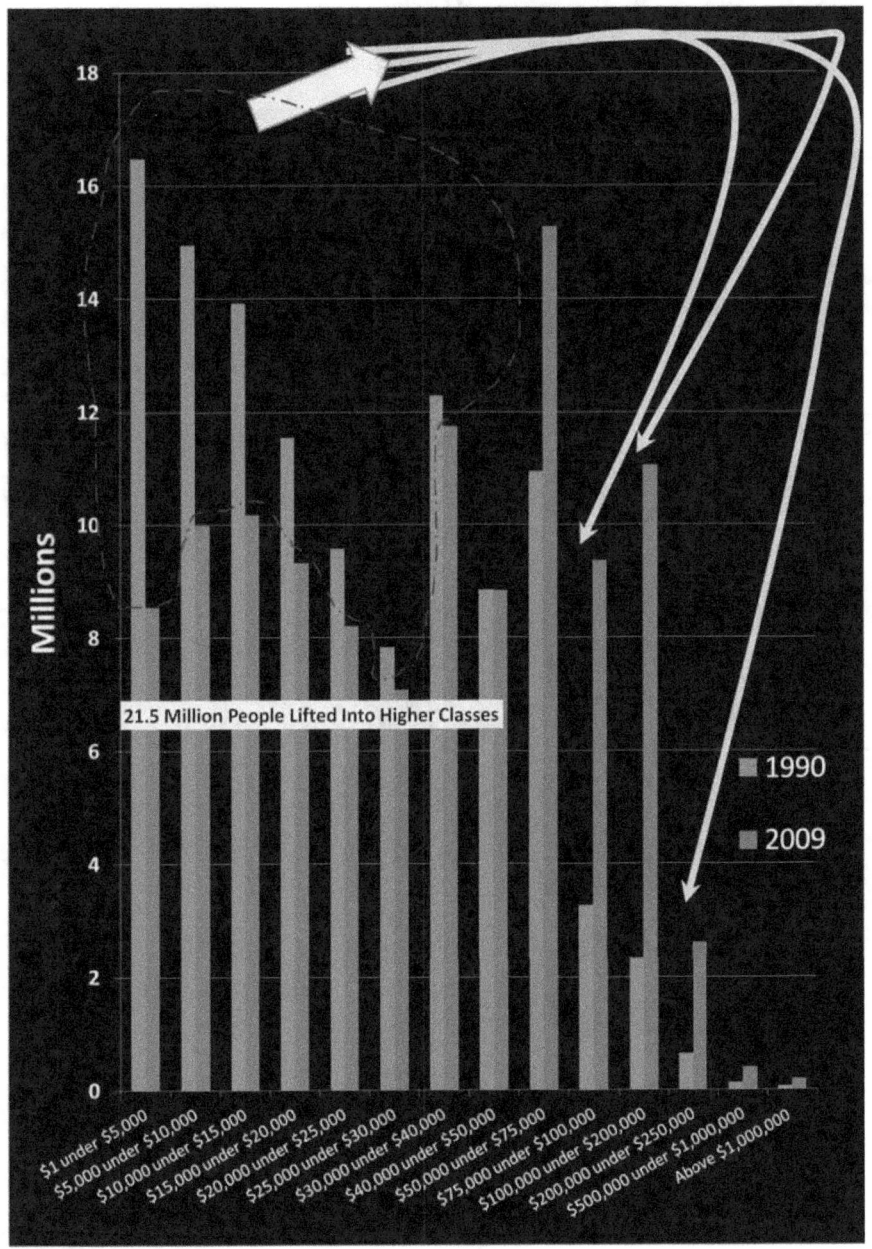

Illustration 38: Graph shows the migration of low income groups towards the upper income brackets in droves throughout the 20 years

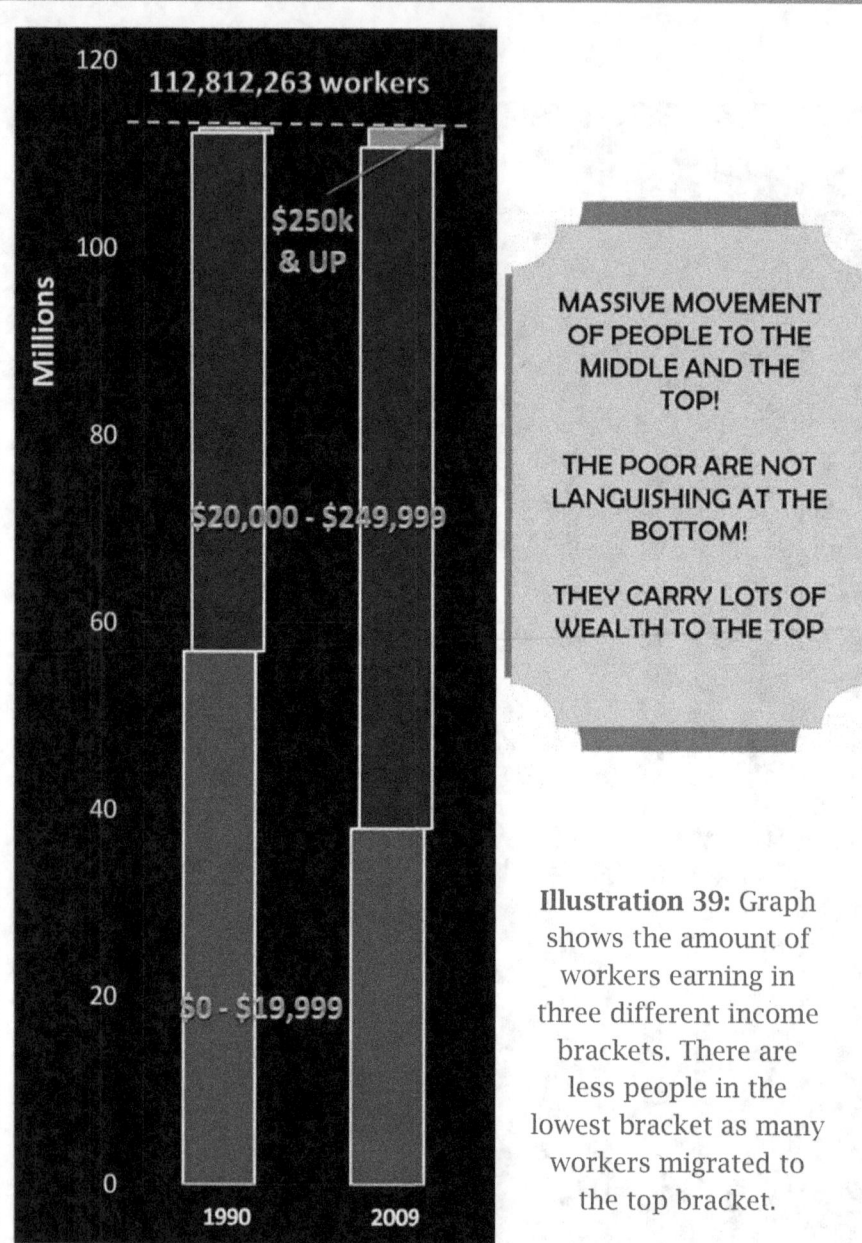

112,812,263 workers

$250k & UP

$20,000 - $249,999

$0 - $19,999

1990　　　　2009

MASSIVE MOVEMENT OF PEOPLE TO THE MIDDLE AND THE TOP!

THE POOR ARE NOT LANGUISHING AT THE BOTTOM!

THEY CARRY LOTS OF WEALTH TO THE TOP

Illustration 39: Graph shows the amount of workers earning in three different income brackets. There are less people in the lowest bracket as many workers migrated to the top bracket.

Now, we are about to arrive at the single biggest item never discussed out there. We are now able to calculate, how many of the bottom individuals, increased their incomes, and by exactly how much.

Take a look at the data.

Illustration 40: Table showing the whole data. The highlighted data is extracted in the next illustration for easy reading

See on next page in 2009

Income bracket	1990 — Number Of People	1990 — Total Income (thousand of dollars)	2009 (CORRECTED) — Correcting No. of people to match 1990 numbers	2009 (CORRECTED) — Modified Total Income for each bracket (thousands of dollars)	Number of people moved to higher brackets	Migration of bottom people to the top carried this much new money into their new home bracket (thousands)
	16,478,272	41,497,039	8,541,836	23,684,543	-7,936,436	
$10,000 under $15,000	14,952,855	111,951,215	9,991,170	77,966,151	-4,961,685	
$15,000 under $20,000	13,922,750	173,376,264	10,174,454	129,830,462	-3,748,296	
$20,000 under $25,000	11,543,228	201,638,041	9,320,662	165,287,742	-2,222,566	
$25,000 under $30,000	9,572,317	214,321,942	8,203,562	186,488,065	-1,368,755	
	7,838,225	215,207,577	7,082,247	197,032,562	-755,978	
$30,000 under $40,000	12,282,786	426,384,692	11,750,052	413,540,763	-532,734	
$40,000 under $50,000	8,837,067	394,730,512	8,826,991	399,727,633	-10,076	
$50,000 under $75,000	10,944,102	657,214,261	15,284,675	950,508,066	4,340,573	269,927,226
$75,000 under $100,000	3,276,142	279,524,997	9,372,577	818,060,018	6,096,435	532,110,816
$100,000 under $200,000	2,036,396	252,138,471	9,664,150	1,304,407,801	7,627,754	1,029,547,542
$200,000 under $200,000	293,166	53,429,119	1,391,282	187,786,667	1,098,116	148,216,916
$200,000 under $250,000	285,944	83,473,127	1,159,811	262,149,878	873,866	197,518,364
$250,000 under $500,000	226,986	66,262,039	920,673	288,777,218	693,686	217,580,889
$500,000 under $1,000,000	131,096	38,269,667	531,735	204,656,660	400,639	154,199,716
	130,252	87,142,014	402,716	277,250,888	272,464	187,578,487
$1,000,000 under $1,500,000	29,060	34,978,215	88,378	108,377,886	59,318	72,741,519
$1,500,000 under $2,000,000	11,581	19,891,323	36,197	63,256,651	24,616	43,018,070
$2,000,000 under $5,000,000	15,331	45,034,350	50,623	151,440,475	35,292	105,577,493
$5,000,000 under $10,000,000	3,184	21,463,938	11,709	80,411,813	8,525	58,546,485
$10,000,000 or more	1,522	33,308,207	6,765	197,556,686	5,243	153,108,133
Total	112,812,263	3,451,237,011	112,812,263	6,488,198,610	0	3,169,671,655

TOP 1%

	IN 2009	
	Number of people moved to higher brackets	Migration of bottom people to the top carried this much new money into their new home bracket (thousands)
$1 under $5,000	-7,936,436	
$5,000 under $10,000	-4,961,685	
$10,000 under $15,000	-3,748,296	
$15,000 under $20,000	-2,222,566	
$20,000 under $25,000	-1,368,755	**ORIGINAL 1990 TOP 1% LINE**
$25,000 under $30,000	-755,978	
$30,000 under $40,000	-532,734	
$40,000 under $50,000	-10,076	
$50,000 under $75,000	+4,340,573	269,927,226
$75,000 under $100,000	+6,096,435	532,110,816
$100,000 under $200,000	+7,627,754	1,029,547,542
$100,000 under $200,000	+1,098,116	148,216,916
$200,000 under $250,000	+873,866	197,518,364
$250,000 under $500,000	+693,686	217,580,889
$250,000 under $500,000	+400,639	154,199,716
$500,000 under $1,000,000	+272,464	187,578,487
$1,000,000 under $1,500,000	+59,318	72,741,519
$1,500,000 under $2,000,000	+24,616	43,018,070
$2,000,000 under $5,000,000	+35,292	105,577,493
$5,000,000 under $10,000,000	+8,525	58,546,485
$10,000,000 or more	+5,243	153,108,133
	0	3,169,671,655

Illustration 41: Table shows the total income carried by the bottom to the top

The large migration to the top by the bottom-earning individuals, who increased their incomes by many multiples, carried with them not billions of dollars, but trillions of dollars to the top! This migration will terribly distort the incomes of the existing Top 1%, towards a much higher level. As an example, the original 1,522 person sitting at the top most bracket of incomes of more than 10 million dollars a year, have to now share their bracket with an additional 5,243 individuals, who are all coming from the bottom 65%. These additional 5,243 individuals carried with them, an amazing 153.1 billion dollars to the bracket, and since these people are coming from the bottom 65%, they carried with them the actual incomes of the bottom 65%, up into the top. The incomes of the poor, is transferred to the top, when the individuals move. By right, these people are the original poor of the bottom 65%, and aptly we should still count them as the original 'bottomers'. If we calculate all of the bottomers' incomes that were wrongly counted as the incomes of the top 35%, the number will be an eye dropping 3.1 trillion dollars! These are all incomes of the poor, now counted as the incomes of the top! How screw up our economists has been? The following are key statistics we calculated from all of the above data.

(Figures in thousands of Dollars)	1990	2009 (CORRECTED)	% Change
Top 1% Incomes	$ 483,252,000	$ 1,082,951,001	124%
Bottom 99% Incomes	$ 2,967,985,011	$ 5,405,247,609	82%

Illustration 42: The table shows the total incomes held by the groups in 1990 and in 2009.

The income of the Top 1% in 1990 is 483.2 billion dollars, and in 2009, 1.082 trillion. It's a 124% change. The Bottom 99% meanwhile, earned 2.967 trillion in 1990 and 5.405 trillion in 2009, an increase of 82%. There is hardly a big difference between the two, but remember, these two are erroneous numbers because they include the original shifted bottomers, who should remain in their own group, rather than being counted as top earners. The next illustration will actually show the correct or proper key ratio if we count the original 1990 Top 1% as the Top 1% in 2009 and the original 1990 Bottom 99% as the Bottom 99% in 2009.

(Figures in millions of dollars)	1990	2009 (CORRECTED)	% Change	2009 (CORRECTED) PROPER (Money migration correction)
Top 1% Incomes	$ 483,252	$ 1,082,951	124%	$ 483,578
Bottom 99% Incomes	$ 2,967,985	$ 5,368,506	82%	$ 6,004,619

Illustration 43: Table shows the proper and 'actual' total incomes held by each group if the migration was not allowed (the poor stays in poor bracket and the rich stays in the rich bracket).

The actual numbers that we have is that the rich's incomes did not grow at all! This is obtained when the 1.082 trillion dollars of the rich, is deducted by 600 billion dollars for the amount owned by the bottom 65% that migrated there.

The next illustration will show the actual, correct ratios between the Top 1% and the Bottom 99%.

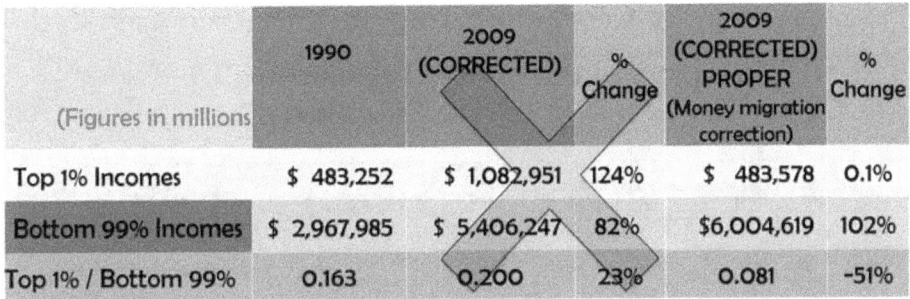

(Figures in millions	1990	2009 (CORRECTED)	% Change	2009 (CORRECTED) PROPER (Money migration correction)	% Change
Top 1% Incomes	$ 483,252	$ 1,082,951	124%	$ 483,578	0.1%
Bottom 99% Incomes	$ 2,967,985	$ 5,406,247	82%	$6,004,619	102%
Top 1% / Bottom 99%	0.163	0.200	23%	0.081	-51%

Illustration 44: Table shows the exact data if the poor remains in their bracket even if their incomes goes up. The bottom or poor people actually getting richer and the rich actually loses a lot of their incomes.

The ratio of Top 1% to the Bottom 99%, is 0.163 in 1990 and subsequently declined by a massive 51%, to 0.081! The share of incomes of the rich, compared to the rest of the population, had declined radically. Essentially it means that the rich are well, getting less of the share of all incomes. The rich are getting richer? Not even close! Look at the erroneous struck out data of 2009 we crossed out; it mistakenly show the rich is getting richer, precisely the source of frustration of many people especially the Occupy Wall Streeters.

Well to those who are obsessed with inflation adjusts thingy, we did the calculations for you. We adjust all of the data, referenced to 2009, so it is of constant 2009 dollars. We however were unable to get a much more detail data for 1990 from the IRS, but managed to get the 1991 detail data, so we used 1991 instead.

To avoid boredom and to make for better understanding, we now present the inflation-adjusted data in a slightly different way as below.

| AGI Brackets | 1991 | | |
	NUMBER OF PEOPLE	TOTAL INCOME (CONSTANT 2009) [thousands]	GROUP
$1 under $5,000	9,932,886	23,048,796	
$5,000 under $10,000	12,239,167	90,628,396	
$10,000 under $15,000	9,125,718	114,723,946	
$15,000 under $20,000	11,018,394	195,071,613	
$20,000 under $25,000	7,868,521	180,248,136	
$25,000 under $30,000	6,484,106	177,231,178	
$30,000 under $40,000	9,691,977	321,589,314	
$40,000 under $50,000	7,873,620	319,933,938	
$50,000 under $75,000	21,163,566	1,217,998,805	
$75,000 under $100,000	11,390,205	1,015,153,507	
$100,000 under $200,000	3,571,629	451,601,028	
$200,000 under $250,000	2,306,274	422,680,070	
	291,634	79,382,936	
$250,000 under $500,000	425,904	183,069,169	
	250,134	107,516,814	
$500,000 under $1,000,000	118,350	117,864,231	
$1,000,000 under $1,500,000	52,019	188,206,684	
TOTAL	113,804,104	5,205,948,561	

To tally with IRS 2009 summary of historical data (09in01etr.xls) in order to get similar Top and Bottom numbers and incomes, returns with negative incomes are not included, as per the IRS data file and explanations

Illustration 45: Number of people and their incomes in 1991 (in constant 2009 Dollar)

Illustration 46

AGI Brackets	2009 Number of People	2009 Total Income (constant 2009) [thousands]	Group
$1 under $5,000	10,447,635	27,218,608	Bottom 99%
$5,000 under $10,000	2,220,335	92,407,278	
$10,000 under $15,000	2,444,512	155,465,805	
$15,000 under $20,000	1,400,228	199,017,560	
$20,000 under $25,000	10,033,887	225,167,737	
$25,000 under $30,000	8,662,392	237,994,230	
$30,000 under $40,000	14,371,647	499,879,773	
$40,000 under $50,000	10,796,412	483,088,798	
$50,000 under $75,000	18,694,893	1,149,068,817	
$75,000 under $100,000	11,463,725	990,337,913	
$100,000 under $200,000	13,522,048	1,801,446,897	
$200,000 under $250,000	1,262,536	280,228,936	
	156,044	34,635,037	
	1,126,087	324,859,787	
$250,000 under $500,000	650,372	265,623,642	Top 1%
$500,000 under $1,000,000	492,567	332,037,478	
$1,000,000 under $1,500,000	236,883	726,910,880	
TOTAL	**137,982,203**	**7,825,389,176**	

Illustration 46: Number of people and their incomes in 2009 (in constant 2009 Dollar)

Illustration 47

AGI Brackets	2009 (Modified) Number of People	Total Income (Modified) (constant 2009) [thousands]	Group
$1 under $5,000	8,616,935	22,449,194	Bottom 99%
$5,000 under $10,000	10,079,012	76,215,101	
$10,000 under $15,000	10,263,907	128,224,121	
$15,000 under $20,000	9,402,609	164,144,466	
$20,000 under $25,000	8,275,687	185,712,447	
$25,000 under $30,000	7,144,514	196,291,402	
$30,000 under $40,000	11,853,358	412,287,733	
$40,000 under $50,000	8,904,598	398,438,977	
$50,000 under $75,000	15,419,058	947,721,839	
$75,000 under $100,000	9,454,980	816,804,750	
$100,000 under $200,000	11,152,631	1,485,786,178	
$200,000 under $250,000	1,041,307	231,125,481	
	128,701	28,566,071	
	928,767	267,935,837	
$250,000 under $500,000	536,410	219,079,417	Top 1%
$500,000 under $1,000,000	406,256	273,855,808	
$1,000,000 under $1,500,000	195,375	599,537,039	
TOTAL	**113,854,104**	**6,454,175,859**	

Illustration 47: The number of people is reduced in equal proportion in order to arrive to similar total of 113.8 million back in 1991

AGI Brackets	1991		2009 (MODIFIED)		2009 ORIGINAL
	NUMBER OF PEOPLE	% OF TOTAL	NUMBER OF PEOPLE	% OF TOTAL	% OF TOTAL
$1 under $5,000	9,932,886	8.7%	8,616,935	7.6%	7.6%
$5,000 under $10,000	12,239,167	10.8%	10,079,012	8.9%	8.9%
$10,000 under $15,000	9,125,718	8.0%	10,263,907	9.0%	9.0%
$15,000 under $20,000	11,018,394	9.7%	9,402,609	8.3%	8.3%
$20,000 under $25,000	7,868,521	6.9%	8,275,687	7.3%	7.3%
$25,000 under $30,000	6,484,106	5.7%	7,144,514	6.3%	6.3%
$30,000 under $40,000	9,691,977	8.5%	11,853,358	10.4%	10.4%
$40,000 under $50,000	7,873,620	6.9%	8,904,598	7.8%	7.8%
$50,000 under $75,000	21,163,566	18.6%	15,419,058	13.5%	13.5%
$75,000 under $100,000	11,390,205	10.0%	9,454,980	8.3%	8.3%
$100,000 under $200,000	3,571,629	3.1%	11,152,631	9.8%	9.8%
$200,000 under $250,000	2,306,274	2.0%	1,041,307	0.9%	0.9%
	291,634	0.3%	128,701	0.1%	0.1%
$250,000 under $500,000	425,904	0.4%	928,767	0.8%	0.8%
	250,134	0.2%	536,410	0.5%	0.5%
$500,000 under $1,000,000	118,350	0.1%	406,256	0.4%	0.4%
$1,000,000 under $1,500,000	52,019	0.0%	195,375	0.2%	0.2%
TOTAL	113,804,104	100.0%	113,804,104	100.0%	100.0%

Illustration 48:
Table shows the modified 2009 numbers are similar in total to 1991, and also similar to its original 2009 ratio

Illustration 49: NUMBER OF PEOPLE

AGI Brackets	1991	2009 [MODIFIED]	1991 to 2009 MOVEMENT OF PEOPLE
$1 under $5,000	9,932,886	8,616,935	-1,315,951
$5,000 under $10,000	12,239,167	10,079,012	-2,160,155
$10,000 under $15,000	9,125,718	10,263,907	+1,138,189
$15,000 under $20,000	11,018,394	9,402,609	-1,615,785
$20,000 under $25,000	7,868,521	8,275,687	+407,166
$25,000 under $30,000	6,484,106	7,144,514	+660,408
$30,000 under $40,000	9,691,977	11,853,358	+2,161,381
$40,000 under $50,000	7,873,620	8,904,598	+1,030,978
$50,000 under $75,000	21,163,566	15,419,058	-5,744,508
$75,000 under $100,000	11,390,205	9,454,980	-1,935,225
$100,000 under $200,000	3,571,629	11,152,631	+7,581,002
$200,000 under $250,000	2,306,274	1,041,307	-1,264,967
	291,634	128,701	-162,933
$250,000 under $500,000	425,904	928,767	+502,863
	250,134	536,410	+286,276
$500,000 under $1,000,000	118,350	406,256	+287,906
$1,000,000 under $1,500,000	52,019	195,375	+143,356
TOTAL	113,804,104	113,804,104	0

Illustration 49: Table shows millions of people are lifted out from their brackets

Illustration 50: INCOME [2009 Dollars]

1991	2009 [MODIFIED]	1991 to 2009 MOVEMENT OF INCOME (thousand)
23,048,796	22,449,194	-599,602
90,628,396	76,215,101	-14,413,295
114,723,946	128,224,121	+13,500,174
195,071,613	164,144,466	-30,927,147
180,248,136	185,712,447	+5,464,311
177,231,178	196,291,402	+19,060,224
321,589,314	412,287,733	+90,698,419
319,933,938	398,438,977	+78,505,039
1,217,998,805	947,721,839	-270,276,966
1,015,153,507	816,804,750	-198,348,757
451,601,028	1,485,786,178	+1,034,185,150
422,680,070	231,125,481	-191,554,589
79,382,936	28,566,071	-50,816,865
183,069,169	267,935,837	+84,866,667
107,516,814	219,079,417	+111,562,603
117,864,231	273,855,808	+155,991,576
188,206,684	599,537,039	+411,330,355
5,205,948,561	6,454,175,859	+1,248,227,299

Illustration 50: Table shows billions and even trillion of dollars moved together when the people move up from their brackets

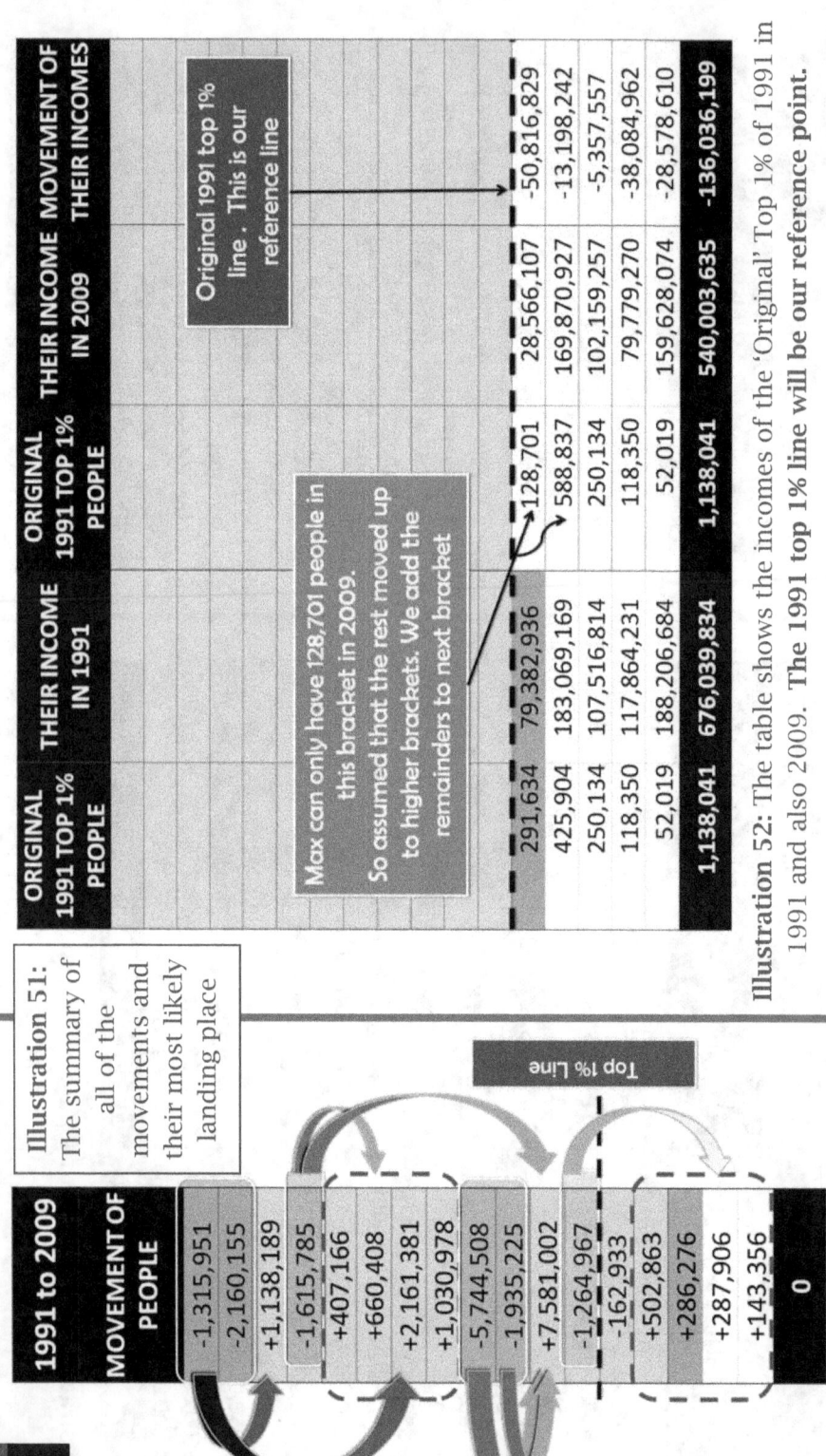

Illustration 51: The summary of all of the movements and their most likely landing place

Illustration 52: The table shows the incomes of the 'Original' Top 1% of 1991 in 1991 and also 2009. **The 1991 top 1% line will be our reference point.**

1991		2009 (MODIFIED)		1991 to 2009
ALL PEOPLE IN THE 1991 TOP 1% LINE	INCOME	ALL PEOPLE IN THE 1991 TOP 1% LINE	INCOME	MOVEMENT OF INCOME
291,634	79,382,936	128,701	28,566,071	-50,816,865
425,904	183,069,169	928,767	267,935,837	+84,866,667
250,134	107,516,814	536,410	219,079,417	+111,562,603
118,350	117,864,231	406,256	273,855,808	+155,991,576
52,019	188,206,684	195,375	599,537,039	+411,330,355
1,138,041	676,039,834	2,195,509	1,388,974,171	+712,934,337

We will use the top 1% line of 1991 to limit the original 1% people. Any increase in the number of people in the Top 1%, must come from the bottom

Illustration 53: The table shows the incomes of all the people that resides in the 1991 top 1% line.

	IN 1991		IN 2009	
	Number of People	Income (thousands)	Number of People	Income (thousands)
Total	113,804,104	5,205,948,561	113,804,104	6,454,175,859
Original 1% of 1991	1,138,041	676,039,834	1,138,041	540,003,635
Original 99% of 1991	112,666,063	4,529,908,727	112,666,063	5,914,172,225

Continue in next table….

When we use the original 1991's top-1% line, we can actually see what those original Top 1% and Bottom 99% in 1991 brought in 2009. Table in the next page will show the exact incomes the Bottom 99% who crossed the line in 2009, carried to the top.

	IN 2009	
	Number of People	Income (thousands)
Original 1991 Top 1%	1,138,041	540,003,635
Original 1991 Top 1% + Bottomers that moved up in 2009	2,195,509	1,388,974,171
Bottomers that crossed the 1991 top 1% line in 2009	1,057,468	848,970,536

Now, this is how much total income the previous Bottom 99% who rose to the Top 1% carried with them in 2009....

Or **$802,833** each 'poor' person

Illustration 54: The tables show how much each of the bottomers is carrying to the top, thus skewing the data for the Top 1%

Let say these newcomers came from the closest bracket that lost 1.3 mil people in 2009 (the $200k - 250k bracket), with average income of $183,274 in 1991

$75,000 under $100,000	11,390,205	9,454,980	-1,935,225
$100,000 under $200,000	3,571,629	11,152,631	7,581.002
$200,000 under $250,000	2,306,274	1,041,307	-1,264,967
	291,634	128,701	-162,933
$250,000 under $500,000	425,904	928,767	502,863
	250,134	536,410	286,276
$500,000 under $1,000,000	118,350	406,256	287,906
$1,000,000 under $1,500,000	52,019	195,375	143,356
TOTAL	**113,804,104**	**113,804,104**	**0**

So, their old income would be
1,057,468 x $183,274 = $ 193,806,373,865

Illustration 55: Calculating the old income of the original 1991 Bottom 99% people who crossed the 1991 top 1% line in 2009.

	IN 1991		IN 2009		% Change in Income
	Number of People	Income (thousands)	Number of People	Income (thousands)	
Original 1991 Top 1%	1,138,041	676,039,834	1,138,041	540,003,635	-20.1%
Original 1991 Bottom 99%	112,666,063	4,529,908,727	112,666,063	5,914,172,225	30.6%
Poverty Line ($6,400)	15,463,121	55,302,833	13,656,441	73,259,261	32.5%
Bottom 1991 that crossed the 1991 Top 1% line	1,057,468	193,806,374	1,057,468	848,970,536	338.1%
New Entrants into the economy	0	0	24,178,099	1,371,213,317	

Illustration 56: Table shows the actual wealth of the Bottom 99% of 1991, in 2009. The poor is not getting poorer, they are getting richer! The original rich of 1991 saw their total incomes, declined. Table also shows the wealth created by new entrants into the economy.

ORIGINAL TOP 1% OF 1991

↓ 20.1%

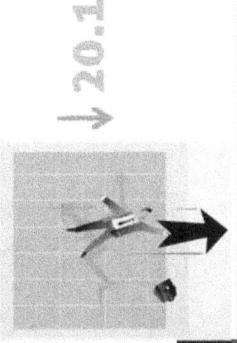

ORIGINAL BOTTOM 99% OF 1991

↑ 30.6%

ORIGINAL BOTTOM 99% OF 1991 THAT CROSSED INTO THE 1% LINE

↑ 338.1%

	IN 1991	IN 2009	% Change in
	Income per Person (USD)	Income Per Person (USD)	Income Per Person
Original 1991 Top 1%	594,038	474,503	-20.1%
Original 1991 Bottom 99%	40,207	52,493	30.6%
Poverty Line ($6,400)	3,576	5,364	50.0%
Bottom 1991 that crossed the 1991 Top 1% line	183,274	802,833	338.1%
New entrants into the economy	0	56,713	

Illustration 57: Everyone grew their incomes, except the 'poor' rich Top 1%ers of 1991! Their incomes declined perhaps due to heavy competition from the bottom? One will not stay rich forever (and long!). The real answer is, it is just the way the statistics are calculated, the Top 1% is too crowded with new people

Regardless of whether the data is inflation adjusted or not, it would still show that the Bottom 99% created most of the new wealth (they are the majority anyway). Data and the many scary studies portrayed by our economists are wrong; the poor is the one who created trillions of dollars of new wealth. So why was the rich named as the creator?

In a later part of this book, we shall show some real examples of who are the actual poor, who made it in life, but then included into the Top 1% group erroneously, but for now, have a look at the summarized number of people who migrated from the bottom, to the top, in the following illustration.

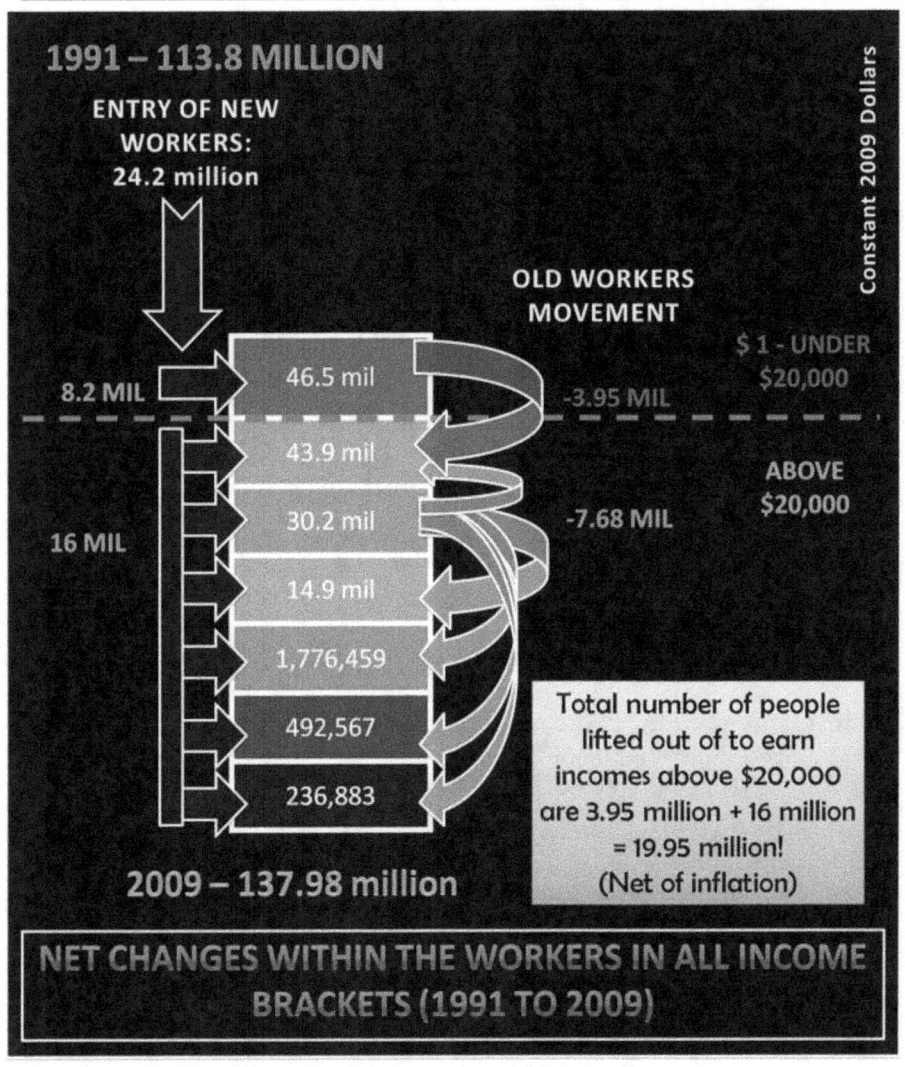

Illustration 58: Net changes within the workers in all income brackets from 1991 to 2009

In Illustration 58, initially they were 113.8 million people (back in 1991). As the years progressed, more and more new people entered the workforce. By the year 2009, 24.2 million new people have entered the workforce and the economy must provide for each one of them a place. A majority of them managed to find a place above the $20,000 a year line (16 million workers) and only 8.2 million 'chose' to reside at the bottom. Meanwhile, the original 113.8 million workers themselves, experienced tremendous movements, when 3.95 million moved out of the bottom bracket and a record 7.68 million, jumped to various higher brackets of the middle and upper incomes. In total, 27 million people changed their lives for the better.

We must stress once more, that it is very apparent that the poor are doing much better than before. They grew their incomes by the most, while adding more people into all of the middle and upper brackets. The majority of the people residing at the top right now came from the bottom; they are the friends and neighbors of the Occupiers themselves.

The following is another interesting fact about the economy. The economy is a machine of wealth generation. If the economy is given ten thousand fresh poor people, it will be able to assign them, given enough time, the following set of incomes:

Fresh entrants into the economy	
Adjusted Gross Income	No of people
All new entrants	**10,000**
No adjusted gross income	513
$1 under $5,000	303
$5,000 under $10,000	1,221
$10,000 under $15,000	1,063
$15,000 under $20,000	818
$20,000 under $25,000	766
$25,000 under $30,000	394
$30,000 under $40,000	555
$40,000 under $50,000	590
$50,000 under $75,000	1,454
$75,000 under $100,000	896
$100,000 under $200,000	1,018
$200,000 under $500,000	306
$500,000 under $1,000,000	60
$1,000,000 under $1,500,000	18
$1,500,000 under $2,000,000	8
$2,000,000 under $5,000,000	13
$5,000,000 under $10,000,000	3
$10,000,000 or more	2

Illustration 59: Table showing the expected distribution of people in the economy given enough time for the capitalistic economy to work its 'magic'

Using a simple definition of poor as those earning less than $5,000 of 1990 dollars, then there will be 816 person sitting in the poor bracket, and 9,184 will be sitting comfortably in the middle and upper brackets. This long-term economic potential will continuously adjusts the existing number of people in each bracket, if those brackets have not reached their long-term potential. The long-term potential was calculated from IRS constant dollars data of taxpayers over a long period of time, where if the economy is given enough time, it will assign 8.1% of the workers, into the poor bracket, and 91.9% into the middle and upper brackets.

In our presented data earlier for 1990, the economic potential was not yet achieved. The economic distribution is shown below (as a number of people in each bracket):

1990 Tax Returns				
	All Returns	Sum of Poor & The Rest	Current Distribution	Preferred Distribution
All returns	113,717,138			
No adjusted gross income	904,876			
$1 under $5,000	16,478,272	17,383,148	15.3%	8.16%
$5,000 under $10,000	14,952,855			
$10,000 under $15,000	13,922,750			
$15,000 under $20,000	11,543,228			
$20,000 under $25,000	9,572,317			
$25,000 under $30,000	7,838,225			
$30,000 under $40,000	12,282,786			
$40,000 under $50,000	8,837,067			
$50,000 under $75,000	10,944,102			
$75,000 under $100,000	3,276,142			
$100,000 under $200,000	2,329,562			
$200,000 under $500,000	644,027			
$500,000 under $1,000,000	130,252			
$1,000,000 under $1,500,000	29,060			
$1,500,000 under $2,000,000	11,581			
$2,000,000 under $5,000,000	15,331			
$5,000,000 under $10,000,000	3,184			
$10,000,000 or more	1,522	96,333,990	84.7%	91.84%

Illustration 60: The number of people in the brackets of the 1990 tax returns were not in the preferred distribution of the economy

The economy will continuously move the people in each bracket, towards achieving the long-term economic potential. What would happen if we allow the economy to reassign the workers according to its long-term potential?

Year XXXX (Economic Potential Achieved)			
	1990	Given Enough Time	Changes
All returns	113,717,138	113,717,138	
No adjusted gross income	904,876	5,836,781	+4,931,905
$1 under $5,000	16,478,272	3,445,416	-13,032,856
$5,000 under $10,000	14,952,855	13,879,313	-1,073,542
$10,000 under $15,000	13,922,750	12,084,528	-1,838,222
$15,000 under $20,000	11,543,228	9,297,354	-2,245,874
$20,000 under $25,000	9,572,317	8,714,837	-857,480
$25,000 under $30,000	7,838,225	4,478,527	-3,359,698
$30,000 under $40,000	12,282,786	6,306,582	-5,976,204
$40,000 under $50,000	8,837,067	6,707,042	-2,130,025
$50,000 under $75,000	10,944,102	16,535,064	+5,590,962
$75,000 under $100,000	3,276,142	10,188,688	+6,912,546
$100,000 under $200,000	2,329,562	11,572,157	+9,242,595
$200,000 under $500,000	644,027	3,484,792	+2,840,765
$500,000 under $1,000,000	130,252	679,664	+549,412
$1,000,000 under $1,500,000	29,060	201,152	+172,092
$1,500,000 under $2,000,000	11,581	94,592	+83,011
$2,000,000 under $5,000,000	15,331	145,709	+130,378
$5,000,000 under $10,000,000	3,184	39,573	+36,389
$10,000,000 or more	1,522	25,368	+23,846

Illustration 61: Table showing the distribution of income once the economic potential is achieved

As you can see, a total of 25.5 million people will be able to move up the rungs. There will be less poor people, and certainly, more of the well to do.

'Unfortunately', the capitalistic economy is burdened with an additional job that is much tougher, that is, there are new entrants into the economy every year, continuously that it must absorbs and assigns them a place as well. The economy performed this job beautifully as well. In reality, it is not the economy that performs; it is the people themselves. A fair and free economy will enable anyone to succeed.

The addition of the new workers will make the economy to be always chasing its long-term potential, but sure enough, given enough time, it will get closer and closer, as our numerous data had shown

Before we close this chapter off, take a simple look at the following illustration which shows how many people were lifted out from poverty, from our 1991 to 2009 inflation adjusted data comparison we did previously (this include the recent economic crisis, otherwise the number will be much higher).

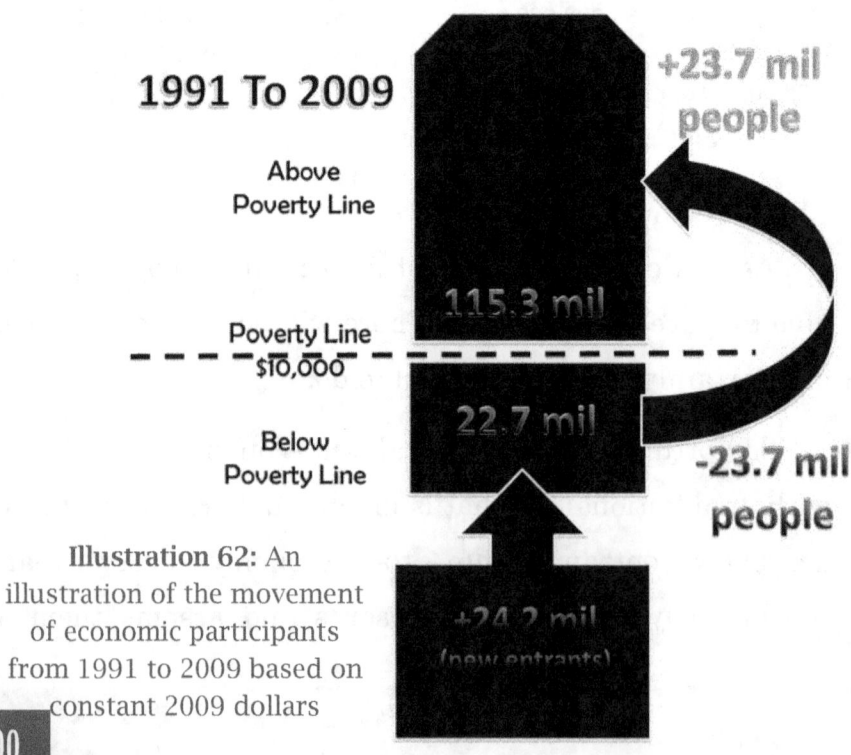

Illustration 62: An illustration of the movement of economic participants from 1991 to 2009 based on constant 2009 dollars

BEST WAY TO COMPARE INCOME

Using minimum poverty line to show affordability

There is a better way to compare the classes. We suggest the use of a "minimum poverty line" to show affordability. After that, there is little point to compare the classes. Did we mention that within the classes, especially the top most and the bottom most, there are massive differences between individuals within each class, when compared to their own peers in their very own class? Please look back at the "Classes Within Class" topic.

This is always the case when comparing income, intelligence, abilities, sports and so forth. Your performance is only dictated by how much you want to achieve. There will always be someone who will have higher IQ score than you have, runs faster than you do, swims faster than you can, are taller than you, or in whatever things you want to compare with. You can of course beat them, but someone else is bound to beat you back. Nobody will be at the top forever, the fastest runner will not be the fastest a few years down the road, and similarly, the rich will not stay rich forever, and the poor will not stay poor forever. What is important is that everyone must keep learning and finding new ways to improve oneself. How good we are compared to someone else (a genius for example), is not important because geniuses are a rarity. They are not the majority. If we are not happy and want society to control everything, it will limit the achievement achievable by society. Would you ask the people with higher IQ to score less so that other people (the bottom scorer) would feel better? Would you ask the athlete in the Olympics to run slower, maybe at the average speed, so that everybody else would feel better? What is the point of limiting people's capabilities? Earning money is also an ability. Those that can create value and can do things more efficiently are rewarded with more money. Limiting that will have an adverse effect to the society as a whole. Stealing their hard work will also have an adverse effect on society.

If everyone can run in your class, that's good enough—how fast each person can run does not matter. The important thing is, everyone can run. We urge everyone to stop comparing how fast each of us can run. Help each other to ensure that all can run, not who is the fastest. In the economy, we have to ensure that as many as possible can afford the basics of life, but beyond that, it is not that important. The basics of life, once obtained, will enable anyone to start pursuing their dreams. That, is what's important.

Again, one of the most basic success criteria of the economy is measured by how many are lifted out of low incomes or poverty, not by how much the top is making compared to yours. Using another analogy, it is similar as to how many people can read (the literacy rate), not how many can solve complicated math that only the top 1% (the brightest) can solve. Society can assist people in getting out of poverty so that they can afford the basics, after that, it is up to that person to go as high as he or she want, IF he or she wants.

Whenever the top most and bottom most are compared, there are a large section of the population, who sits in the middle, being ignored (the elephants). The middle section is actually the majority and it is essential for them to enjoy better lives.

YEAR	2 people		
1959........	947	1983 6/.....	3,242
1960........	962	1984........	3,381
1961........	971	1985........	3,499
1962........	981	1986........	3,569
1963........	994	1987 7/.....	3,699
1964........	1,008	1988........	3,852
1965........	1,024	1989........	4,038
1966........	1,054	1990........	4,255
1967 1/.....	1,084	1991 8/.....	4,433
1968........	1,131	1992 9/.....	4,569
1969........	1,192	1993 10/....	4,707
1970........	1,263	1994........	4,831
1971 2/.....	1,317	1995........	4,967
1972........	1,362	1996........	5,117
1973........	1,448	1997........	5,237
1974 3/.....	1,606	1998........	5,317
1975........	1,753	1999 11/....	5,432
1976........	1,856	2000 12/....	5,618
1977........	1,976	2001........	5,785
1978........	2,125	2002........	5,878
1979 4/.....	2,363	2003........	6,008
1980........	2,682	2004 14/....	6,168
1981 5/.....	2,959	2005........	6,378
1982........	3,141	2006........	6,584
		2007........	6,770
		2008........	7,026
Data from Census Bureau		2009........	6,996
		2010........	7,109

Illustration 63: Table showing the minimum threshold income in dollars for a person to be classified under poverty from 1950 to 2010. This threshold is far higher than the worldwide established standard. The World Bank defines poverty as having income of $1.25 a day or $456/year income. So, are those people living under this US poverty threshold really are poor?

PART 2:
HIDDEN STATISTICS

Now we hope you understood why the OWS's rich and the poor gap is actually "much ado about nothing". It occurs due to wrong comparison methods which lead to terrible interpretations.

We will show some of the statistics that they conveniently "forgot "to show everyone in this section of the book.

Our data are all correct and interpreted correctly. No hiding and no BS.

BIGGEST CONTRIBUTORS TO TAXES

It is no secret that the top few percent of the population paid the most taxes compared to the rest. Check out just how much and whether there is equality and accountability in our nation finances.

Tax Share Burden

The truth is, the top 1% paid the most taxes into the coffers of the government, ensuring enough money for everyone else. Check out this article, "Top 1% Paid More in Federal Income Taxes Than Bottom 95% in '07" at http://economix.blogs.nytimes.com/2009/07/30/top-1-paid-more showing a nice graph of declining tax share of the bottom 95% and the increasing share of the top 5%. In later part of this section, you will see plenty of graphs, just as damning, on the 'free loaders' who demand everything and never think of paying.

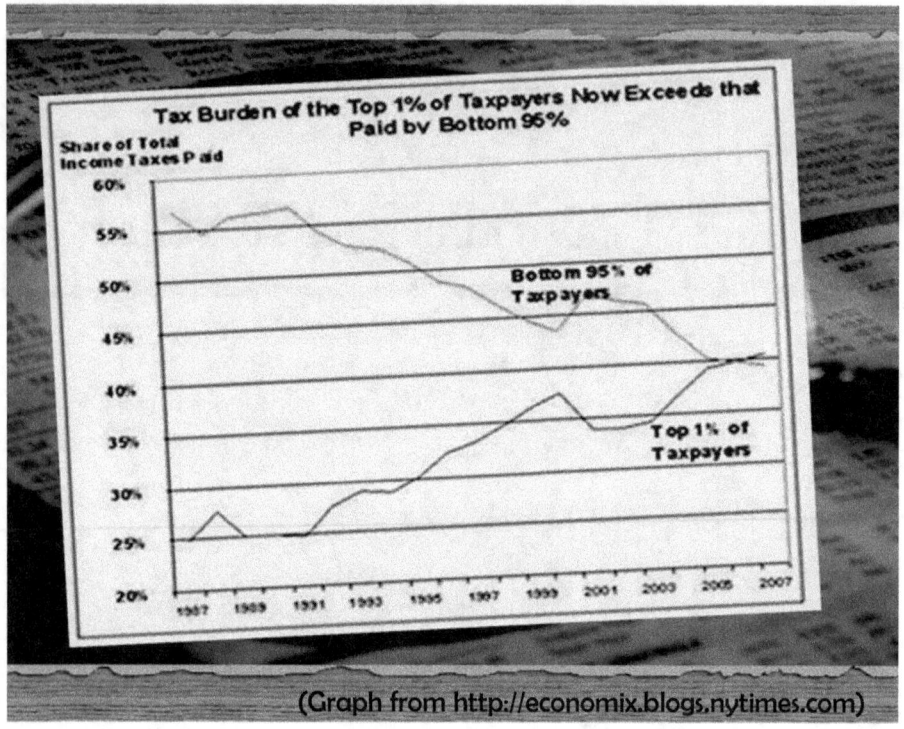

Illustration 64: Graph is from economix.blog.nytimes.com. This is taken for illustration purposes only.

According to the Internal Revenue Services (IRS), the top 1% paid disproportionately higher share of income taxes at 37% of the total. That's 37 times more than the rest (assuming each, one percent of taxpayers should be paying exactly one percent in taxes).

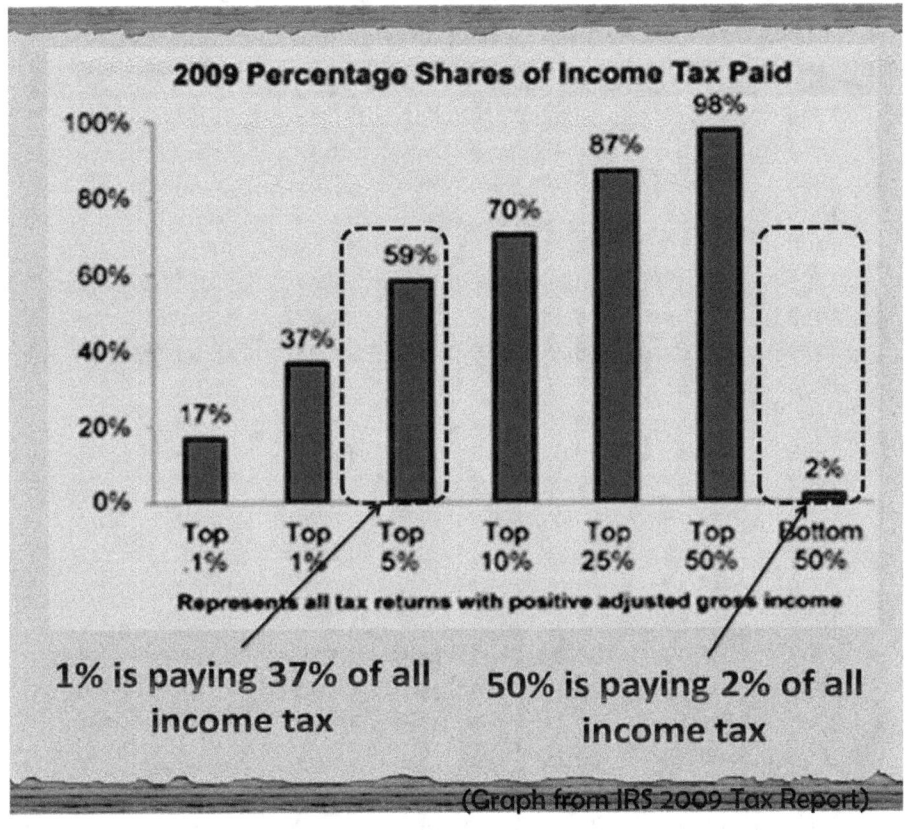

Illustration 65: Graph is from the IRS 2009 Tax report. The top 1% is shouldering 37% of all tax burden. They do not shoulder 1% of the tax burden but 37 times more (if equal share for each American) but still can only cast 1 vote each.

Let us look into the IRS data in depth and show the fact of the matter, that the top 1% is not shirking their responsibility in paying taxes as accused.

TOTAL INCOME TAX SHARE (PERCENTAGE)

	Top 1%	2-5%	6-10%	11-25%	26-50%	51-100%
1986	25.75	16.82	12.12	21.33	17.52	6.46
1987	24.81	18.45	12.35	21.31	17.01	6.07
1988	27.58	18.04	11.66	20.56	16.44	5.72
1989	25.24	18.70	11.84	21.44	16.95	5.83
1990	25.13	18.51	11.72	21.66	17.17	5.81
1991	24.82	18.56	12.44	21.47	17.23	5.48
1992	27.54	18.34	12.13	20.47	16.46	5.06
1993	29.01	18.35	11.88	20.03	15.92	4.81
1994	28.86	18.66	11.93	20.10	15.68	4.77
1995	30.26	18.65	11.84	19.61	15.03	4.61
1996	32.31	18.66	11.54	18.81	14.36	4.32
1997	33.17	18.70	11.33	18.47	14.05	4.28
1998	34.75	19.09	11.20	17.65	13.10	4.21
1999	36.18	19.27	11.00	17.09	12.46	4.00
2000	37.42	19.05	10.86	16.68	12.08	3.91
2001	33.89	19.36	11.64	18.01	13.13	3.97
2002	33.71	20.09	11.94	18.16	12.60	3.50
2003	34.27	20.09	11.48	18.04	12.65	3.46
2004	36.89	20.23	11.07	16.67	11.85	3.30
2005	39.38	20.29	10.63	15.69	10.94	3.07
2006	39.89	20.25	10.65	15.47	10.75	2.99
2007	40.42	20.20	10.59	15.37	10.52	2.89
2008	38.02	20.70	11.22	16.40	10.96	2.70
2009	36.73	21.93	11.81	16.83	10.45	2.25

Illustration 66: Table shows the share percentage of federal income tax of each income class

The Top 1% as well as the Top 5% is paying more taxes, despite their 'supposedly' lower imagined tax rates (this is another contentious issue at the moment). Why are they paying more? This is none other than because they are making more money — much more money than the rest. We prefer to reword it as, "they are creating more wealth for all of the economy to enjoy". The Bottom 95% residents? Well, they are experiencing lower and lower share of taxes. Yet they are making serious false accusations on the rich; painting them as evil and greedy lot, stingy and irresponsible, but the fact is, the lower someone is on the income ladder, the less the person is contributing towards supporting America. Even more shocking, their contribution is getting lesser and lesser over the years.

Each income class below the top 5% are shouldering less of the tax burden in the year 2009 compared to 1986.

INCOME BRACKET	1986	2009	% Change
Top 1%	25.8	36.7	42.6
2-5%	16.8	21.9	30.4
6-10%	12.1	11.8	-2.6
11-25%	21.3	16.8	-21.1
26-50%	17.5	10.5	-40.4
51-100%	6.5	2.3	-65.2

Illustration 67: Table shows tax burden share by income class in 2009 compared to 1986

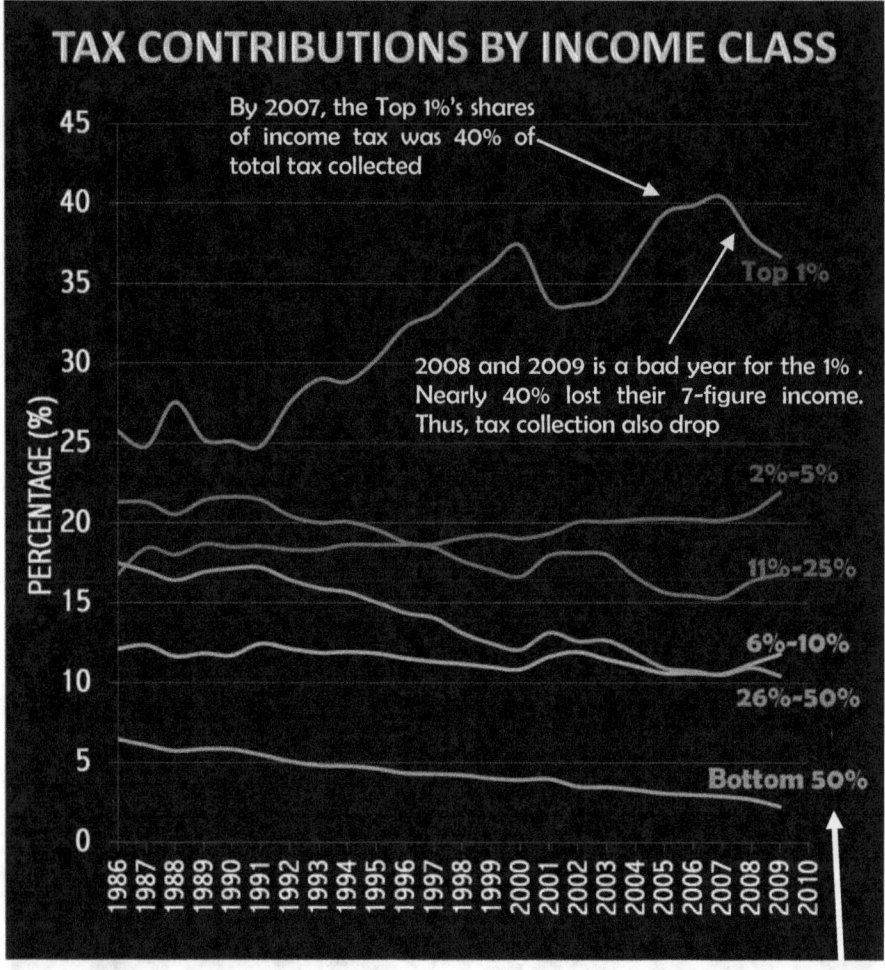

TAX CONTRIBUTIONS BY INCOME CLASS

By 2007, the Top 1%'s shares of income tax was 40% of total tax collected

2008 and 2009 is a bad year for the 1%. Nearly 40% lost their 7-figure income. Thus, tax collection also drop

Top 1%

2%-5%

11%-25%

6%-10%

26%-50%

Bottom 50%

Illustration 68: Graph shows that the top 1% share of the federal income tax has increased from 25% to 37% while the bottom 50% is now only supporting 2% of federal taxes. Table comparing tax burden share by income class in 2009 compared to 1986

By 2009, the bottom 50%'s shares of income tax has dropped by 65%

As you can see from the graph, tax burden (percentage of all tax collected) borne by the Top 1% of tax payers (about 1.4 million taxpayers) has increased by 43%

since 1986 while the tax shared by the Bottom 50% of tax payers consisting of at least 69 million people has decreased by a staggering 65%. Accusing a particular group in the economy of paying less taxes is one thing, but accusing that particular group of paying less taxes, while your own group is the one that actually paying less, is simply not acceptable! Stop accusing others, if you are not paying your own fair share. Everyone must chip in and only those who really deserve help are helped. Paying tax is a patriotic thing to do and is a source of pride for citizens. It is pathetic and not honorable to keep whining and not contributing, especially when they are given the chance to improve. Those of you who pay taxes, should be proud and make sure the government makes full and good use of your money.

The upper middle-income earners tax burden also increased in the double digit, not just for the Top 1%ers. Collectively, the middle-income earners are shouldering almost the entire leftover tax burden that is not already forced on the top 1%'s shoulder. We put the upper-middle income group as those who earn above $100,000 a year, thus putting them into the Top 2%-12% of all earners. As you can see on the next graph, collectively the Top 10% is currently paying a full two-third of all income taxes collected by the IRS.

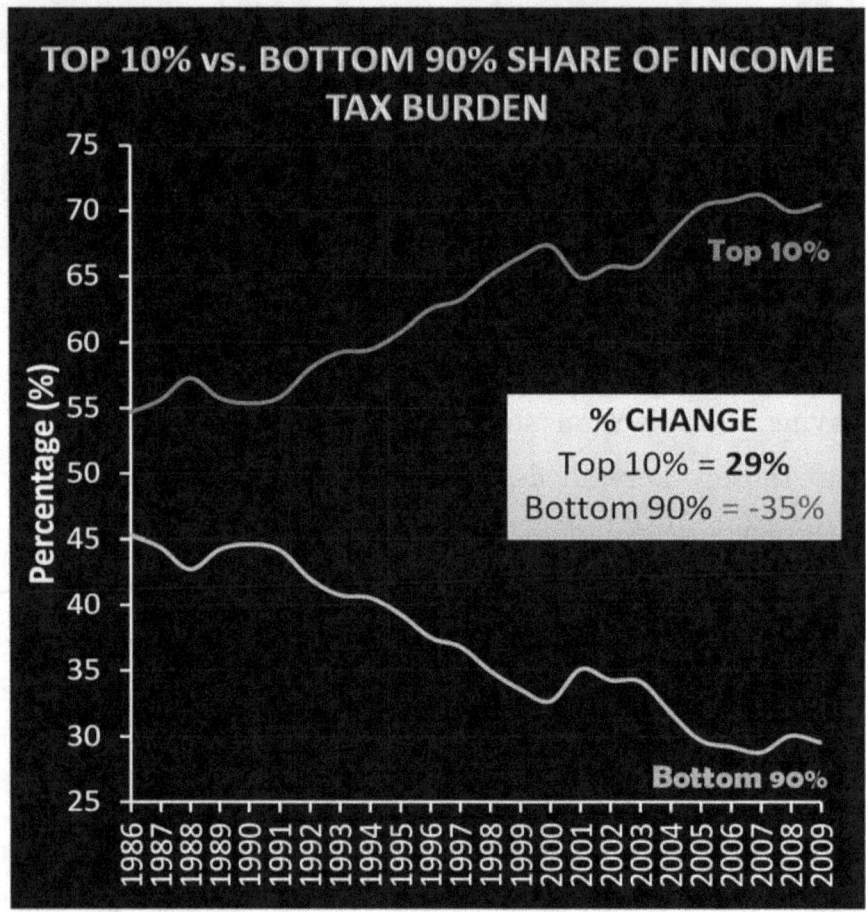

TOP 10% vs. BOTTOM 90% SHARE OF INCOME TAX BURDEN

Top 10%

% CHANGE
Top 10% = **29%**
Bottom 90% = -35%

Bottom 90%

Illustration 69: Graph shows the Top-10% vs. Bottom-90% share of the federal income tax. In 2009, those earning above $100,000 is 12.7% of all 138mil tax filers.

Well, for the 99% obsessed people, we will also show the comparison of 1% vs. 99% graph, just so they don't go red in the face shouting saying that we are side skirting their issues. (You must know by now that the 1% line is somewhat stupid, data represented by that line can also be concluded in the wrong way and there are better ways to compare income levels).

YOU DON'T REPRESENT US—ANSWERING OCCUPY WALL STREET

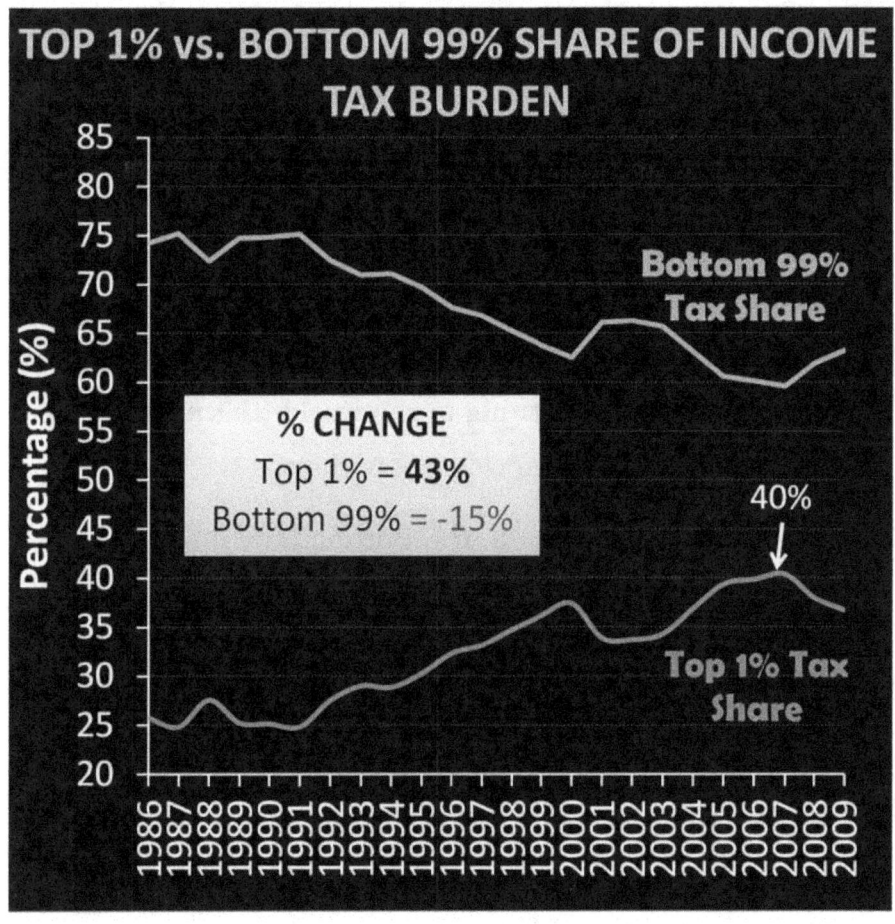

Illustration 70: Graph shows the Top-1 vs. Bottom-99% income tax shares burden. It still shows that the Top 1% burden has increased by 43% since 1986, whereas the 99% has declined by 15%. In fact, at the height of the boom, in 2007 the Top 1% shoulders a whopping 40.4% of the income tax burden (a 57% increased in 20 years)! That one-percent of all income earners is shouldering nearly half of all the income tax collected in the USA. How is this not paying their dues?

The data do not lie, and we are sure they will brush off this issue. For the government to balance its budget, everyone must chip in, contribute their fair share, and stop pointing fingers. Government should assist, but only to those who really need it. Not all in the Bottom 99% need all kinds of help from the government. Some help can be declined, and should be declined. It is not always yours to take. Do not be greedy because there is always a price to be paid. As we already mentioned clearly in our book series, there is nothing in the world that is truly free. All must be paid for, one way or another.

By looking at the data, the Bottom 50% must increase their tax contribution by 300%, just to go back to the level they were paying in the 80s. Else, they have to force their government to shrink spending by eliminating many social "free-rides" like free education (public school), Social Security, Medicare, Medicaid, Government Pensions and so forth. The Top 1% would not feel this cut at all, as they have their own money to cover themselves.

We are however not a fan of big taxes, as we know the government is not prudent in managing OPM (other people's money) and in Book 3 of the 259 Trillion Vs 5 Trillion series, we did propose on how to manage the budget without resorting to large tax increases.

How Much Tax Do Each Of The Classes Pays

Now, let us look at the amount each person in each income class pays in taxes.

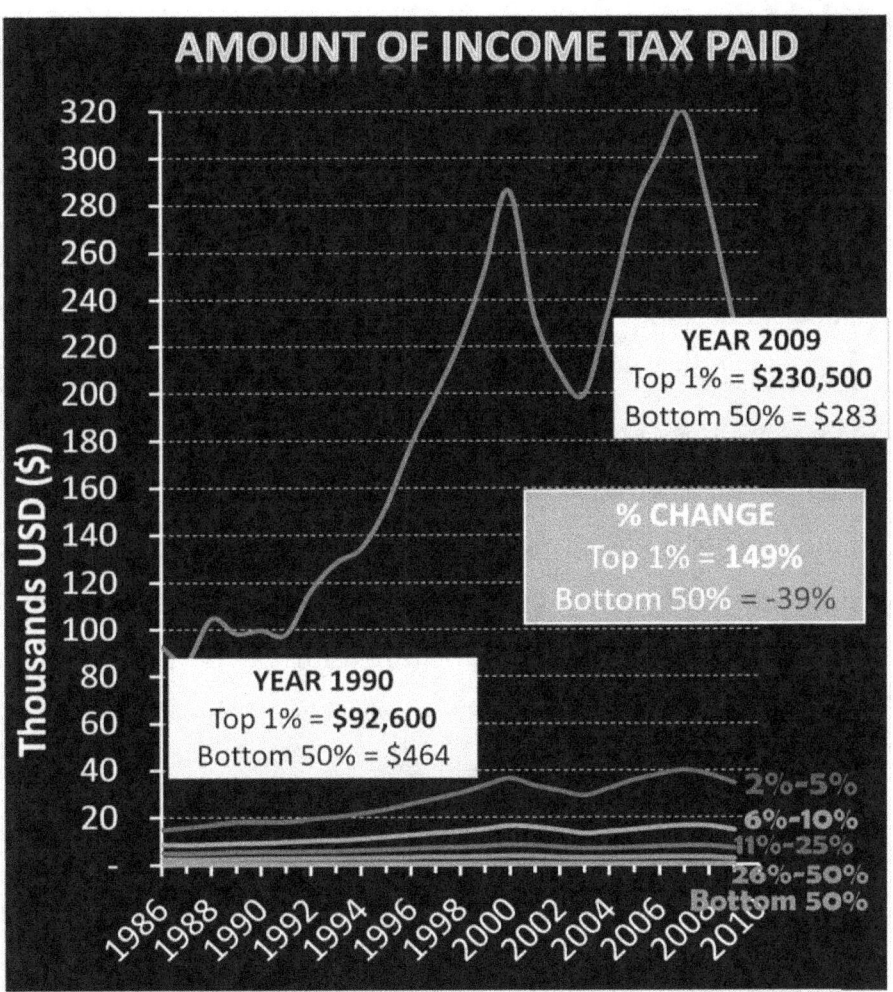

Illustration 71: Graph shows the average tax paid in dollars, for each person in their respective bracket

Income Bracket	Taxes Paid In 1986	Taxes Paid In 2009	Change in Tax Paid
Top 1%	$ 92,559	$ 230,496	149%
2-5%	$ 15,122	$ 34,400	127%
6-10%	$ 8,711	$ 14,821	70%
11-25%	$ 5,111	$ 7,042	38%
26-50%	$ 2,520	$ 2,622	4%
Bottom 50%	$ 464	$ 283	-39%

Illustration 72: Table comparing the average tax paid by each person in each income class in 2009 compared to 1986

The Top 1% increased their tax contribution by the most, increasing by 149%. That's about 2.5 times as what it was back in 1986. The Top 2-5% also increased their tax contributions, by 127%. All groups, contributed more, except the Bottom 50% — its contributions declined by a massive 39%! Each person paid $464 back in 1986, and no doubt, they are now the very same parents of today's children, and yet their grown up children are now paying only a lowly figure of $283. If we correct these numbers for inflation, it will be even lower.

We expect the bottom 50%, to contribute fairly to the country. They are raking in too much government assistance, and contributing lesser and lesser. Government assistance is not a birthright; it is only possible if the government can afford it!

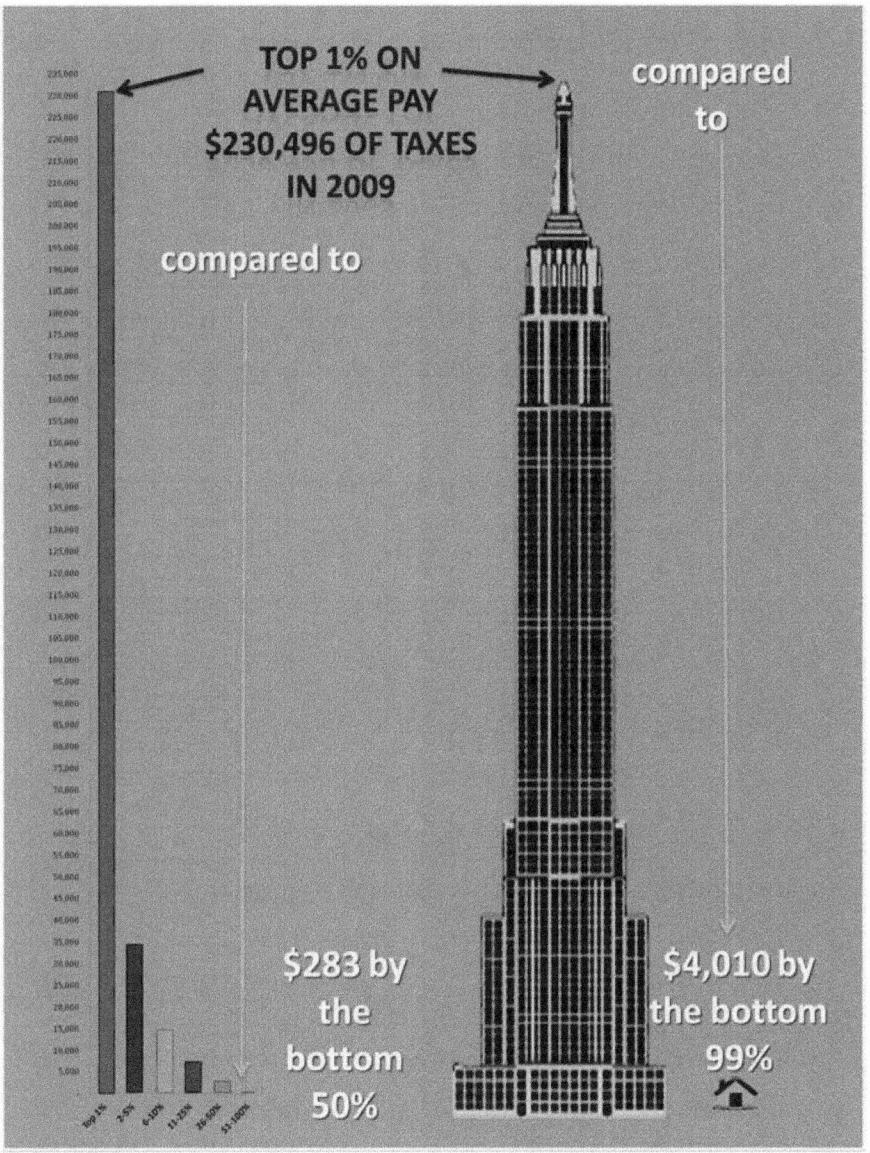

Illustration 73: Graphs shows how far apart the average tax paid by each income groups.

In 2009, the Top 1% paid an average of $230,496 in taxes while the Bottom 50% paid only $283

These same OWS supporters themselves will later regret their action of supporting the movement in the first place, when their actions resulted in the opposite effect from what they advocate. Those smart and hardworking people, who contribute significantly more to society than anyone else in general, will be frustrated and may even leave the country for good. There is no benefit in this 'practice' of selectively targeting the rich, simply because they 'control' more. The rich can simply move their money to tax haven countries or sunnier and friendlier places, resulting in a permanent loss of wealth in the nation.

We will be very concern if the Top 1%, who are making the most money as well as controlling the most assets in the country (only on per capita basis), is also not paying the most tax to the country. The fact is, they are already contributing the lion's share of the 'income pie' of the government. Thus there is little cause of alarm at the moment. During the financial crisis, all segments of the population were affected, and of course it hit the rich disproportionately more. The rich is more exposed and risked more of their wealth while trying to make the world better, therefore they are hit more if the economy declines, or rewarded more if the economy performs well. However, most of the rich are also more financially educated and able to judge and react better to protect their wealth, for if they fail, the whole country will go down with them. The rich also happened to shield other economic participants by absorbing most of the losses themselves, protecting the larger public (refer to data in "The Risk Takers" section) during each economic crisis.

Well, the obtuse will say that of course the rich are paying more in taxes because they earn more than the poor do. They will then change the subject and go on to say that the rich are paying lower tax rates— so, let's see if the tax rate percentages will make the OWS right 'again'. They were saying that the rich is taxed less in percentage compared to the Bottom 99%. According to them, the Billionaire's secretary paid more in taxes than the Billionaire did himself! (Referring to Warren Buffett). Buffett contributed more in dollar terms, than his secretary did. If he wanted to pay more, he can and should.

So let's confirm whether this accusation is correct or not.

Tax Rate Of Each Income Group

Look at the following illustration.

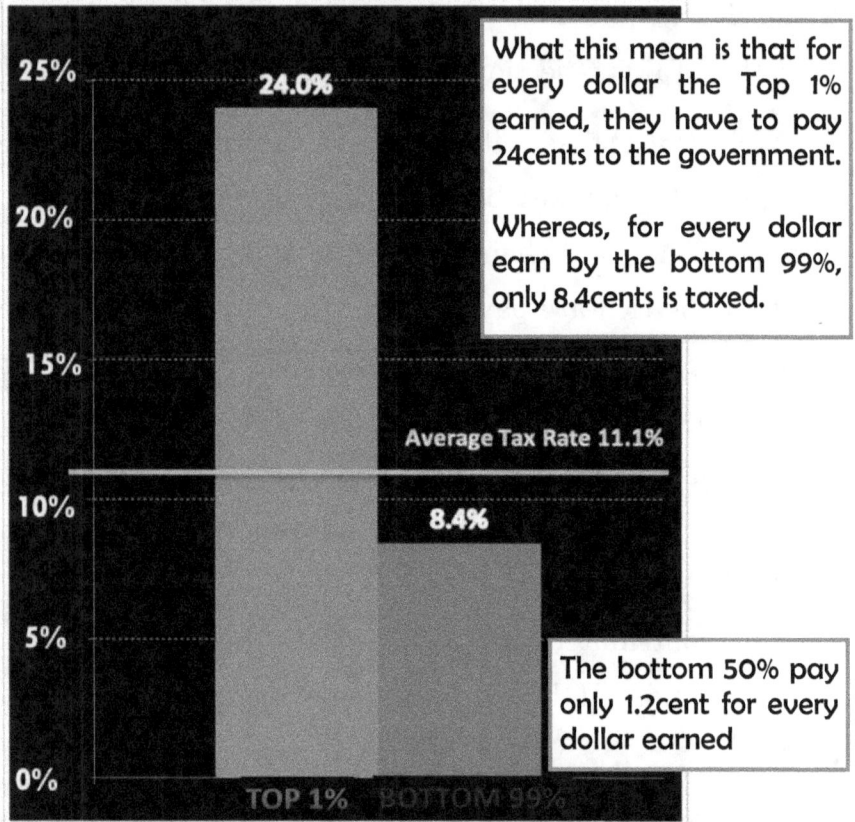

Illustration 74: Graph shows 2009 average tax rate paid by the top 1% and the bottom 99%

Lo and behold, the Top 1% is taxed at a rate of 24%, which is way above the national tax average of 11.1% in 2009. But wait! What about the bottom 99%? They are taxed at a rate of only 8.9% (which is 20% below the average rate) and if you look even further and eliminate the medium income earners and get to the bottom groups (the bottom 50% of about 69 million people), then the rate drop drastically to a low of 1.8%! That is not including the bottom of the bottom, of about 2 million people, who pay at a rate of 0%. Yes, NO TAX whatsoever. When federal aid is included, a large swath of even the bottom taxpayers, are not paying a dime, at all! That is unacceptable. Asked a lot and not giving any in return? Are they really that poor? We found one study from the Heritage.org which mentioned that today's poor are not poor at all, they can afford big houses, big cars, some even with more than one car, they have air conditioners, microwaves, and get this, even big screen TVs. (More on this in the next topic on why the bottom most income earners in the IRS data may not be as poor as we think they are).

The reason OWS says they represent the bottom 99% is because the data and statistics of the bottom 50% is abysmal. By including the rest of the middle income and upper income (the 2-5% are those earning six figure incomes) into their group, then their abysmal statistics become much better. The OWS do not represent this 2-5% or the 10%. They do not even represent the bottom people. What they represent is anybody's guess, but it could have similarity with early Nazism, socialism or communism.

As an example, if we include the Top-49% into the Bottom-50% thus creating the "Bottom 99%", then the average tax rate jump 400% to 8.4% instead of the infinitesimal amount of only 1.8% for the bottom 50%. The OWS is smooching and scrounging stats from the very people that they supposedly hate... the "rich", since the 2-10% group is by definition, a rich group in itself.

We also found that many in the Bottom 50% are actually well to do individuals — there are millions of them (details in "WHY THE BOTTOM MOST CLASS INCOME EARNERS IN THE IRS DATA MAY BE RICHER THAN WE THINK"). So, what exactly are they so angry about?

By the data provided here, thus far, it seems the rich people in the Top-5% bracket are the ones that should be complaining. They do not get many exemptions in their taxes (as certain exemptions are abolished at certain income level) and at the same time, they pay those taxes at much higher rates. They contributed to Social Security at higher amounts, but when they finally retire and are eligible to withdraw their share, their benefits are taxed yet again if their income level is above a certain amount. Well, all of those plus many more, and yet they are accused of all the wrong things.

Table 1. All Returns: Sources of Income, Adjustments, Deductions and Exemptions, by Size of Adjusted Gross Income, Tax Year 2009
All figures are estimates based on samples—money amounts are in thousands of dollars)

Social Security Benefit

Size of adjusted gross income	Total [1]		Taxable	
	Number of returns	Amount	Number of returns	Amount
	(107)	(108)	(109)	(110)

# of Returns	Amount of benefits	# of Returns	Taxable Amount		
				0,332	174,649,879
				4,272	35,951
				5,760	48,981
				3,229	193,804
16,667	481,336	16,666	409,158	6,525	247,308
				7,637	675,515
7,305	220,894	7,302	185,417	5,065	2,065,697
				5,335	3,905,578
10,338	315,347	10,338	288,045	5,262	11,621,909
				7,094	15,876,791
2,477	77,299	2,475	65,672	6,573	48,199,575
				4,764	37,715,258
1,430	47,298	1,430	40,203	8,437	41,361,386
				1,379	4,401,188
$250,000 under $500,000				249,213	6,589,364	249,194	5,600,665
$500,000 under $1,000,000				70,804	2,037,875	70,795	1,731,779
$1,000,000 under $1,500,000				16,667	481,366	16,666	409,158
$1,500,000 under $2,000,000				7,305	220,894	7,302	185,417
$2,000,000 under $5,000,000				10,338	315,347	10,338	268,045
$5,000,000 under $10,000,000				2,477	77,299	2,475	65,672
$10,000,000 or more				1,430	47,298	1,430	40,203
Taxable returns, total				14,909,734	387,533,587	13,413,785	165,587,366
Nontaxable returns, total				9,679,950	169,554,636	1,906,677	9,062,514

Virtually all individuals with a 7-figure income (99.98%) who received social security benefits paid income tax on the benefits received. 85% of their social security paychecks are taxed at their average tax of 24%. In terms of equality, this is not just. They already contributed to social security tax at higher amount but when they received their benefits they are taxed...just because they have income? And their money are given to the bottom 99%?

What more should these people be accused of?

On average each received $2,491 and $2,112 is taxed.

How fair is that?

Illustration 75 & 76: Table shows that 85% of the social security benefits received by the rich (old people above 65) are taxed.

There are also many entitlements that the rich forgo, free public amenities that they did not utilize, giving the bottom, more than what they should be having.

Another reason why it is not true that the billionaire is paying less taxes than his secretary, is because his income has already been taxed twice.

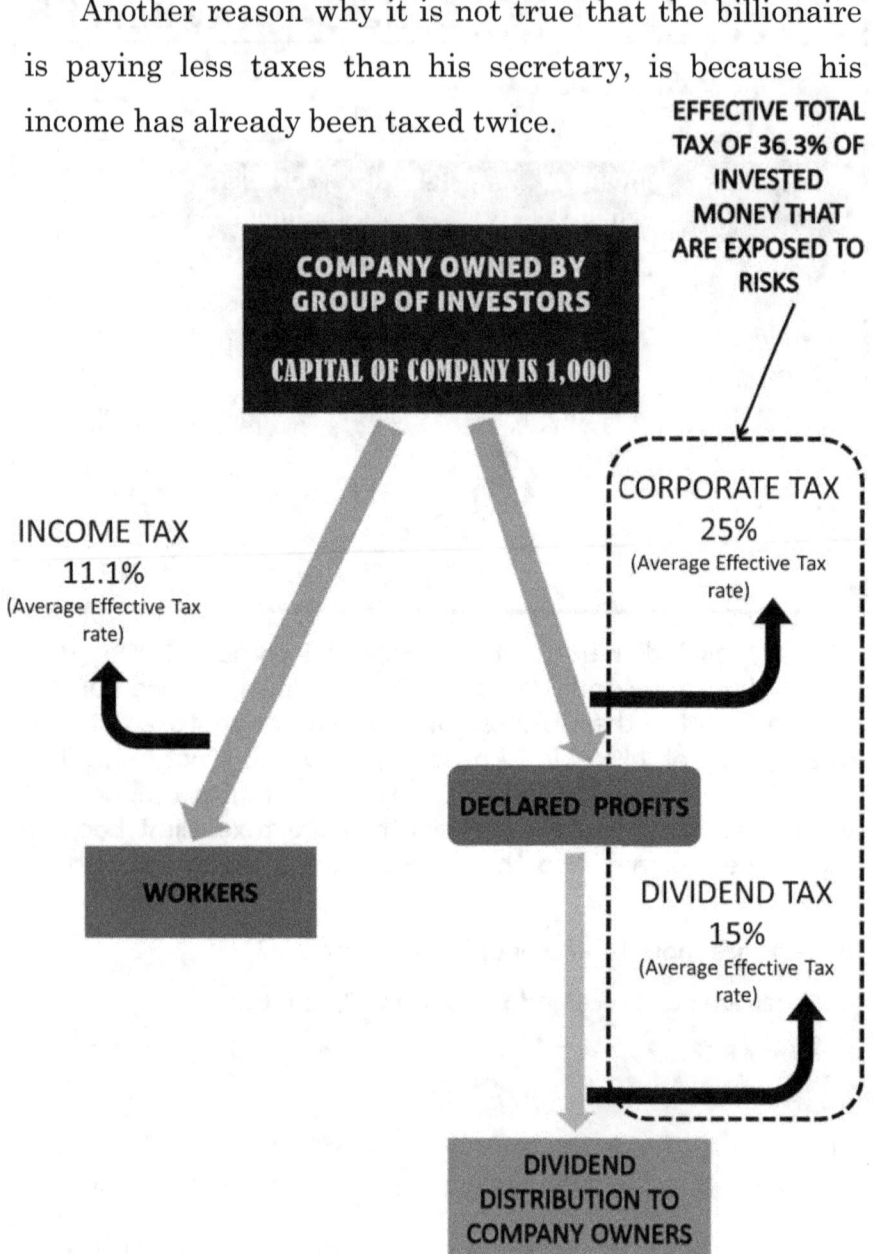

Illustration 77: How returns on invested money is taxed, compared to income tax on wages

The effective total tax on the invested money by the investor is 36.3%, which is more than triple than the workers average income tax rate of 11.1%. This point is not highlighted by the media at all, or the economists and professors. Perhaps they are blind, or just want to deceive you.

Now let us go through a more complicated version of the flow of money between the owners and its corporation. You will be surprised just who will be hit by the proposed higher tax on dividend and corporate tax.

A group of people, pool their savings to fund a new company. These are the company owners. They include the millionaires, the billionaires, other individual investors, mutual fund managers, pension fund managers and many more. Together they invested 1,000 into the company. The company generates profit of 100 a year, which is a 10% gross profit. The profit is taxed by the government at the standard 25% corporate tax rate, leaving only 75 as net profit. This money is then partly reinvested into the business in order to grow it further, in the hope of more returns in the future. This leaves only 50 for distribution to the owners as dividend. Before the declared dividend reaches the owners, the government steps in one more time and tax the distribution at the

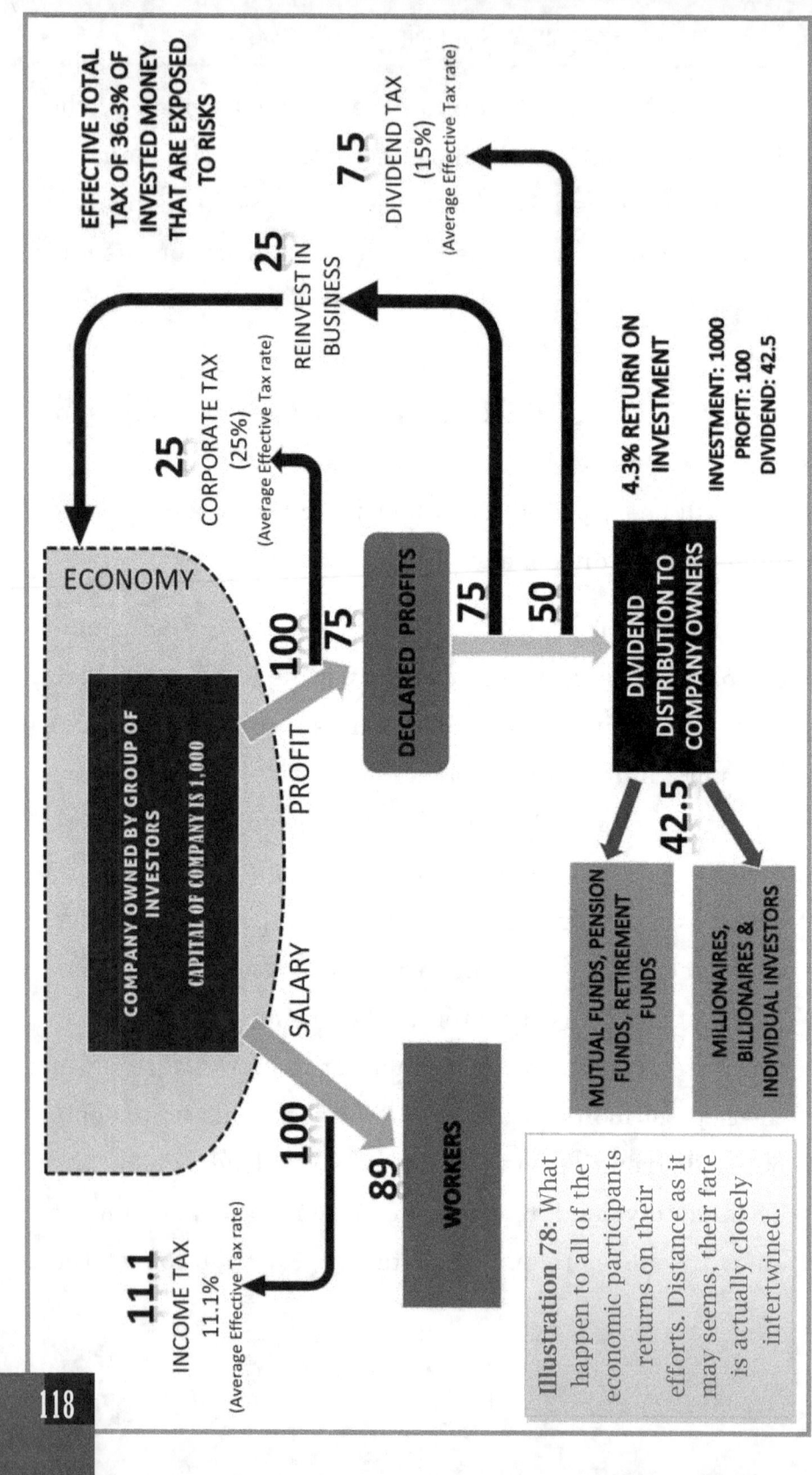

Illustration 78: What happen to all of the economic participants returns on their efforts. Distance as it may seems, their fate is actually closely intertwined.

118

standard 15% dividend rate. When it finally reaches the owner, only 42.5 of the original 100 are left. The dividend is distributed between the owners and their net returns on their 1,000 investment?

4.3%!

This is just a little bit higher than other type of investments out there, such as fixed income securities, CDs and government bonds. If the return is lesser than this, the group of investors may not even form the company in the first place and would rather park their money into safer investments with the same amount of returns.

Now imagine if the tax rate on corporations and especially the tax on dividends of investors are increased just to please the general public, who is under the impression that the low dividend rate is unfair, while in fact, the actual effective tax rate is already more than triple than the average effective individual income tax. What would happen to the net return of the investors?

If we increase the corporate tax to 45% and the dividend tax to 42%, the return to the investors would drop by almost half, yielding only 2.2% a year, which could be lower than other type of investments. Their new effective tax rate on their invested money will jump considerably to 68.1%— a full two third. The investors would close shop and invest their money elsewhere, but first they would try increasing the selling prices of their goods so they can make more profit, and at the same time they would try to reduce the salaries of their. Assuming they are successful, the profit of the company will go up say to 200, but their net return will only claw back to its previous level of 4.3% a year net.

The impact of the high taxes is significant however to the general economy. The group that will be hurt the most is none other than the general workers themselves (whether they are also investors or not). They will be facing the prospect of lower salary and high product costs. The supposedly high government taxes on the 'rich' business owners, ultimately hit the rest of the population harder than on the 'rich' themselves. A large part of the population, the majority middle class composing at least 60% of the population, will also be hit by lower returns on their retirement funds due to the lower dividend rate.

This is one of the reasons why governments should only tax the public according to real needs, and not to waste fund unnecessarily. If will inhibit investments and depress economic growth.

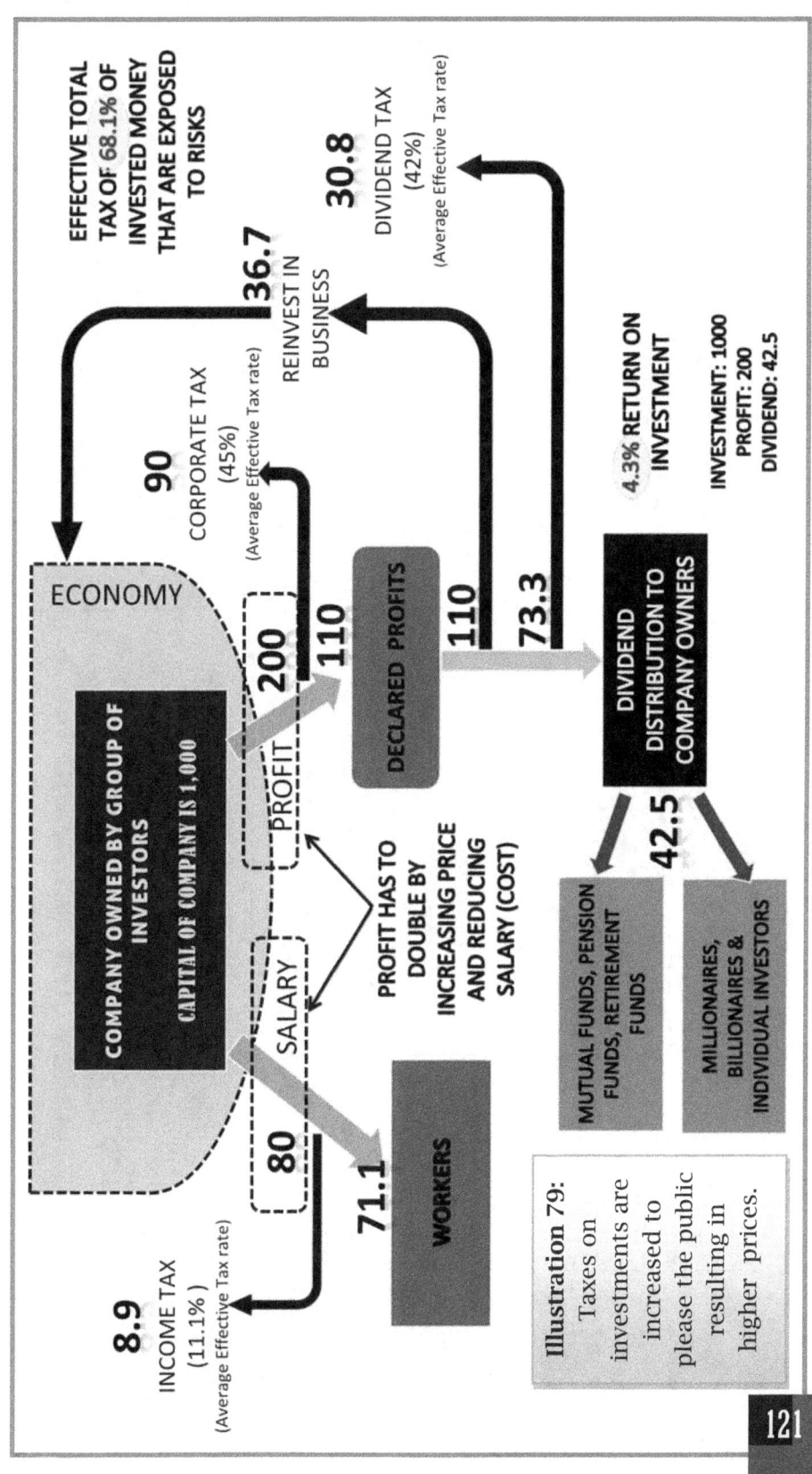

EFFECTIVE TOTAL TAX OF 68.1% OF INVESTED MONEY THAT ARE EXPOSED TO RISKS

30.8
DIVIDEND TAX (42%)
(Average Effective Tax rate)

36.7
REINVEST IN BUSINESS

90
CORPORATE TAX (45%)
(Average Effective Tax rate)

4.3% RETURN ON INVESTMENT

INVESTMENT: 1000
PROFIT: 200
DIVIDEND: 42.5

ECONOMY

COMPANY OWNED BY GROUP OF INVESTORS

CAPITAL OF COMPANY IS 1,000

200
PROFIT

110

DECLARED PROFITS

110

73.3

DIVIDEND DISTRIBUTION TO COMPANY OWNERS

42.5

MUTUAL FUNDS, PENSION FUNDS, RETIREMENT FUNDS

MILLIONAIRES, BILLIONAIRES & INDIVIDUAL INVESTORS

PROFIT HAS TO DOUBLE BY INCREASING PRICE AND REDUCING SALARY (COST)

SALARY

80

71.1

WORKERS

8.9
INCOME TAX (11.1%)
(Average Effective Tax rate)

Illustration 79: Taxes on investments are increased to please the public resulting in higher prices.

121

Percentage of All Population That Pay Income Taxes

So how many of the tax filers actually pay income tax? The Bottom 99% cry foul of the tax system, saying it is not fair to them, however the truth is very far from that. Take a look at the following data on tax returns, again for the year 1990 and 2009, almost two decades apart.

Table 1a.--Individual Income Tax, All Returns: Sources of Income, Adjustments, a Constant 1990 Dollars, by Size of Real Adjusted Gross Income, Tax Year 1990 [1]
[All figures are estimates based on samples--money amounts are in thousands of dollars]

Size of real adjusted gross income	Number of returns	Adjusted gross income (less deficit)
	(1)	(2)
All returns....................................	113,717,138	3,405,427,348
No adjusted gross income.............	904,876	-45,809,664
$1 under $5,000.............................	16,478,272	41,497,039
$5,000 under $10,000.....................	14,952,855	111,951,215
$10,000 under $15,000...................	13,922,750	173,376,264
$15,000 under $20,000...................	11,543,228	201,638,041
$20,000 under $25,000...................	9,572,317	214,321,942
$25,000 under $30,000...................	7,838,225	215,207,577
$30,000 under $40,000...................	12,282,786	426,384,692
$40,000 under $50,000...................	8,837,067	394,730,512
$50,000 under $75,000...................	10,944,102	657,214,261
$75,000 under $100,000.................	3,276,142	279,524,997
$100,000 under $200,000...............	2,329,562	305,567,590
$200,000 under $500,000...............	644,027	188,004,834
$500,000 under $1,000,000...........	130,252	87,142,014
$1,000,000 under $1,500,000........	29,060	34,978,215
$1,500,000 under $2,000,000........	11,581	19,891,323
$2,000,000 under $5,000,000........	15,331	45,034,350
$5,000,000 under $10,000,000.....	3,184	21,463,938
$10,000,000 or more......................	1,522	33,308,207
Taxable returns.............................	89,862,434	3,298,920,383
Nontaxable returns........................	23,854,704	106,506,965

Illustration 80: Table from IRS 1990 Tax File.

Table 1. All Returns: Sources of Income, Adjustments, Deductions and Exemptions, by Size of Adjusted Gross Income, Tax Year 2009
(All figures are estimates based on samples—money amounts are in thousands)

Size of adjusted gross income	Number of returns	Adjusted gross income less deficit
	(1)	(2)
All returns, total	140,494,127	7,626,430,723
No adjusted gross income	2,511,925	-198,958,452
$1 under $5,000	10,447,635	27,218,608
$5,000 under $10,000	12,220,335	92,407,278
$10,000 under $15,000	12,444,512	155,465,805
$15,000 under $20,000	11,400,228	199,017,560
$20,000 under $25,000	10,033,887	225,167,737
$25,000 under $30,000	8,662,392	237,994,230
$30,000 under $40,000	14,371,647	499,879,773
$40,000 under $50,000	10,796,412	483,088,798
$50,000 under $75,000	18,694,893	1,149,068,817
$75,000 under $100,000	11,463,725	990,337,913
$100,000 under $200,000	13,522,048	1,801,446,897
$200,000 under $250,000	1,418,580	314,863,973
$250,000 under $500,000	1,776,459	590,483,429
$500,000 under $1,000,000	492,567	332,037,478
$1,000,000 under $1,500,000	108,096	130,149,237
$1,500,000 under $2,000,000	44,273	76,148,200
$2,000,000 under $5,000,000	61,918	182,986,391
$5,000,000 under $10,000,000	14,322	97,493,167
$10,000,000 or more	8,274	240,133,885
Taxable returns, total	81,890,189	6,777,684,912
Nontaxable returns, total	58,603,939	848,745,811

* Estimate should be used with caution because of the small number of sample returns on which it is based.

Illustration 81: Table from IRS 2009 Tax File.

Look carefully at the total number of tax returns filed. In 1990, it was 113 million. In 2009, the number of tax returns filed grew to 140.4 million. It is a big increase — but take a closer look at the "taxable tax returns". This is the number of people who actually have to pay taxes on their income (which already adjusted to correct for losses and other deductions). In 1990, it was 89.8 million, but the number of people who actually paid taxes in 2009, instead of going up in tandem with the increase in the number of filers, dropped to only a dismal 81.8 million. This is a very large, unacceptable drop. The crux of the issue — many people are not paying taxes anymore, compared to the year 1990. Therefore, the tax burden is shifted further up, and the rich must contribute more to compensate. Despite fewer of the Bottom 99% paying taxes, they complained of being taxed too much and not getting much in return. The percentage of filers who have to pay tax in 1990 was 89.8/113.7 = 78.9%. If the same percentage is going to have to pay taxes in 2009, an additional 29 million individuals will have to pay tax (making the total to 110.8 million). This humongous number of people relieved from paying taxes is depriving the government of important revenues. There is no justice in this and there is certainly no pride involved. Everyone must pay his or her dues, no matter what. We opined that the poor should continue to pay taxes, despite being granted assistance from the government (even if the government assistance is larger than the amount of taxes they pay). The reason is simple, if you pay for the government's expenses; you will care more on how it is expended. Instead of asking ever more, you will realize that someone else, a real person, and this person have to work extra hard, just to pay for your additional requests. One day, this person could be you; therefore, everyone will think twice before making illogical requests for assistance from the government. The government cannot create new wealth, people do.

The government by itself, cannot be left alone on its own because it is so gullible and naïve; the politicians are more concerned about their votes and reelections, who pays for it, is of little worry to them, thus making them easily swayed by the 'needy voters' to give away ever more. We need to stop treating government money as free money coming from one very big and rich uncle. The truth is, government's money is obtained from individuals, whether directly or not. The more money we took in, the more we are taking from others. They could be your neighbors, your parents, your friends, heck, even your own children and their future children (future debts to be paid by them). Start treating government assistance as a debt that you would want to repay. This is real justice and you will be proud you did.

Let's check what percentage of the individuals in each class that are actually paying their dues. In 2009, those in the $1 to $19,999 bracket, only 20% of them actually pay a cent or more in taxes. 80% of them paid not a cent.

At the top most brackets, as you might suspect, virtually all of them pay their dues (99.4%). The bottom most bracket contributed a mere 0.4% of all taxes, in contrast to those at the top most, who earned more than a million (0.2% of all tax payers); they paid a hefty 20.5% of all taxes.

1990

Amount collected: $447,061 Million

INCOME BRACKETS	ALL RETURNS FILED	RETURNS WITH TAXABLE INCOME (AFTER CREDIT)	% PAID TAX
$1 to $19,999	57,801,981	34,297,791	59.3%
$20,000 to $99,999	52,750,639	52,405,408	99.3%
$100,000 - $999,999	3,103,841	3,098,664	99.8%
Above $1 million	60,678	60,571	99.8%
TOTAL	113,717,139	89,862,434	79.0%

2009

Amount collected: $865,863 Million

INCOME BRACKETS	ALL RETURNS FILED	RETURNS WITH TAXABLE INCOME (AFTER CREDIT)	% PAID TAX
$1 to $19,999	49,024,635	9,961,694	20.3%
$20,000 to $99,999	74,022,956	54,650,204	73.8%
$100,000 - $999,999	17,209,654	17,042,877	99.0%
Above $1 million	236,883	235,413	99.4%
TOTAL	137,982,203	81,886,368	59.3%

Illustration 82: Tables show a summary of taxable filers after tax credits are applied. Also note that in 2009, there were more credits given, enabling many in the lower brackets to reduce or negate their tax responsibilities on their incomes. However, the top two brackets contribution is maintained at above 99%.

The data is so amazing; the scale of the decline was enormous. In 1990, 41.7% of those who earned less than $20,000 did not pay a dime in taxes. In 2009, the number nearly doubled, to 79%. For the low to middle-income bracket, in 1990, 99.3% paid their dues, contributed to the economy and incomes of the government.

However, in 2009, the number declined significantly, only 74% paid their dues. This is despite a very good real increase in the average annual income of all individual tax filers, which rose to $38,171 in 2009, from $34,371 back in 1990. In 1990, virtually everyone who earns more than $20,000 a year paid his or her taxes, while an amazing 59.3% of the bottom most bracket of less than $20,000 a year, also pay taxes. However, the numbers then dropped precipitously to only 20.3% in 2009, dragging along the next bracket (of $20,000 to $100,000) as well, which dropped from 99.3% to only 73.8%. Even in an inflation adjusted terms, the numbers are just as horrible. For the upper middle income and the top most brackets, there is no change in the percentage of people paying taxes, it was almost always 100% for both years, and we are sure they are immensely proud of it.

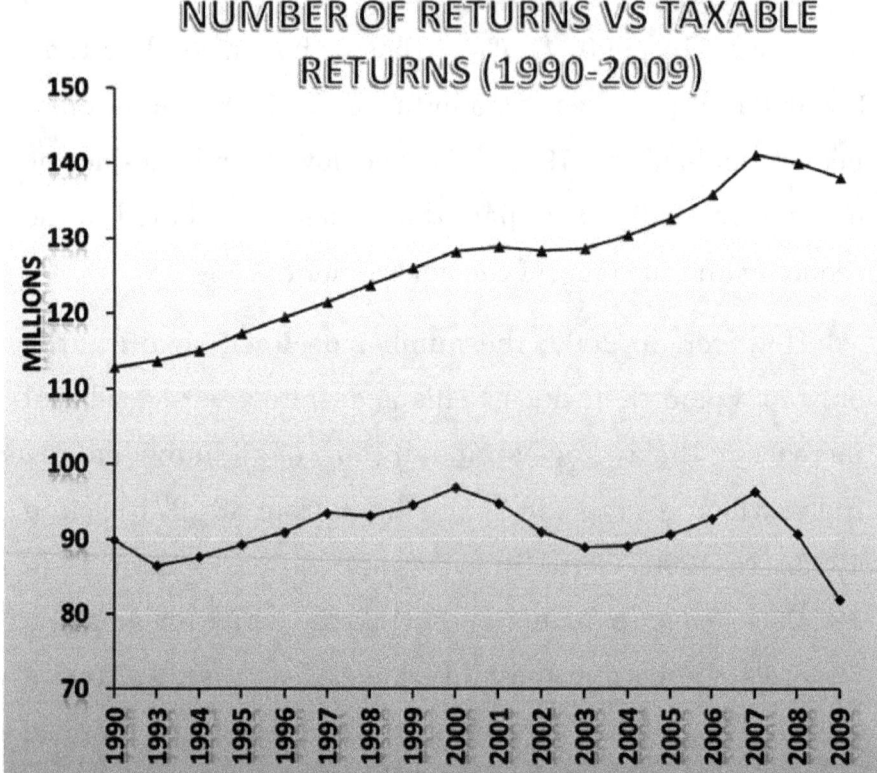

Note: Data based on IRS historical numbers which deduct the negative income filers from the total

Illustration 83: From 1990 to 2009, the number of filings increased 21% but number of taxable returns declined and dropped to the lowest level in 2009.

Everyone loves refunds, so let us talk a bit about refunds before we summarize our findings. In 2009, there are 46.5 million people earning below $20,000 a year. Only 9.9 million have to pay tax and on average, they paid $380 each. However 81% of these tax filers, or 37.7 million people, received an average tax refund of $1,978 each! As a group, each is calculated to have paid only $51 in taxes, but received $1,008 in refunds.

They paid no income taxes at all in the end, yet have the guts of complaining of how much they are paying every month out of their paychecks, conveniently forgetting the tax refunds at the end. If someone who pay taxes every month, and later get every cent of it, plus more, but complains about unfairness of the tax system, is simply not a respectable person. More than 83% of the Bottom 47% received refunds from the IRS and if any of them complain about unfairness, they should really look at themselves in the mirror and actually ask what contributions they plan to give to the country, and the world.

If you have taken from others, just **when** are you going to pay it back?

Summary of Tax Statistics

Let us summarize the abundance of tax data presented:

The Top 1% shoulders 37% of the total tax paid to the government. The top 10% shoulders 70% of the tax burden while the Bottom 90% covers the remaining 30% (Year 2009). The tax burden of the Top 1% had increased by 43% compared to 1986 while the Bottom 99% had theirs reduced by 15%. Further down the chain, the bottom 50% only contributed 2.25% of the tax burden (down a jaw dropping 69%).

The Top 1% pay on average 24% tax on their income, and the Bottom 50% only 1.8% tax rate! The whole Bottom 99% is paying at a rate below the national average tax. In addition, even though the national tax rate is on the decline, the top 5% tax rates are the only one that is not decreasing from year 2003 onward.

Each person at the top 1% contributed $230,496 to taxes while the 99% contributed $4,010 in taxes each. The bottom 50% however, only contributed $283 in tax (or about 77 cents per day!).

Hence, it is absolutely not true that the rich, the Top 1%, are not paying their fair share. They do. There is one group, which obviously does not pay its fair share, —the Bottom 50% themselves.

The Bottom 50% always complains that their taxes are high, and the government is not helping them enough. However, they forgot that there are many exemptions in the USA tax code and sometimes after EIC (Earned Income Credit), they can get refunds or reduce their overall tax payments. Many expenses can also be deducted in the US tax code to minimize the tax burden. The OWS and the disgruntled are all possibly coming from the bottom group, yet they are complaining of many things, despite already getting most of the assistance and paying little taxes, if any.

2009

INCOME BRACKETS	ALL RETURNS FILED	RETURNS WITH TAXABLE INCOME (BEFORE CREDIT)	RETURNS WITH TAXABLE INCOME (AFTER CREDIT)
1 to 19,999	49,024,635	16,349,246	9,961,694
20,000 to 99,999	74,022,956	70,406,196	54,650,204
100,000 - 999,999	17,209,654	17,169,649	17,042,877
Above 1 million	236,883	235,649	235,413
TOTAL	140,494,128	104,160,740	81,890,188

INCOME BRACKETS	NUMBER OF PEOPLE BENEFITED FROM CREDIT	%
1 to 19,999	6,387,552	39.1%
20,000 to 99,999	15,755,992	22.4%
100,000 - 999,999	126,772	0.7%
Above 1 million	236	0.1%
TOTAL	22,270,552	21.4%

INCOME BRACKETS	AMOUNT OF TAX PAID (thousands of dollars)	AVERAGE TAX PAID ($USD)
1 to 19,999	$ 3,869,854	$ 388
20,000 to 99,999	$ 215,507,856	$ 3,943
100,000 - 999,999	$ 469,070,922	$ 7,523
Above 1 million	$ 177,500,065	$ 753,994
TOTAL	$ 865,948,697	$ 10,575

Illustration 84: Tax credit helped the bottomers immensely and exempted more than 22mil with incomes of less than $100,000 from paying income tax.

The number of people actually paying any taxes as percentage of the tax returns has been on a steady decline. This is despite 29 million new workers (tax filers) added from 1990 to 2009, and in 2009, the number of people that need to pay income tax drop to the lowest level in as many decades.

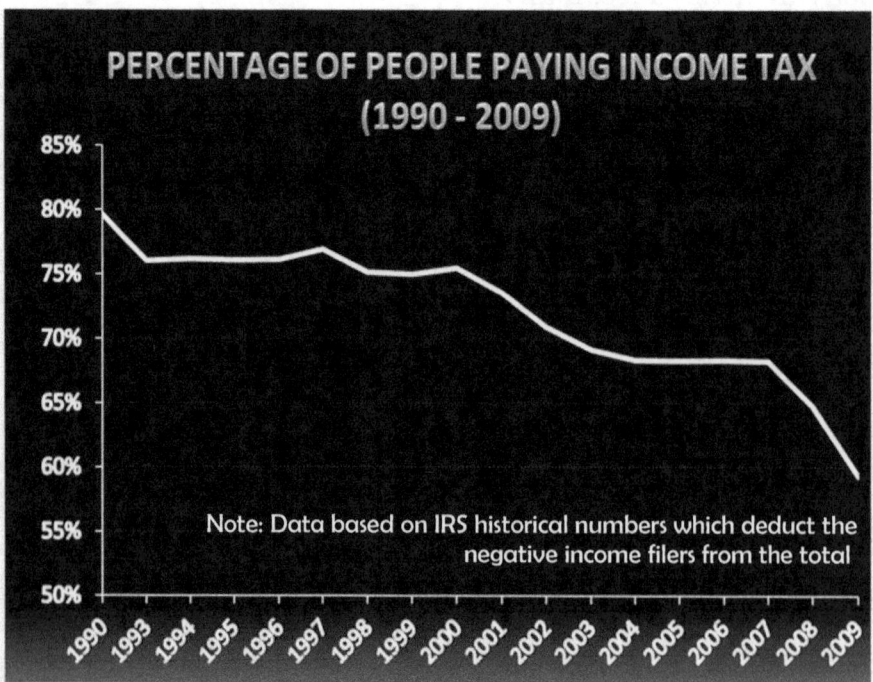

Illustration 85: Percentage of people actually have to pay income tax has been on the decline and dropped to the lowest level in 2009.

The rich is not getting richer, and certainly, they are not getting richer at the expense of the poor. Therefore taxing the rich more, is not the answer. In order to reduce the pressure on the federal government financial standing, everyone including the poor must pay adequate taxes, while government expenditures need to go down and "pork" projects reduced. Capitalism works but it must be balanced by the human side. More on this topic in **Book 3** of our **259 TRILLION VS 5 TRILLION** series.

By regulating how much the rich can make or by taking away the poor's incentives to become rich (incomes above $200,000 was taxed at an unbelievable rate of 94% in the year 1944), will discourage anyone from trying further once they have reach a certain income. They would stop innovating etc., which will limit what the government can get (tax), and the rest of the population (product and services) will not benefit. Limiting wealth creation, by eliminating initiatives and hard work, will do no one any good. If everybody is rewarded the same, why would anyone want to work harder or come out with better products and services?

Why are the rich rewarded and most importantly, entrusted by society to manage a substantial part of the resources of the country? The short answer is that they are rewarded by the rest of the population only when they managed their resources, risk and results wisely and by working hard to create wealth for society. The rich would not become rich (not the swindle artists) if they waste and

destroy these resources.

Will you let a stupid, moronic person in charge of the country's military?

On the other hand, will you select a nasty, crooked fellow to become the president of the country? Will he sell out the country to foreigners? Will he stupidly or crookedly, steal the nation's wealth? What kind of silly deals these silly people are going to make?

The price to be paid is very dear, and it is a risk that cannot be taken. Try giving people things that they do not deserve, and stand ready to see they spoil it. Try giving a beautiful car to someone who cannot drive, then just wait and see he destroys it. Try giving an airplane to someone who cannot fly, and stand ready to duck when he crashes the plane. Society gave the poor instant wealth by lotteries and Powerball, and gasps every time history repeats itself when these people blew it all off.

The point is, wealth must be earned. It is not easy to manage and only capable people can manage it. Wealth is a trust given by society to the select few, chosen when they successfully upgraded the wealth of the masses, showing their mettle, skills and capabilities. That is why when wealth is inherited (not due to hard work, knowledge and perseverance); the inheritors tend to lose that wealth in a short time. The rich do not stay rich forever unless they add value to the economy and the society. Remember what we wrote in **Book 1**? There are no good, forever lasting storage of wealth out there and money is liquefied wealth created for easy trade of goods and services. The only good store of wealth is knowledge and the ability to adapt to change; whatever changes the society and economy throws at you.

WHY THE BOTTOM MOST CLASS INCOME EARNERS IN THE IRS DATA MAY BE RICHER THAN WE THINK

Yes, it is exactly as what is written; don't be misled! We bet they "forgot" to tell you these!

Data from the IRS showed that a large portion of the population, declared incomes of less than $5,000 a year, including millions more that reports zero or negative income. Well, this is highly unlikely and when we analyzed the IRS data, we found that 34% of the zero income filers, earned dividend incomes, worth 5,581 dollars, so they probably holding assets worth north of $186,000 each (at dividend income of 3% a year). Well, these people are hardly poor at all! In fact, their dividend incomes per year cannot be matched by those of the next higher bracket, and so are the next, and the next, all the way to the upper middle class of $200,000 to $250,000. Only this bracket can beat the dividend incomes of this 'zero' income bracket who are sitting at the bottom most.

Old retired couple, who are earning say about $11,000 a year from dividend alone (exclusive of Social Security incomes), are probably holding stocks worth $367,000 or more. If other assets are included such as houses that were fully paid for, this couple could well be millionaires. However, after just the standard deductions, they would have landed inside the "$1 to Under $5,000" bracket, and be put at the bottom most income bracket. Then the economists and their friends will crow about it, about how many poor people there are, forgetting that those people are actually far from being poor.

There is another group of people, who declared zero income in their tax returns. When we really analyzed this group, we concluded that it is impossible for someone to earn zero income for a period of one year. Even a homeless and out of work person, can earn more than zero in a course of one year. Seriously, zero everyday for 365 days? These people are characterized by the IRS as those who made some losses, and they filed in order to obtain certain benefits. They are not the bottom most group of people; they actually came from higher brackets.

So we traced their roots, and we found that 31% of the no 'adjusted gross income' group reported they received salaries worth $31,000 a year, which is 9 times more than the next higher bracket. This is right at the bottom of the middle class bracket, and cannot be considered as 'poor'. On top of their wages, they also have other type of incomes, making their total income to be well into the middle class territory.

Then, what about those having negative incomes?

Therefore, all data must be analyzed in their proper context otherwise, it will mislead everyone.

Many people mistaken the very poor who are under poverty, are composed of those at the bottom most of the income ladder, and they earn the minimum wage. Contrary to what many people think, those who earn the minimum wage, hardly qualify as those living in poverty.

Those who earn the federal minimum wage will earn about $17,160 a year, far higher than the poverty threshold of $7,000. Therefore, an able-bodied person who is willing to work hard will earn at least the federal minimum wage, and would not be considered as a person who is living in poverty. So if the minimum wage guarantees anyone to have an income higher than the poverty level, then why is there people living in poverty? Mainly, we found that many of them do not work full time, or they are composed of simple part timers such as university students who only work on some days or the weekends. Most likely, these workers chose to work this way and therefore earn less during the year, despite being paid at least the federal minimum wage. Therefore, they are not at the poor bracket because they are forced to, but it is by choice. This will alas, skew any economists' data, unless they correct for the number of part timers (available in the IRS database). In our case, we know clearly why the poor is earning less than the minimum wage, so there is no confusion on our part, and thus our conclusions.

Now . . . . .
Let's Answer Their
Other Unfounded
Accusations Directly!!

PART 3:
CONUNDRUM THAT ISN'T

RICH ARE GETTING RICHER, WHILE THE POOR ARE GETTING POORER FALLACY

This statement is found to be false. It is impossible to occur in real time. Occupy Wall Streeters (OWS) had followed and cited erroneous and terribly misleading studies on distribution of incomes, especially on CEO pay. Find out below.

After much analysis, we concluded that the general statement of the 'rich are getting richer' while 'the poor are getting poorer' is not correct. It is a fallacy perpetuated by ill-informed people, for it is indeed a conflicting statement by itself. The rich cannot be richer, unless the poor also gets to be richer. Otherwise, where will the rich sell their useful products and services? If the products they sell help society, of course the whole society will be richer. Just like when a corporation is getting more successful and making more money in its business, it will reward its employees more, including the janitor. The richer the rich gets, the richer the 'poor' will also get.

The recent financial crisis illustrates the fact that once society stray from a sincere and honest path, trying to get rich the easy way by buying products from the rich 'crooked' up owners that do not add value to the society as a whole, the whole country will end up poorer. Buying multiple houses for instance, or purchasing multiple cars with little economic return, is dangerous to the economy as a whole due to misallocation of resources and destruction of wealth, despite such purchases rewarding the builders, the manufacturers and others who are owned by the so-called 'rich'. The Bottom 99% should stop buying things they don't really need and instead divert their precious resources into improving themselves and then invest their money into 'society improving' endeavors, not into short cuts, get rich quick schemes promoted by some of the 'rich' gurus—Property Guru, Gold Guru and the Insurance and Fund Manager Guru. Whenever you are presented with any money making scheme, check and verify where the new wealth is to be created. If you cannot find it, bail out at once!

The Bottom 99% should really think twice for faulting the Top 1% of their imagined 'predicament'. Today's Bottom 99% is far better off, than say a generation ago. They are far, far better off compared to two generations or more ago. These Bottom 99%ers are now, 'far richer' than what they used to be, because the inventors/owners from within their own group had provided good quality products and services as tools for creating new wealth for themselves.

In the 1890s, Founder Thomas Edison sold GE's first lightbulbs. Back then, in order to pay for an hour of light powered at the equivalent strength of today's 100 watts, the average worker would have to work a full hour. By 1960, the time period decreased to a mere eight minutes. And by 1992, it was down to less than a second when using a compact fluorescent bulb.

(From GE citizenship Report 2012)

The rich get richer, but the poor do even better. Between 1980 and 2000, the poor doubled their consumption. The Chinese are ten times richer and live 25 years longer than they did 50 years ago. Nigerians are twice as rich and live nine more years. The percentage of the world's people living in absolute poverty has dropped by over half. The United Nations estimates that poverty was reduced more in the past 50 years than in the previous 500.

In the United States, rivers, lakes, seas, and air are getting cleaner all the time. A car today emits less pollution travelling at full speed than a parked car did from leaks in 1970.

Reader's Digest (April 2012)
For more, read "The Rational Optimist " by Matt Ridley.

Illustration 86: Other quotes from other writers that shows that we are better off today, and we should be optimist and work hard for the betterment of the society as a whole.

The inventors/owners will not become rich the way they are now unless they are rewarded by the Bottom 99%, who paid out of their pockets from the newly created wealth (wealth, assets and money are explained thoroughly in Book 1 and 2 of the 259 Trillion Series) whenever they use the products and services of those inventors/owners. Remember the famous light bulb inventor? If instead of a light bulb, he invented the upside down umbrella, would he be rewarded as handsomely? (He would probably be laughed at and ridiculed even).

WHAT IF EDISON INVENTED THE UPSIDE DOWN UMBRELLA INSTEAD OF THE LIGHT BULB?

Your worth consists in what you are and not in what you have

Quote from: www.brainyquote.com   -Thomas Alva Edison

Illustration 87: Thomas Alva Edison would not have been a well known figure and rich as well if he did not deserve it. He invented a lot of innovative products and also one of the founders of a company that still exist today (and thriving). He was rewarded by society because he deserved it. He did not steal anybody else's portion. A lot of the rich worked hard for their fortune; yes even Rothschild did.

However, since he invented something that revolutionized and helped the public, he was amply rewarded. By the way, he is one of the two founders of General Electric. GE is also included in our case study of high CEO pay in the later parts of this book.

Now, imagine two different small towns, each has a billionaire of its own. Town A has one billionaire who is stupid and careless, while Town B has one brilliant billionaire who wants to improve the society for everyone's benefit. The billionaire in Town A, who is stupid and careless, will devise many short cut schemes for getting richer, which the bottom 99% will happily subscribe to those schemes in the hope that they will become just as rich. That billionaire will also devise new projects, such as building bridges to nowhere and many others, which everyone will gladly declare as 'development'!

That billionaire is risking a lot of his own wealth to push through his 'schemes', however he is not smart and in the process, he will lose all of his wealth, but not before the bottom 99% who bought every product of his, lose everything they have first. The end result— the whole town will end up poorer. When the rich is getting poorer, the poor will end up even poorer. Wealth is destroyed in this instance. Town A's wealth is destroyed in the process by the action of its own residents, rich and poor.

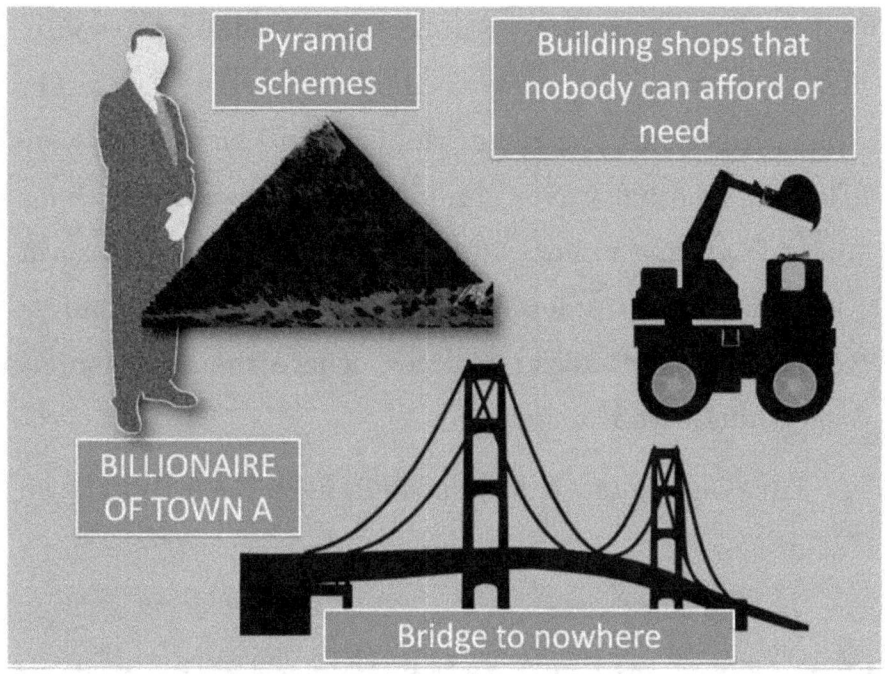

Illustration 88: A not so smart billionaire in Town A with his stupid money making scheme and useless endeavors.

Now, how about the smart billionaire, who devises clever schemes that actually generates new wealth for the town's people? What will happen to this other small town? The billionaire smartly analyzed of what are needed by the small town and invests in good real estate by building factories instead of bridges to nowhere, then provide free trainings to the poor, so they can work in her high tech factories. The poor in the town will end up richer once they are working in the new factories, producing goods that are needed by the economy. The billionaire will end up richer as well, because her factories will make new profits, or to be exact, brand new wealth. The whole town, as a whole, will end up richer. The richer the rich become, the richer the poor will become as well. There is no other way around it. It is not possible to have the rich getting richer, while the poor is getting poorer at the same time (unless you are living in a communist countries or dictatorial regimes, where the elite control everything with iron fists).

An example of wealth distribution of Town B is shown below:

BEFORE THE SMART BILLIONAIRE OPENS A FACTORY			
Residents Distribution	Population	Individual Income	Total Income
Poor	10,000	15,000	150,000,000
Rich	1	150,000,000	150,000,000
Poor + Rich	10,001		300,000,000

Total Income Distribution Ratio	
Rich to Poor Ratio	1
Rich to the rest Ratio	1

Illustration 89: A billionaire lives in a town where the rest of the population only have jobs paying $15,000/year.

Initially the town with the smart billionaire with 10,001 inhabitants is having the following distribution of income:

The poor is making only $15,000 each for a total of $150,000,000 in the poor category ($15,000 X 10,000 people). The sole rich person is making $150,000,000 as well. The income distribution between the rich and the poor is therefore one to one.

The smart billionaire took the risk to invest and build a new factory, employing a thousand of the poor people in the town, paying each of them a good middle class salary of $55,000 a year; of course after providing them with good trainings, resulting in a permanent upgrade of their knowledge and skills. Now what will happen to the famous ratios that everyone love to argue about?

Will the rich be getting richer, while the poor get poorer?

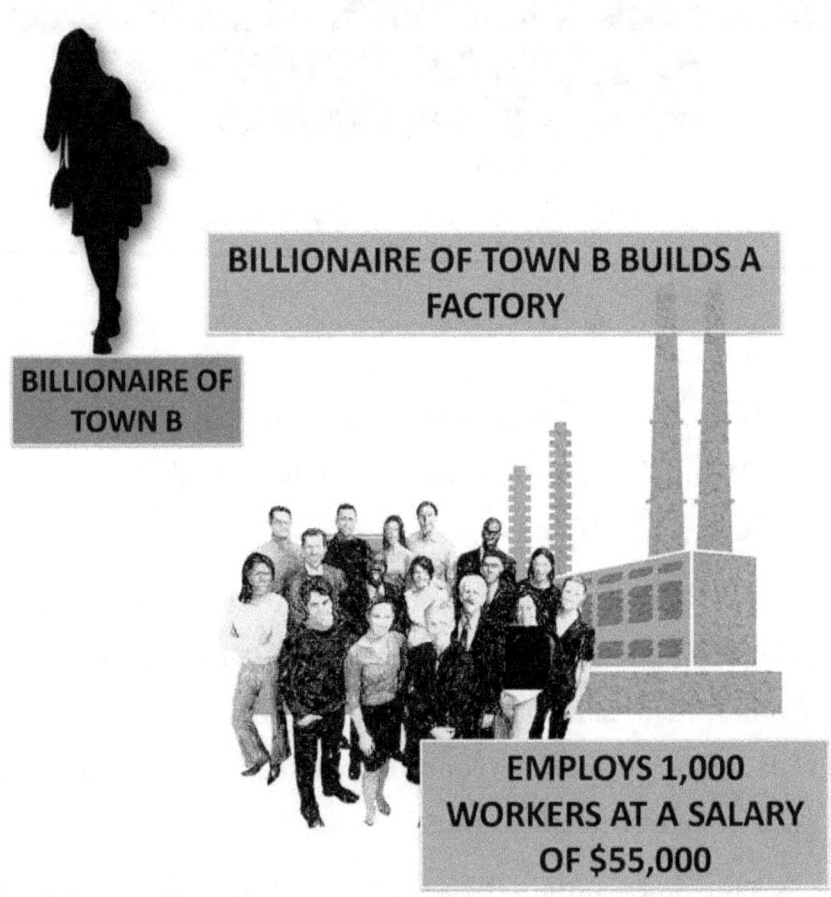

BILLIONAIRE OF TOWN B BUILDS A FACTORY

BILLIONAIRE OF TOWN B

EMPLOYS 1,000 WORKERS AT A SALARY OF $55,000

Illustration 90: A smart billionaire in Town B opened a factory and employed a thousand workers, permanently increases the incomes of the town's people

AFTER THE SMART BILLIONAIRE OPENED A FACTORY CREATING MANY JOBS FOR THE TOWN'S PEOPLE			
Residents Distribution	Population	Individual Income	Total Income
Poor	9,000	15,000	135,000,000
Middle Class	1,000	55,000	55,000,000
Rich	1	180,000,000	180,000,000
Poor + Middle Class + Rich	10,001		370,000,000

Total Income Distribution Ratio	
Rich to Poor Ratio	1.33
Rich to the rest Ratio	0.95

Illustration 91: Tables show the impact of a higher paying jobs to the key ratios

9,000 STILL AT OLD JOB OF $15,000

The remaining 9,000 of the poor are still making $15,000 each, but 1,000 of the town's poor population are now making a good $55,000 a year. The distribution of income will now be the following:

Poor = 9,000 X $15,000 = $135,000,000   Oh No! The poor seems to be getting poorer!

The Rich = 1 X $180,000,000 = $180,000,000. Oh No, No, No! The rich seems to be getting richer!

The income distribution ratio between the bottom 99.99% and the top 0.01% has now worsened, from one-to-one, to one to 1.33. That mean every dollar the poor makes, the rich will make 1.33 dollars. According to most economists and politicians and just about every other person out there, the rich is getting richer at the expense of the poor. It seems the incomes of the poor are being transferred directly to the sole rich person in the town. Well, if you really understand the numbers, this is not the case at all.

Look at each of the poor person's income, the income is still $15,000 each, thus even though the gap seems to have increased according to the key ratios, the rich person (Billionaire of Town B) did not take any of the poor person's income, but rather from the new wealth she and the 1,000 upgraded workers had created. Nobody is taking from the poor, because the poor continue to make exactly the same amount of money as they were before. This fact is explained clearly in **Book 3** of the **259TVS5T** series.

There is now a large and sizable middle class in the town. This is not normally mentioned out there, and thus they are entirely overlooked. The town's overall income has increased tremendously, due to the new factory. An important key ratio rarely calculated properly by everyone else— the ratio of the 'original' poor and rich combined with the new middle class, is performed by us. We did the calculation and it showed a lower figure than one, at 0.95. The way we measure income distributions today, fail to properly reflect the movement of people from each class, and could not explain exactly why the rich are making more.

The income distribution of the economic pie (as explained in **Book** 3) of Town B is getting larger due to new wealth created by the building of the factory and the products it is churning out.

How many of us remember what will happen to a small town when an important factory or a whole industry closes? The town will decline in stature, crime rate may go up, and the local administration will be strapped of money for lack of incomes. People will start migrating out, in search of better lives. The same effect can be seen in a large metropolis; Detroit is one good example.

In our example above, the populace that is not working at the new factory is considered poor, but their number has shrunk. The gap between the poor and the rich will be shown to be very large, according to our economists. You may be itching to present us with your solution on what to do with the poor by now, but let us. Since the town is now much richer overall, the town can now afford to provide aid for its poor, in order to move them up the rung. With the new wealth created, the town can now afford to train and upgrade a new batch of its low -income workers, to work in another new factory. Do you honestly want to prevent the rich from getting richer, and by that, making the whole country poorer overall? There is no logic in this, therefore careful consideration must be taken and that truth, justice, honesty and equality must prevail.

Currently there is a continuing explosive growth of IT; the world is changing into requiring more 'knowledge based workers' that are supposed to be smarter, using their brains in their work, not just spending their energy making something repeatedly, over and over like robots. These knowledge workers can modify and tweak a process, in order to make it more efficient, cheaper and faster. When a process fails, they will find a new solution. Knowledge based economy is the new future, where efficiency will go up a full notch or even more, for, the knowledge workers are capable of producing a great deal more than their previous brethren. More profit and therefore more wealth will be created. It is the goal of society; and the bottom rung of society's workers must therefore always strive to go up a notch in their performance, getting richer in the process. Society must assist them, whenever new wealth is created.

Every time you are buying goods and services, you are casting a vote in the economy. You may not realize it, but our collective votes will direct the economy into producing the things that are being demanded by the participants. If everyone is rich in the economy and cost reduction is not an issue but quality is, then prices of goods will go up and in return, the quality will go up. If this is what is exactly demanded by the market participants, then that is exactly what the economy will deliver. However, if the market demands cheap substitute and quality is of little importance then that is what they will get from the 'rich'.

The rich are significantly more rewarded in the economy because they are willing to take risks, on society's behalf. The rich are more exposed to risks, and they can lose a lot, if not all of their wealth if they build or manufacture the wrong items, things and services that are not demanded in the economy. Hence, it is not a surprise if the rich strike it right and is heavily rewarded, because this is the way it is, for nobody will be willing to risk his or her wealth otherwise. If anyone who do not want the rich to be richer, then they should stop buying the products of the  rich, but risk becoming poorer themselves in the process if the products are important. However, do not buy the thousands of dollars of watch (Rolex, Tissot) when a $20 watch would tell the same exact time, if you are poor. Buying an expensive watch will not create any value to you or make you richer in the process.

Thus, as we have mentioned in the first topic, the poor is not getting poorer while the rich is getting richer. When your parents or your siblings, or even your friends get richer, you will too. They will offer you valuable information on how to be rich as well. Their assistance is important, but please only asks them to assist you non-monetarily; otherwise, you will not grow richer. The economists who first made the statistics of 1% vs. 99% do not understand that nobody stays at the same income bracket for the rest of their lives. How they have misled all of us! Well, until now that is.

We have definitive evidence from the IRS showing that the rich never stays at the top for long. The group's participants are constantly changing. In fact, the poor are the ones that become millionaires. Please find and read about the many billionaires, millionaires or society changing inventors that usually come from poor and humble background and made their way to the top (we included some of these stories in this book). The economy is fair. If you create something of value, society will reward you and once your creation is no longer valuable, then society will move on (remember products that were once the most sought years ago but nobody want them now?). Thus, to remain rich, new creation of value or competitive pricing must be done.

In the course of 20 years of incomes profile from IRS's trove of data, we saw that the bottom bracket is getting less crowded when nearly 9 million people successfully moved up, despite the entry of more than 29 million new workers into the economy in the course of those 20 year period. The following illustration illustrates that fact.

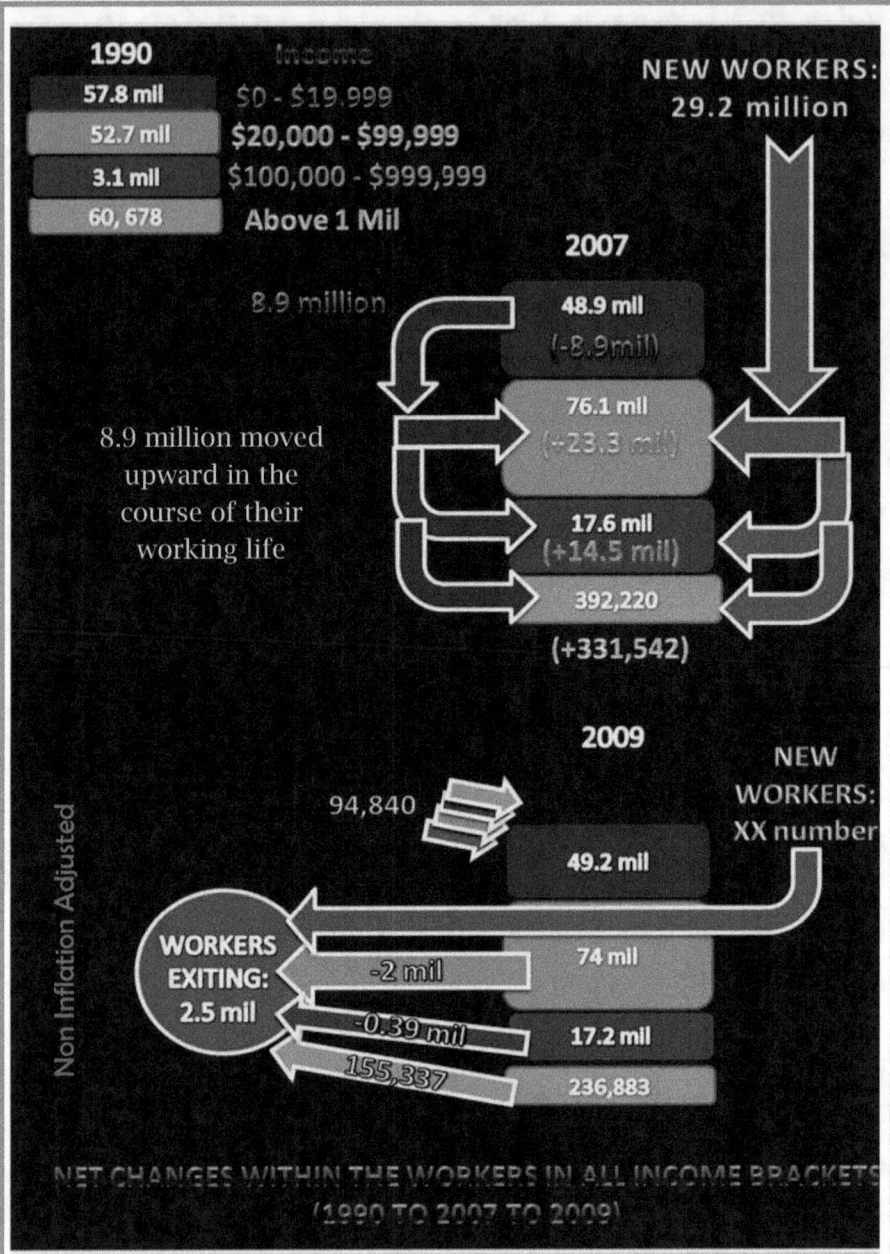

Illustration 92: Mass migration of workers into the upper classes, permanently changing the status of once "poor" people to rich or even "filthy" rich within 18 years. Not that the rich becomes richer but the poor joining the ranks of the rich.
The 2007 crisis affected the rich far worst than the bottommost, with 40% of seven figure income earners either went bankrupt or got poorer.

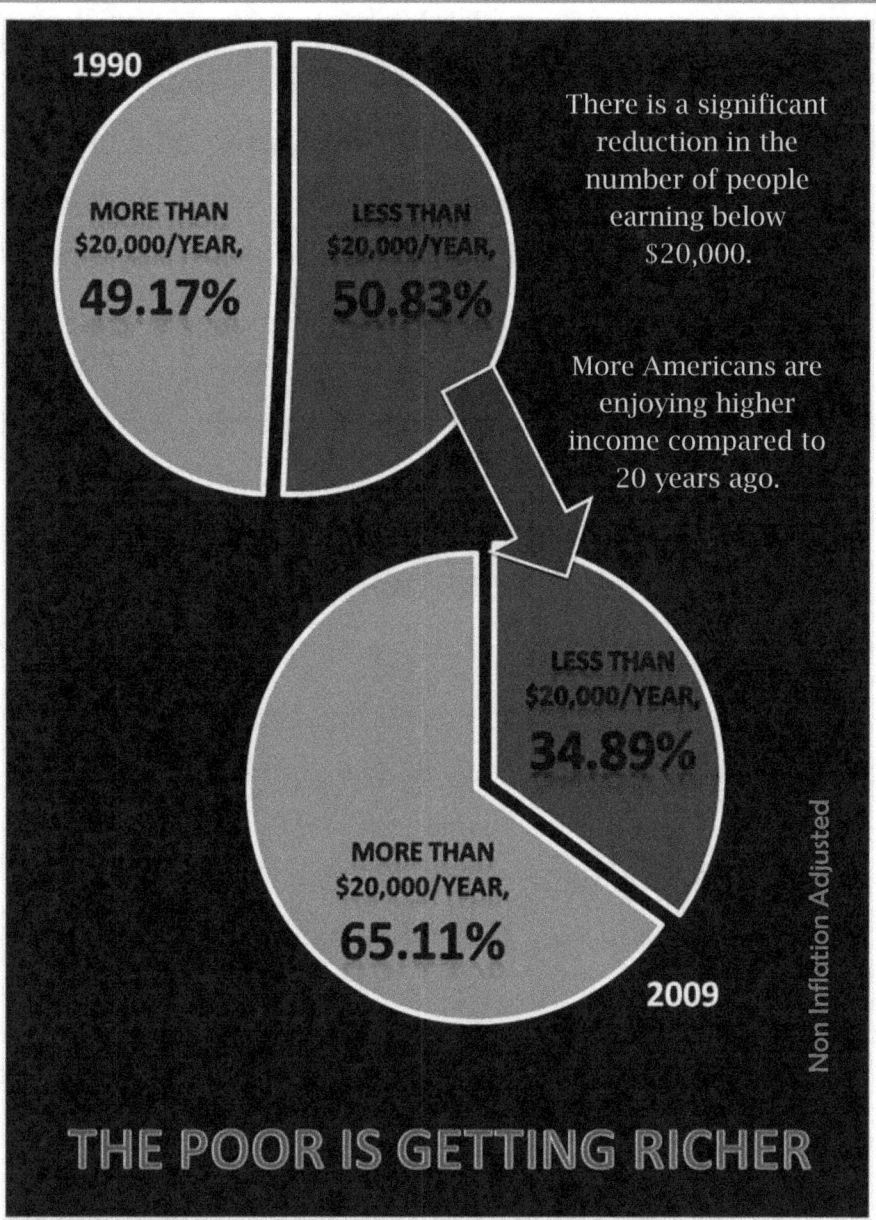

Illustration 93:
We hope this is big enough for the OWS & their supporters for imprinting in their mind (for inflation adjusted data, refer to earlier illustrations).

As if one source of data is not enough, now let's look at another reliable source of income data, this time from the Bureau of Labor Statistics. It is another dependable source of data repository and provided a wealth of good information, if one knows how to analyze them properly! The best part is, they both show the exact same thing; despite their dissimilar methods of collecting data. We summarized their data for you in the following wonderful graph (and by the way, BLS data is referred extensively in **Book** 3 of our **259 TRILLION VS 5 TRILLION** book series).

So who say the rich keeps getting richer? Clearly, the rich are obtaining less income per person, than back in 1968! The reason is very simple; remember the problem of averages? Here, there are simply too many new entrants into the upper income group, making the average lower. In essence, the rich is getting well, poorer. Just do not forget that graphs depicting incomes (increasing or decreasing) over many years do not measure the same group of people but the average of the incomes of those years. The poor of 1968 would probably be in the middle income or upper income or even in the millionaires group!

The BLS data is inflation adjusted using the 2010 CPI -U-RS.

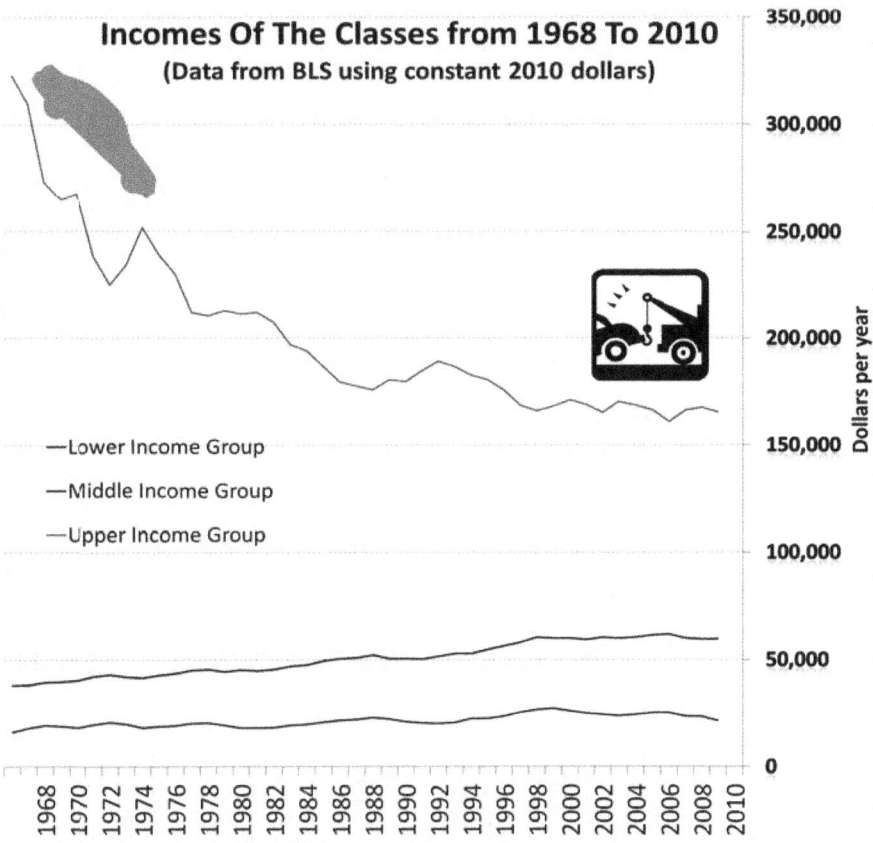

Illustration 94: Data from Bureau of Labor Statistics shows large declines of the incomes of the upper bracket while the rest of the population registered steady increases. Our data from IRS also show a similar trend

When Forbes Magazine started compiling the list of the world's billionaires back in 1987, the richest man on the planet then was Yoshiaki Tsutsumi from Japan, with wealth amounted to 20 billion dollars.

In 1988, his wealth declined to 18.9 billion, and in 1989— it was down to 15. A few years later, he was displaced by the first American, Bill Gates, who became the new richest man in the world. Subsequently, Yoshiaki's fortune dropped even more — to less than 10 billion and continued to drop, and drop. By the year 2007, he was knocked out from the billionaire list for good due to his fortune shrinking to less than a billion.

Thus, the rich and the poor come and go. Some go up and some go down, in a constantly changing landscape. The lucky 'uppers' and the poor 'downers' are not the same people all the time.

A large chunk of the fortunes of rich people especially the billionaires, are not liquid. Their fortunes are mostly tied to their companies. Their fortunes intertwine on its perceived value by investors depending on the profitability of the companies. When the public start abandoning their products, their companies' value would fall as investors jump ship.

This is in contrast with when more people perceive their products as the best and keep coming back in droves (just like what happened to Apple stocks since the release of the first iPod and iPhones and the return of Steve Jobs), and their fortunes would soar. The billionaires rarely have much liquid. They prefer to stand behind the companies they believed in or the companies that they had built.

They are much like a captain of a ship who will be the last one to leave and would rather go down with their sinking ship. It is what they were 'created' for.

Thus, when the stock markets turned around in the year 2010 onwards, their shares also went up and with that, they are able to recoup  their large losses from the previous stock markets' crash. This is why we are seeing that these people recapturing most of the new wealth 're-created' in the economy recently. It is not that they are getting richer while leaving the rest behind; it is that they are simply recouping their previous losses, their original incomes which they had lost. Read more about billionaires in "The Risk Takers" section.

Just remember, rich people are human too, and so are the poor. There can be rotten apples in each, but there are far many more good and incredibly honest people within each group. If the rich are wasteful, then indeed they will be penalized eventually, and their fortunes, lost. If the poor work hard and add value, they will strike it rich too.

There are no limits to what one can achieve.

THE BOTTOM 99% IS CONTROLLING MORE WEALTH TODAY THAN EVER BEFORE

Actual data shows the bottom 99% has increased their wealth holding of USA

An interesting fact that is never mentioned out there is that since 1990, during the longest economic expansion in America's history where 20 trillion dollars of new wealth was created, only a few hundred billions or perhaps a few trillions went to the top 1%, the majority of the wealth goes to the bottom 99%. In fact, our calculations adapted from the IRS data showed that the share of all wealth in the country controlled by the top 1%, actually declined by 2.8% from 1989 to 2007 (search for Personal Wealth Data of IRS, Statistics Of Income Division).

The data showed by OWS supporters and the others probably showed the share of the rich had gone up instead of going down, but not by much— however we disagreed with their calculations.

First, the distribution of new wealth that was created must be accounted in its gross form, not the net form. The reason is if someone who receives a million dollars from his hard work, and later buys a house worth three million dollars, paying with the cash in hand of one million and covering the remainder two million with a loan, is calculated as having a net wealth of only one million dollars regardless. Nonetheless, this person is now controlling wealth totaling three million dollars. Despite the poor's low net wealth, their gross wealth is actually rather significant. From the wealth that they controlled, incomes will be generated; provided the money is invested in wealth generating assets (houses are mostly not, unfortunately). In spite of this fact, whether we calculate the net or the gross wealth data, the numbers still show that the top 1% control on the nation's wealth declined by at least 2.4 percentage points during that period, and more, if we include the period up to 2009.

The following are the gross wealth's share of the population over the period from 1989 to 2007, and then on to 2009. IRS data showed that the top 1% was controlling 4.9 trillion dollars of wealth back in 1989, for a 20.8% share of the gross wealth of the nation, which was 23.6 trillion dollars.

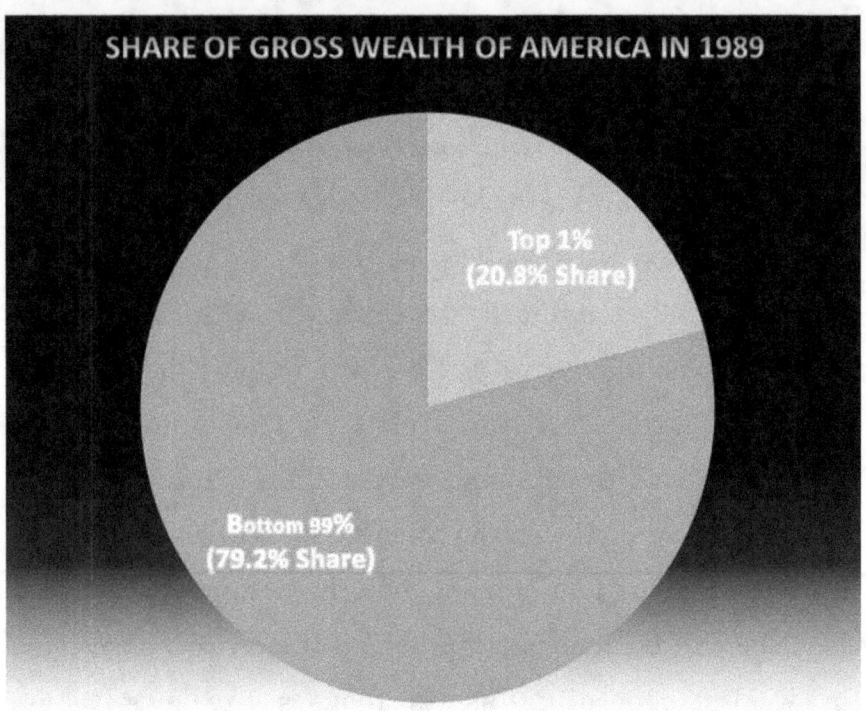

Illustration 95: Share of all wealth in America between the Top 1% and the Bottom 99% in 1989. Data obtained from the Federal Reserve and the IRS.

Contrary to what many award winning economists and pundits claimed, in 2007 the Bottom 99% actually increased the wealth they controlled, by several percent, thereby reducing the wealth level controlled by the Top 1%. Do not believe their misleading calculations because they have no clue of what they were calculating. Their conclusions are crazily misleading, until people fight over their heads due to that. Use our data and our conclusions freely and contest their outrageous conclusions!

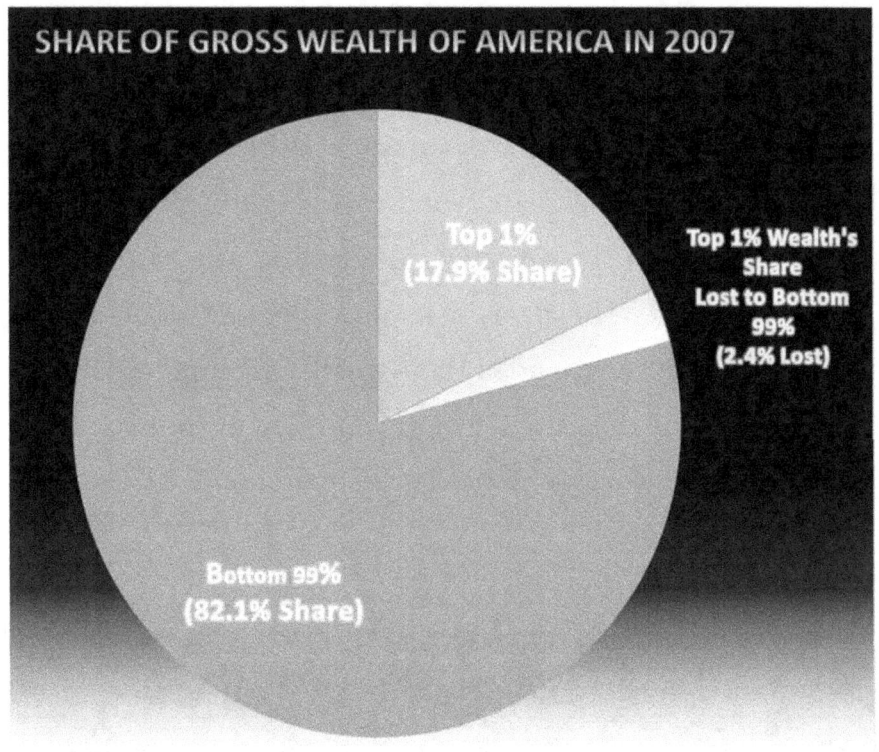

SHARE OF GROSS WEALTH OF AMERICA IN 2007

Top 1%
(17.9% Share)

Top 1% Wealth's
Share
Lost to Bottom
99%
(2.4% Lost)

Bottom 99%
(82.1% Share)

Illustration 96: Share of all wealth in America between the Top 1% and the Bottom 99% in 2007. Data obtained from the Federal Reserve and the IRS.

By 2007, the Top 1%'s share of 14.1 trillion dollars out of the nation's overall gross wealth of 78.5 trillion was down to only 17.9%. We do not know how those economists and those OWS arrived at their numbers, perhaps they can reveal their references to us for scrutiny. Gross wealth of the country is obtained from the Federal Reserve, 'Flow of Funds' for 1989 and 2007.

But wait! We portrayed the data as if the Bottom 99%

has taken over the wealth of the Top 1%. It is as if they grow their wealth at the expense of the Top 1%. Is this really true? Well, this was surely would be a confusing scenario for the OWS and their friends, and they will go gaga once again if we portray the rich as the one that is grabbing more. However, it is not confusing to us at all. The Bottom 99% expanded their wealth holding by several percent, not at the expense of anyone else in the economy. The reason is very simple. The economic pie had grown larger— by a lot.

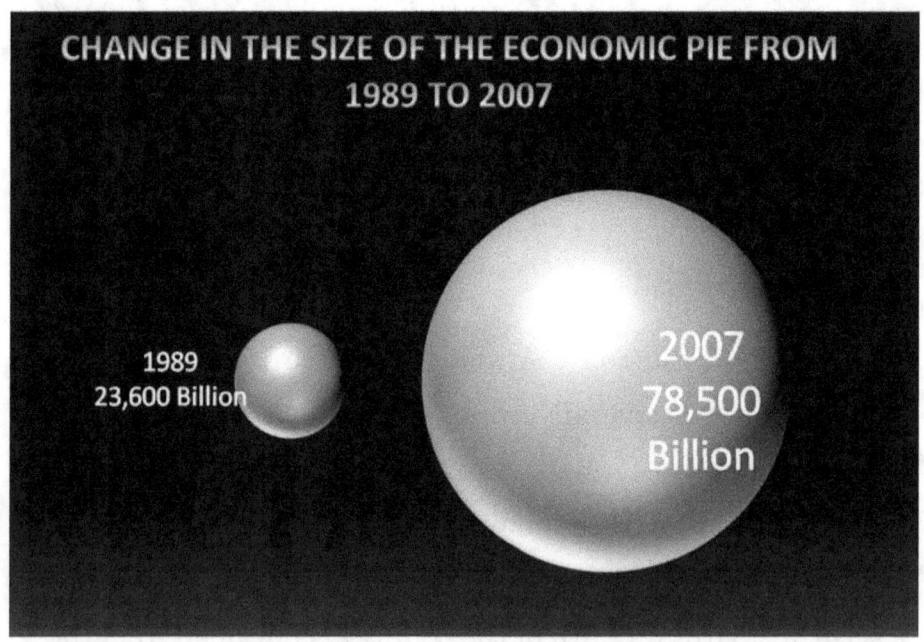

Illustration 97: Size of the economic pie has grown many times in size from 1989 to 2007. Data obtained from the Federal Reserve.

The wealth of America (as estimated by the Fed and the IRS), has grown many times over its previous size, back in 1989. It was only 23.6 trillion dollars then; but subsequently grew explosively to 78.5 trillion dollars in 2007. The Bottom 99% simply made more wealth, than the Top 1% during the period, and therefore added to their wealth— no one is taking from the other.

The mathematics of the economic pie was discussed in our **259 TRILLION VS 5 TRILLION** book series (in **Book 3**).

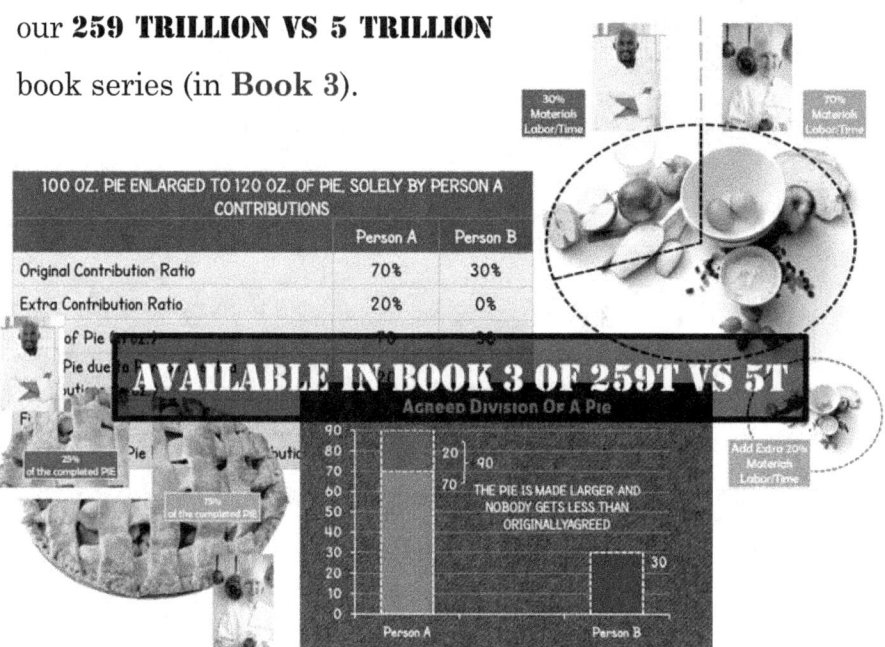

Now let us see for ourselves, what happen to the economic pie, in 2009, this time using a bar chart to see the big changes that occurred due to the financial crisis of 2008.

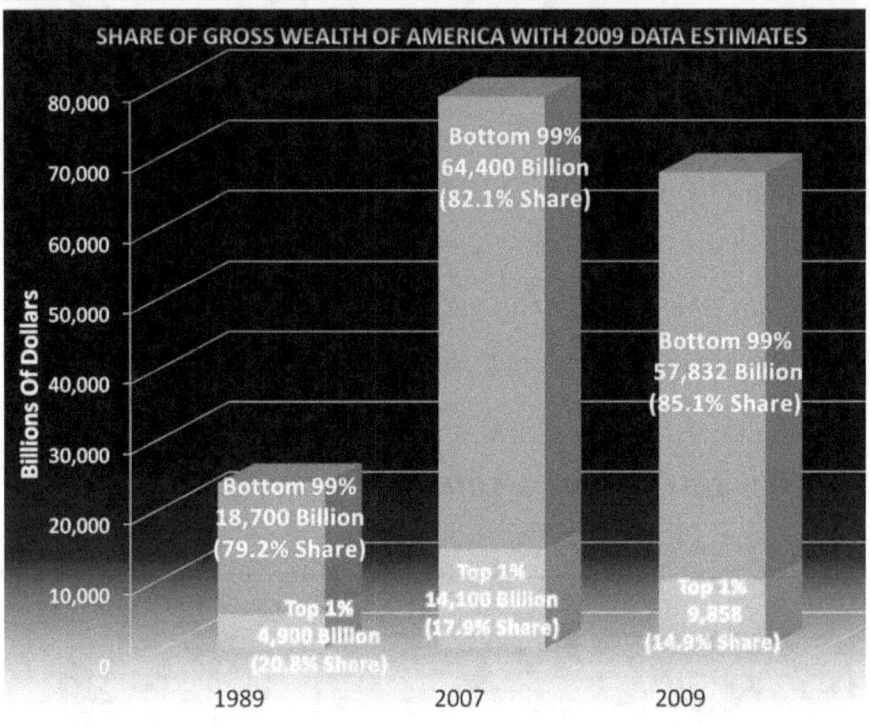

Illustration 98: Size of the economic pie and the share of the classes. Steep drop suffered by the Top 1% in 2008 resulting in further shrinkage of its share of the pie. Data obtained from the Federal Reserve with our own estimates.

In 2009, the decline of the rich intensified due to the economic crisis. We estimated from actual gross wealth data obtained from the Federal Reserve, the Top 1% share of the gross wealth declined to only 14.9% when they took a large hit on their wealth during the downturn. The Bottom 99% expanded their share of the gross wealth of America further, making the pro OWS and their likes, to be shooting their own feet because in effect, they are the one who are taking more, not the rich.

Again, the issue of the rich is controlling more and more of the nation's wealth is unfounded. They are based on half-truths and incorrect data presentation. This valuable set of data also confirmed the fact that the rich won't be getting richer, unless the poor are getting richer too. When you buy a computer, it is not only the chip manufacturer who would benefit, you will as well. It is a two way street and whenever the rich goes up a notch, you will too, and often, you will make more than them.

How about the tax burden of the rich and the poor alike? Are they shouldering the expenses of the nation fairly and in proportion to each other, or one party is paying for most of it, or if not, all of it?

Earlier at the beginning part of this writing, we mentioned that the Top 1% is already being burdened by a large disproportionate tax whereby each individual in the top 1%, are paying an average of 37 times the typical leveled tax for each individual taxpayer in all income brackets. This is however impossible to be achieved, because the rich do make more than the poor of course, and they will be bound to be paying more, even if the tax rate is the same for everybody.

In a flat taxation system, where everyone is taxed at the same rate, someone who makes more money will naturally be paying more in taxes. Someone making

$100,000 a year and is taxed at 20% would be paying $20,000 in taxes. But another person who is making one million dollars will be paying 10 times more taxes at $200,000, although they both are having the same rate of 20%.

To make matters worse, in a progressive taxation system, the more money an individual make, the higher the tax rate will be, causing the total tax to be very high. For example, if the tax rate for income above one million is 55%, a person who is making 10 million dollars will be paying $200,000 + 55% x $9,000,000 = $5.15 million dollars. That is more than 50% of the person's total income. Well, the major question is, can the government make a better use of this money than the taxpayer can? Well, it depends. This is where the taxpayers and the voters alike must make a judgment call. There is a real danger that too high of a tax, can hinder productivity and economic growth, and the rich, may simply go overseas and earn their incomes there. Based on our proposal for eliminating the national debt (in **Book** 3 of **259 TRILLION VS 5 TRILLION** series), the current tax system must be maintained and in fact, increased slightly, across the board to ensure enough income for the government, until such a date presented in the proposal.

When we mentioned earlier that the Top 1% is paying

37 times the average taxes paid by the average worker, we did not mention that if we compare the top 1% and the bottom 50%, the difference in the actual taxes paid is mind-boggling. The top 1% is paying an incredible, 815 times more than the bottom 50% in 2009, having quadrupled from its 1989 difference of 200 times. In other words, for every 10 dollars the poor is paying in income taxes, the rich will have to pay 8,150 dollars! To add salt to injury, the bottom 50% is actually paying less and less taxes, while the rich is paying more and more. This is contrary to claims by OWS and their supporters that the poor is paying more taxes. No, they do not. This is similar to someone who throws stone and point the finger to someone else — an unhealthy culture of blaming someone else for their own problems.

We have now destroyed the accusations made against the Top 1% of the nation, unfairly accused of things they never did, in fact, the accusers are the one who paid less than they did previously (or not paying any taxes at all). The rich had created immense wealth to be enjoyed by everyone; they are not at fault for the problems of this country. In fact, since the economic crisis started, the Top 1% of the nation had to live with a colossal reduction of 700 billion dollars in their yearly incomes, while the bottom 99%, hardly lost any of their income. Apparently the rich has shielded the bottom 99% from being hit too much, making the recent 2008 financial crisis, as truly a crisis of major proportion for the Top 1% (Refer to below short argument/hypothesis on how the rich is protecting the rest of the economic participants in "The Risk Takers" section).

It is clear that when the rich is getting poorer, the whole nation will be poorer as well (as predicted). However, the rich is taking it harder than the rest, sacrificing a significant chunk of their wealth and incomes in the process (business owners even take out personal loans or use their personal wealth to cover losses, should they still fail, only then they lay off their workers and close shop). When things are going in reverse, that is when the rich are getting poorer, the poor will also be getting poorer. This fact is clearly illustrated in our data (so when it goes back up; when the rich is getting richer, so will the poor).

Instead of being thanked, the Top 1% is being bullied into accepting humiliation and wrong accusations. We urge everyone to stop and think hard, and find those crooks amongst the population, while educating all economic participants on financial knowledge and management.

Here are some additional interesting facts, this time on yearly incomes, not on accumulated wealth.

For every dollar the top 1% makes, seven dollars are created at the bottom 99%. The economy is a wealth generating machine benefiting everyone.

The original bottom 99% made on average $26,575 each in 1990, and subsequently made $53,764 in 2009. It is an increase of 102%. The top 1%? They saw no change in their income level at all and stagnated at $428,00 a year.

In inflation adjusted term, the original top 1% actually suffered a shrinkage of their income, from $594,038 (in 2009 dollars) down to only $241,021 a year. The original bottom 99% proper, increased their income from $40,207 to $53,087 each a year. Now who is actually getting richer and richer all the while?

In 1990,

•3.1 million people made more than $100,000 a year
•64.3 million people made between $15,000 to $100,000 a year
•46.3 million people made less than $15,000. These are the people who are living in poverty.

In 2009,

•A record 17.4 million people made more than $100,000 a year
•A record 85.4 million people made between $15,000 to $100,000 a year
•A record low of 37.1 million people made less than $15,000.

Illustration 99: Some income statistic

It is apparent that the economic machine of the USA lifted millions of people from poverty, into the middle and the top brackets. On top of that, the middle class is also lifted into, well, the top brackets as well. It is a superb achievement never accomplished before, anywhere else. The labor force changes are summarized below (once more, for your reading pleasure!):

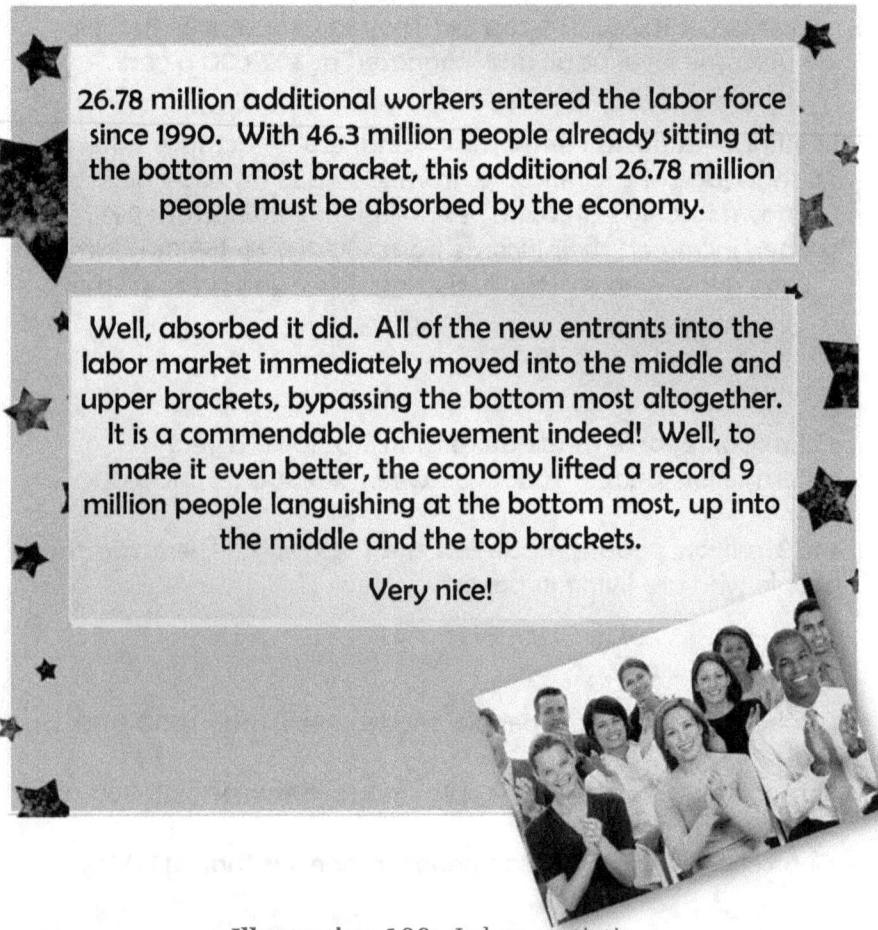

26.78 million additional workers entered the labor force since 1990. With 46.3 million people already sitting at the bottom most bracket, this additional 26.78 million people must be absorbed by the economy.

Well, absorbed it did. All of the new entrants into the labor market immediately moved into the middle and upper brackets, bypassing the bottom most altogether. It is a commendable achievement indeed! Well, to make it even better, the economy lifted a record 9 million people languishing at the bottom most, up into the middle and the top brackets.

Very nice!

Illustration 100: Labor statistic

Even in inflation adjusted terms, every income brackets of the economy prospered, as will be shown by the following series of graphs. When adjusted for inflation, the incomes of all levels of society went up, faster or higher than inflation, netting them real and substantial income increases.

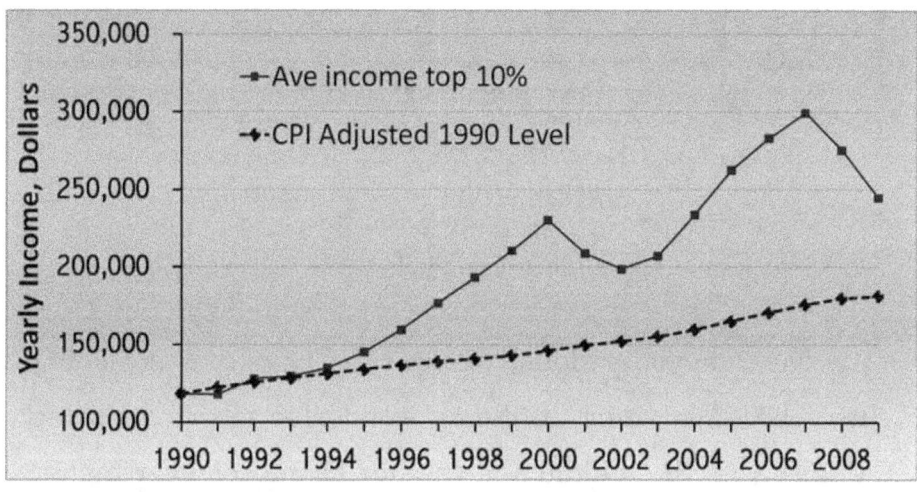

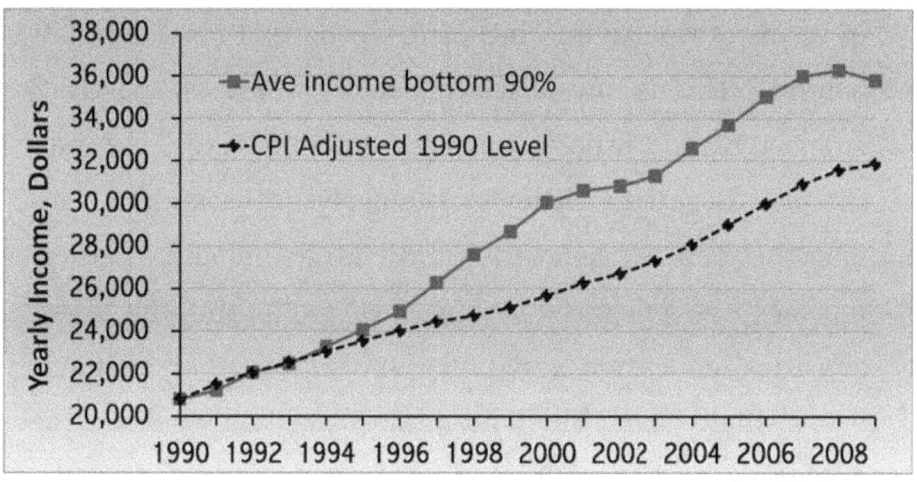

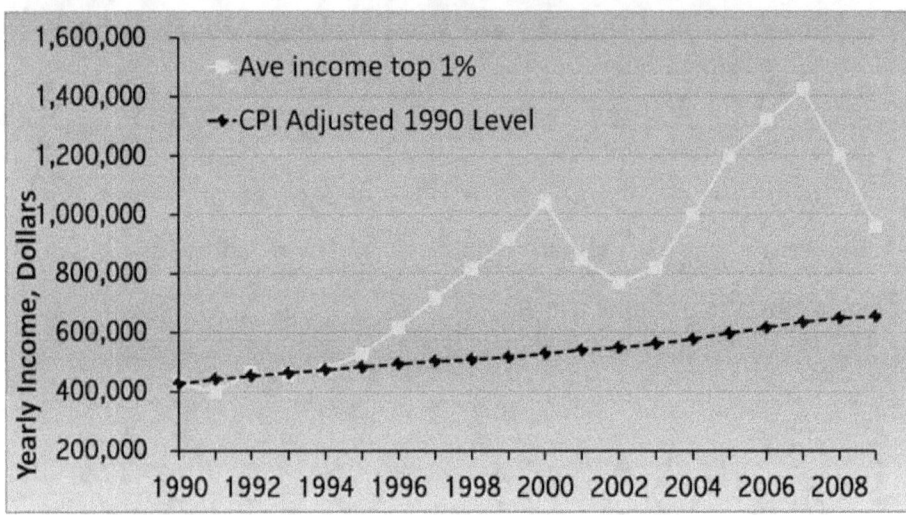

Illustration 101: Both the Top 10% and the Bottom 90% experienced an increase in income even after inflation is factored in. The Top 1% also is also similar. So, all is well at the income level for all classes

Now, do you seriously think the economy is not doing its job? We think it did a wonderful job in creating wealth. As the middle and the top 1% moved ever higher in terms of wealth and incomes, the bottom most 'felt' left behind. This is only a feeling, made worse by the OWS supporters and other economists and the like. Not just the poor is getting richer by themselves, the middle class and the Top 1% is transferring large amount of their incomes to support the bottom most group, through taxes, charities, education assistance and many other avenues, every single year. The bottom most need only ask for the assistance and learn from the assistance provided by the rich, in order to lift themselves out. One thing we learned is that people must want to be lifted out, otherwise it will not happen. Therefore, stop whining and join those who are already in the middle and the top, towards your own goals!

The rich and poor alike, created more wealth for themselves, which benefit themselves. Arguing who is making more and how much, is really pointless, because everyone actually benefits and made more. The Occupy Wall Street movement is either being misled and is mistakenly attacking the wrong group or have a hidden agenda. We suggest they target the 'crooks' instead, not the Top 1%ers.

When a large amount of wealth, is distributed to a very large group of the population, numbering in the tens of millions, the distribution of wealth seems to be small, despite the very large absolute amount involved. A poor person, who is making a thousand dollars and receives a thousand dollars in aid, either from the government or anyone from the society, has double his or her wealth or income. That is very lucky indeed and the distribution of wealth in this way is very significant. Such gifts must not be wasted on useless items, but instead be directed into improving one's own capabilities such as education and upgrade of skills.

America is the only country that we know of, that taxed its citizen's earnings from abroad, even if they had paid taxes on it. This will tilt the reported incomes of the rich further up. Nobody mentioned that the rich, those sitting at the top 1%, are now earning a larger chunk of their incomes, from overseas ventures. This is similar to public companies that are doing business globally. By earning incomes globally, they are earning it from a much wider base; it is no longer "Gross Domestic Incomes" and should not be counted into the GDP as well. Other comparisons such as the CEO pay also cannot be made only to average USA workers income alone as shown by OWS supporters and the rest. The right way to compare CEO pay is explained in the next topic – "ANSWERING THE ACCUSATION OF HIGH CEO PAY".

Further, remember that the older you become, the more your income will be. The OWS and their kind are ignorant of this fact. People who start work in their early 20s, normally earns $24,000 a year or so, but will earn considerably higher years later, and in fact, it will reach its zenith decades later— just before they retire. This is the normal way of progression for the majority. With more skills and more experience, a worker's pay would go up to reflect that.

However, there are people who would not command

higher salaries or incomes, as they get older, because they do not deserve it. They do not work hard, never acquire any useful skills and are generally not nice workers. If your friend was flipping burgers 10 years ago and still is flipping them today, without any improvement in quality and quantity, then why should he or she be paid more today than his or her initial salary of 10 years ago? There is no justice in paying your friend more, unless there are more vacancies and less workers around, of which both were not true today. There are many new workers entering the labor force, your friend will be up to a very fierce competition! Your friend either would lose his or her job, or would have to be content for lower pay. In order to be paid more, your friend must do two things, otherwise your friend do not deserve it. Higher quantity or quality, or both. Paying your friend more, is unjust, because the burgers will cost more for no obvious improvement, and it will costs ordinary people, including well, the poor themselves more dollars for the exact same burger. Therefore an increase must be justified, otherwise, it will be unfair to millions of people within the economy, and this will surely comes around and bite them back in terms of higher prices just about everywhere else.

Rewards must be just, and justified. Only deserving people who perform well in society should be rewarded.

Some people (mostly the rich) would however bypass these middle-income salary-type works. They would risk everything they have; they innovate, market, and "bulldoze" their way to the top or they would fail miserably, tumbling down to the bottom. These are the risk takers, their way is different, and their rewards are more. Not many people have the guts and the perseverance to do it.

America now has record number of old and retiring workers due to longer lifespan, so this may distort the data either way (to the top or the bottom) and is worth to look at. If anyone willing to do this study, please share it with us. The young adults, who are supporting the OWS and earning fewer dollars now, will move up the income ladder over the years and will exit or graduate from the work force, probably at the top most bracket. We are sure these same people will find it odd that just a few years before, they were the noisiest "kids on the block" who complained vehemently about those top income individuals, but now they find that they themselves become one of them. They should think twice before shooting their own foot with wrong understanding of factual data and make a fool of themselves.

These Top 1%ers are typically older individuals of the population, and it is not a surprise that they tend to make more money than the rest. The young and the poor are fighting their own fathers and mothers, grandfathers and grandmothers, and whether they like it or not, one day, they will be sitting in the same bracket just like their parents once did. We wonder how these people will think of the OWS then.

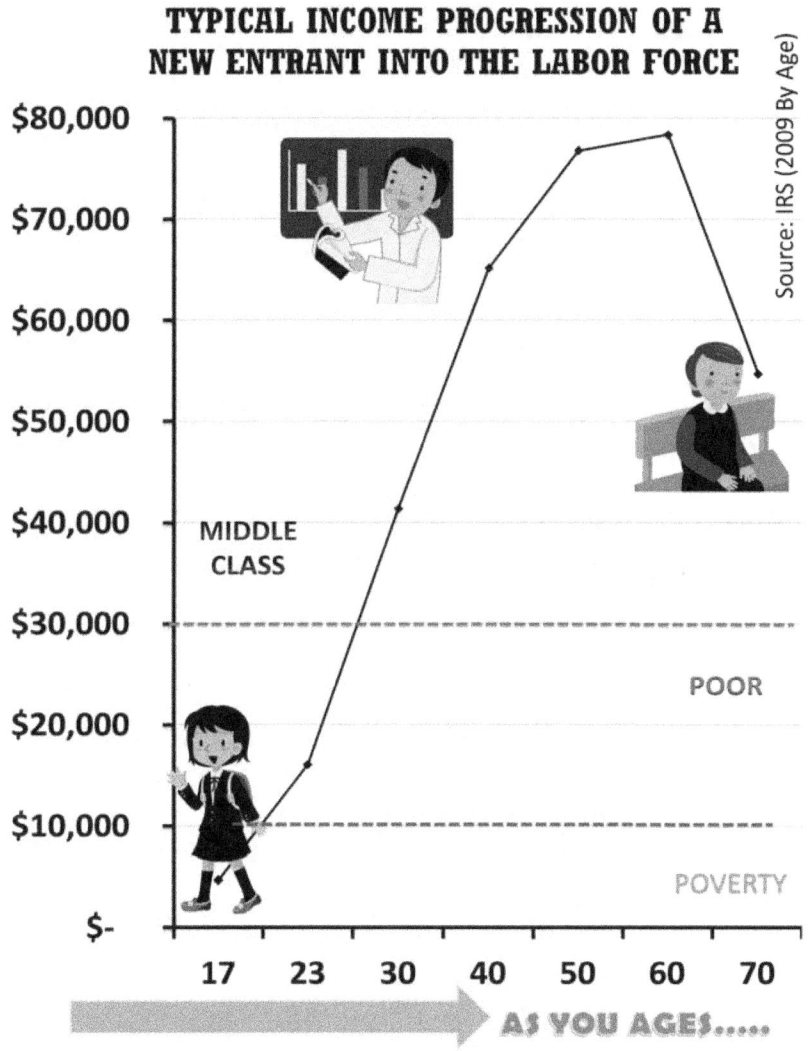

TYPICAL INCOME PROGRESSION OF A NEW ENTRANT INTO THE LABOR FORCE

Source: IRS (2009 By Age)

MIDDLE CLASS

POOR

POVERTY

17 23 30 40 50 60 70

AS YOU AGES.....

Illustration 102: You don't stay poor for long in the economy. Virtually all economic participants start at the bottom of income and is characterize as poor, but they move up within just a few years.

ANSWERING THE ACCUSATION OF HIGH CEO PAY

High CEO Pay? You will understand why it is not the case, as explained below. Subtle and clever data manipulation misled the public.

Remember the 20 trillion? We mentioned about it in our animatic **259 TRILLION VS 5 TRILLION** book series (Look for it in Book 2!). The 'fancy' statistics presented and published by those who do not understand enough of the workings of the economy showed that the income of the rich, jumped significantly compared to the poor. This seems to be the case, but in reality, it is not true. The wealth of the rich is a subset of the wealth of all of the poor, combined, for without the poor, there are no rich people. They could not exist without the poor. The 'poor' is only relative to the rich, they may not be poor in every sense, but seems to be when compared to the rich. This 'relativity' can be a big source of agitation for America's poor. They should try comparing themselves to the poor of other countries, those who make just a few dollars a year, not even enough to feed their own selves, never have any kind of telephone, of course never owning a big screen TV (because they have no electricity connection at all) and certainly, many more. Their work hours? Could it be longer than America's poor? If we put just one of them inside America, will the person become rich very quickly for working so hard?

Well, back to the 20 trillion — it was the amount of wealth created during the longest economic expansion in the 1990s, and how much do you think went to the Top 1%? There is one study published by United For a Fair Economy (cited by many Occupy Wall Streeters, making this as their major bullet against high CEO pay) which cited that from 1990, CEO's pay has increased by 298% while the average worker's pay grew only 4.3%. In terms of the average worker's pay, the CEO pay grew to 350 times their workers' pay.

[Bear with us, this study is flawed and by the end of this topic you will understand why]

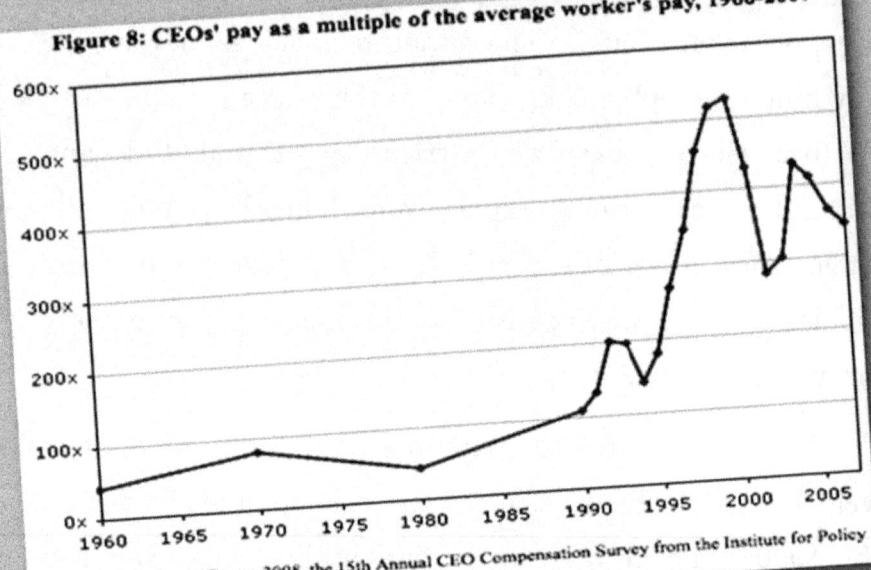

Figure 8: CEOs' pay as a multiple of the average worker's pay, 1960-2007

Source: *Executive Excess 2008*, the 15th Annual CEO Compensation Survey from the Institute for Policy
... for a Fair Economy.

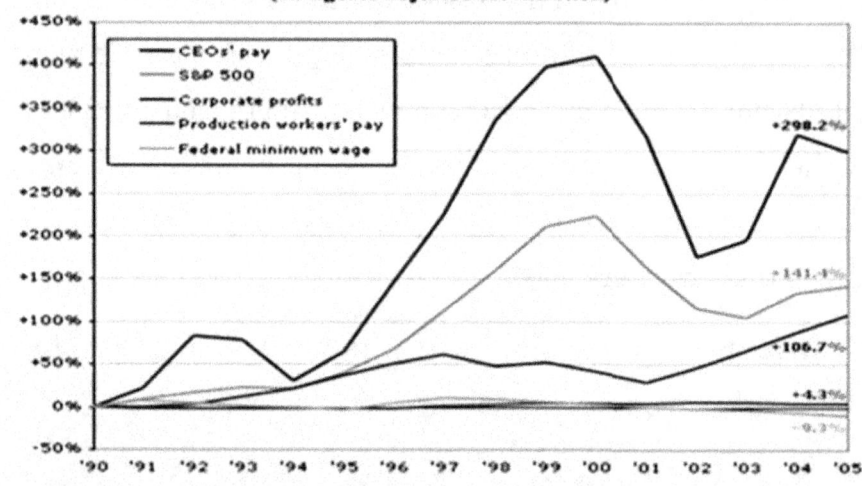

Figure 9: CEOs' average pay, production workers' average pay, the S&P 500 Index,
corporate profits, and the federal minimum wage, 1990-2005
(all figures adjusted for inflation)

Source: *Executive Excess 2006*, the 13th Annual CEO Compensation Survey from the Institute for Policy
Studies and United for a Fair Economy.

Illustration 103: Graph is taken from http://
www.businessinsider.com/what-wall-street-protesters-are-so-angry
-about to illustrate the study which is highly selective. Visit the
link for the author's view.

This study cited by OWS supporters is a terribly misleading study, presenting their data in a very erroneous fashion. For example, CEO pay is calculated by adding their salary, bonus, restricted stock options and other perks, while for the average workers' pay, their pay is only calculated based on hourly wages multiplied by average number of hours in a week, multiplied by 52 to make the number for a year. Where are the bonus, and other perks such as Social Security, Medicare and other portions that are paid by the employer? Also medical insurance, education, paid vacation and many other benefits were not included as well. This can easily skewed their 'study' significantly. Now, even if all of those are included, their study will still be very erroneous for one very big reason, selectivity of data with misrepresentation.

We can also make similar selective study, for example, we can compare the highest paid childcare provider (nanny) in the USA and compare it to nannies in other countries or with their peers in the USA to show inequalities. For your information, there are nannies that are making six-figure incomes. But is that fair? Do they deserve that high pay? 99% of other nannies may think so, because it comes with the job requirements. The same goes with CEOs.

The median CEO pays as reported by the United States Bureau of Labor Statistics is ONLY $165,080 in 2010. This is far lower that what OWS and other studies want us to believe. There are more than 250,000 CEOs in America, and we bet that (the CEO survey conducted by the Institute for Policy Studies and United For Fair Economies) did not include all CEOs.

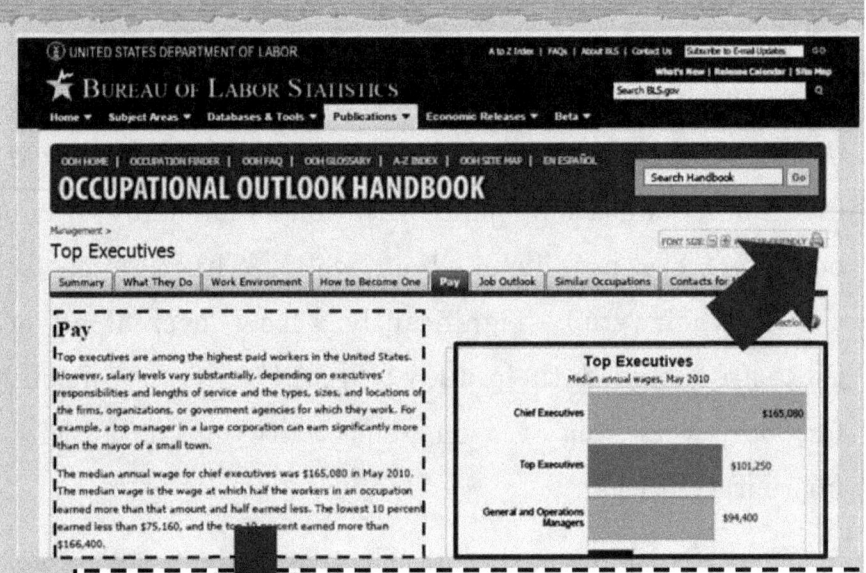

Pay

Top executives are among the highest paid workers in the United States. However, salary levels vary substantially, depending on executives' responsibilities and lengths of service and the types, sizes, and locations of the firms, organizations, or government agencies for which they work. For example, a top manager in a large corporation can earn significantly more than the mayor of a small town.

The median annual wage for chief executives was $165,080 in May 2010. The median wage is the wage at which half the workers in an occupation earned more than that amount and half earned less. The lowest 10 percent earned less than $75,160, and the top 10 percent earned more than $166,400.

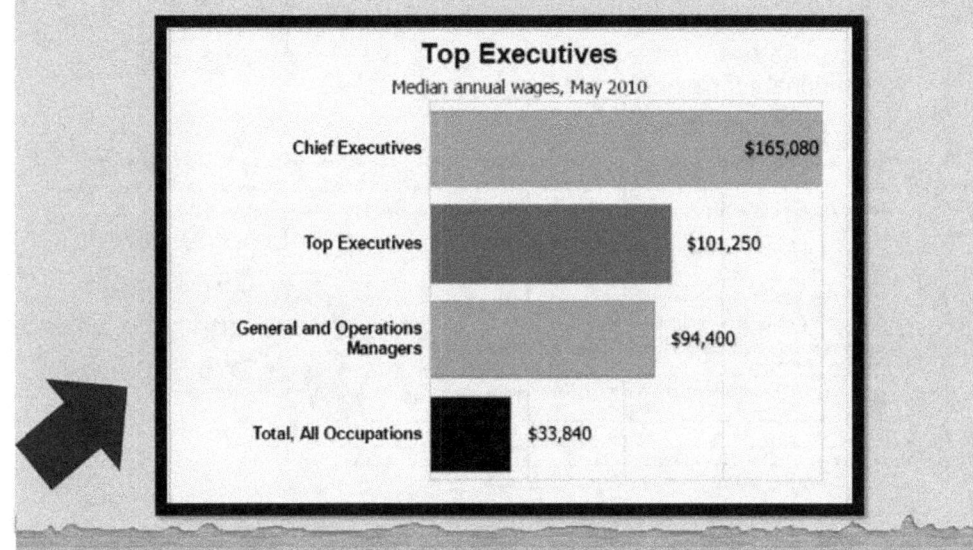

Illustration 104: Bureau of Labor Statistic reported that the median annual wages for CEO is $165,080 in May 2010. The survey includes all CEO which numbers in hundreds of thousands which is a stark contrast with picking top highest paid CEO by the 'other" study..

In our opinion, the BLS data is far more accurate than the random or limited surveys conducted by these studies mentioned. The real situation on the ground is different than what they are portraying. During the longest economic expansion, everyone grew richer, and we confirmed that the poor especially, did a lot better than most people. Corporations made the most profit ever recorded then, their workers rewarded handsomely, their shareholders too, but not so for their CEOs. In this part of the book, we will show how CEOs fared, compared to their workers in general.

Occupational Employment and Wages, May 2011

11-1011 Chief Executives

Determine and formulate policies and provide overall direction of companies or private and public sector organizations within guidelines set up by a board of directors or similar governing body. Plan, direct, or coordinate operational activities at the highest level of management with the help of subordinate executives and staff managers.

Employment: 267,370

Mean annual wage: $176,550

National estimates for this occupation: Top

Employment estimate and mean wage estimates for this occupation:

Employment	Employment RSE	Mean hourly wage	Mean annual wage	Wage RSE
267,370	0.5 %	$84.88	$176,550	0.4 %

Percentile wage estimates for this occupation:

Percentile	10%	25%	50% (Median)	75%	90%
Hourly Wage	$36.47	$52.56	$80.25		
Annual Wage	$75,860	$109,320	$166,910		

(US Bureau of Labor Statistics)

Industries with the highest levels of employment in this occupation:

Industry	Employment	Percent of industry employment	Hourly mean wage	Annual mean wage
Management of Companies and Enterprises	21,340	1.12	$100.63	$209,320
Local Government (OES Designation)	18,740	0.34	$52.61	$109,440
Elementary and Secondary Schools	13,58	0.16	$66.70	$138,730
State Government (OES Designation)	8,850	0.39	$48.43	$100,510
Depository Credit Intermediation	7,460	0.44	$86.32	$179,550

(US Bureau of Labor Statistics)

Illustration 105: Bureau of Labor Statistic reported that the median annual wages for CEO is $176,550 in May 2011. For other tables (top paying industries, highest concentration of employment and others) visit the www.bls.gov.

The number of CEOs vary significantly depending on how CEOs are categorized; there are more than 5 million companies in the United States, so clearly not all of them are called 'CEOs'. To make things even worst, it is possible to be even more selective in choosing whom to compare with or what— we found that many studies only surveyed the pay of CEOs of publicly traded companies in the US, thereby selecting only around 6,000 companies in total (compared to 5 million plus companies, public and private overall, a mere 0.12% of the total). Just when we thought that their erroneous and misguided presentations could not get any worse, well— it does! This selectivity is pushed even further, when more pronounced and hyped studies continued on selecting only the largest of those publicly traded companies, those top few hundred or so, of the largest corporations in the world (not just in the US). The end result, is a disastrous kind of comparison with the average workers' pay.

Therefore, we will provide the solution and how to present the comparison of CEO pay and their employees properly. We challenge these people to go and make the following calculations. First, each CEO must be compared to their own workers only. Their pay cannot be compared to other companies' average workers because of their different profitability and nature of business. CEO is paid more when the company is doing well, and we deduce, their workers will enjoy similar windfall as well. However, it is not correct to compare a highflying CEO pay in a very profitable company, with a not so profitable company's average worker pay, somewhere in the US. It will be very misleading and mathematically, erroneous. It is not apple to apple comparison, but to rotten egg instead!

Second, the total payment towards all labor costs within the company is compared to that of the CEO. Make these calculations, and present it! A company such as IBM or General Electric with more than one hundred thousand workers, is spending billions in workers' pay, and is only paying their CEO's in the tune of millions of dollars. Those who are making these calculations must take note of how many of their employees are residing out of the US, and although they are paid lower compared to their American colleagues, but when compared to their country of residence, their pay could be larger than the comparable locals. If they dare not make these calculations and reveal it, or perhaps they are incapable of analyzing the data to present to the world, no fear, because we can do so! It is a pain to do, but it is worth it.

We found that the ever-higher CEO pay is actually the reverse; it is ever shrinking!

Let's go through the data, together. It is rather long,

but we dug out all the CEO pay packages of select companies, and then compare their pay to their workers' pay. We dug out the number of employees they have and what are their total expenses for their employees and related expenses. Our data may not be perfect, but it does reveal the important fact that we are looking for.

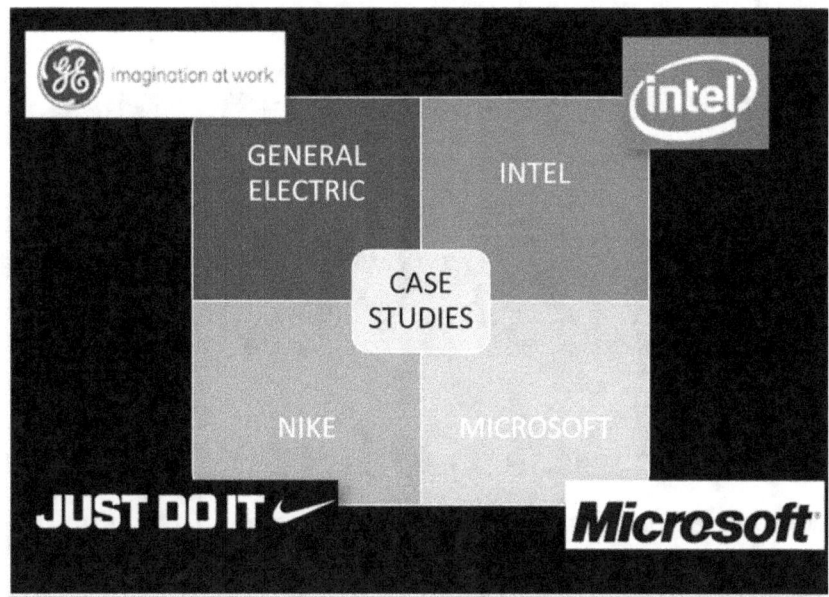

Illustration 106:

We chose four well known USA companies as case studies for the CEO pay. This is a better study of CEO pay compared to what is out there.

In fact, if you do this to all public listed companies (good and reliable companies), you will see that our conclusions are correct. There are companies where the ratio is on the increase of course, but the increase would be small and not to the tune of 350x as per the "over-hyped" studies by the OWS supporters.

Case Study #1

First, we will start with a company that is so synonymous with America — GENERAL ELECTRIC.

GENERAL ELECTRIC		
	1993	
Sales Total	$60,562,000,000	
Workforce	222,000	
Net Profit as of Sales	$4,315,000,000	
Sales per employee	$272,802	
Other costs and expenses	$13,774,000,000	
CEO Compensation	$8,025,534	
Other costs and expenses - CEO pay	$13,765,974,466	
Costs & Expenses Per Employee	$62,009	
CEO Pay/ Sales	0.0133%	percent of sales
Worker's Pay/ Sales	22.73%	percent of sales

Illustration 107: Summary of sales, labor and cost for GE in 1993

Back in 1993, GE paid its CEO (Jack Welch) a compensation package totaling $8,025,534 (based on data filed with SEC). The total revenue of GE at that time was USD60.5 billion, making the CEO pay over the total sales to be 0.01325%. GE listed its costs of employment and other costs and expenses as USD13.78 billion, and with 222,000 strong employees on its payroll, their various costs of employments over their own sales number was therefore about 22.7%.

Now let us move on to the year 2007, at the height of the 'Irrational Exuberance'.

GENERAL ELECTRIC

	2007
Sales Total	$173,000,000,000
Workforce	327,000
Net Profit as of Sales	$22,208,000,000
Sales per employee	$529,052
Other costs and expenses	$40,297,000,000
CEO Compensation	$14,209,267
Other costs and expenses - CEO pay	$40,282,790,733
Costs & Expenses Per Employee	$123,189
CEO Pay/ Sales	0.0082%	percent of sales
Worker's Pay/ Sales	23.28%	percent of sales

Illustration 108: Summary of sales, labor and cost for GE in 2007

GE registered a massive revenue of USD173 billion with a very significant increase of workers to 327,000. The CEO pay was $14,209,267 for that year, which is a mere 0.0082% of total sales. This is a significant decline from the 0.01325% ratio recorded in 1993. The CEO pay has shrunk, when compared to his 1993's pay, but his responsibilities— did not. The CEO (Jeff Immelt) now have to manage one hundred thousand more workers than before, a bigger company than before and a much more complicated and tough, global business environment with difficult and nasty competitors. The pay for workers and others plus related expenses was USD40.3 billion (at 23.28% over sales), which is an increase from its 1993 ratio.

(1993)
PAY/SALES: 0.0133%

(2007)
PAY/SALES: 0.0082%

Images: Courtesy of GE

Illustration 109: From 1993 to 2007, the CEO pay/sales declined by 38%

In fact, if you take Jeff Immelt's salary in 2007 (all of it) and give it to each of GE employees, then each employee will get $43.45 for that year! Hardly making a difference to the employee annual salary at all. It is similar to the shareholders, not a dent in their dividend returns.

What Jeff Immelt brings into the company is more valuable.

It is clear that when a true comparison of the CEO and its workers' pay is made, it will yield a result that is the opposite of what the OWS and other studies concluded to have happened.

The following illustration handily show what happened to GE all these years, and what its CEO pay should be, if they simply maintain the same ratio as in the 1990s, where CEO pay was cited by OWS and others to be low compared to their workers. We will compare the actual and proposed rate for the year 2007, where CEO pay is at its highest.

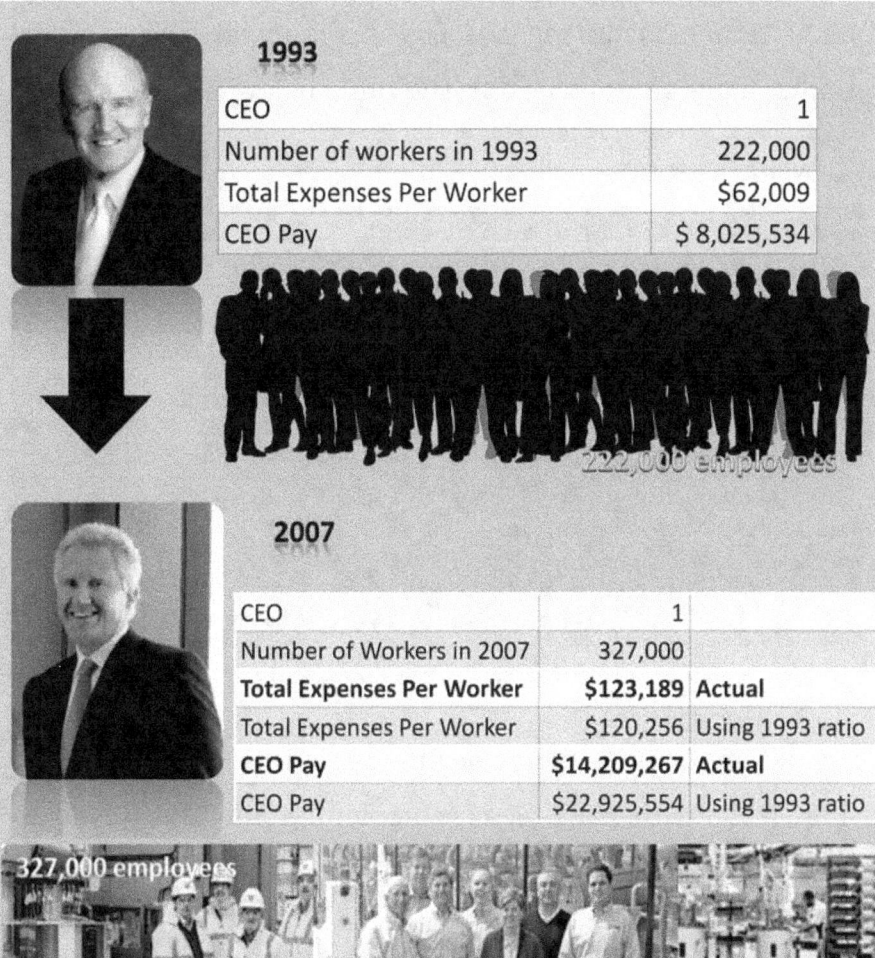

1993	
CEO	1
Number of workers in 1993	222,000
Total Expenses Per Worker	$62,009
CEO Pay	$ 8,025,534

222,000 employees

2007		
CEO	1	
Number of Workers in 2007	327,000	
Total Expenses Per Worker	$123,189	Actual
Total Expenses Per Worker	$120,256	Using 1993 ratio
CEO Pay	$14,209,267	Actual
CEO Pay	$22,925,554	Using 1993 ratio

327,000 employees

Images: from GE Annual report 2007/ Jack Welch (GE Website)

Illustration 110: If based on the 1993 ratio, Jeff Immelt's pay should have been 23mil. Instead he only received 14mil, a 38% pay cut even though his sales grew by 186% and with more than 100,000 extra employees.

Even though the current CEO of GE grew his company's revenue by 186% and with 100,000 more staffs to manage, his pay took an effective 38% cut.

We also decided to obtain the numbers for the year 2009, which is during the Great Financial Crisis. The findings are summarized in the table below.

GENERAL ELECTRIC		
	2009	
Sales Total	154,438,000,000	
Workforce	304,000	
Net Profit as of Sales	11,025,000,000	
Sales per employee	508,020	
Other costs and expenses	37,354,000,000	
CEO Compensation	9,885,240	
Other costs and expenses - CEO pay	37,344,114,760	
Costs & Expenses Per Employee	122,842	
CEO Pay/ Sales	0.006%	percent of sales
Worker's Pay/ Sales	24.18%	percent of sales

Illustration 111: Summary of sales, labor and cost for GE in 2009

When GE's revenue declined, so was the CEO pay. This is what responsible corporations would do. Rewards are based on performance and profit. Every sales person knows this.

Illustration on the next page shows the overall comparison between the years:

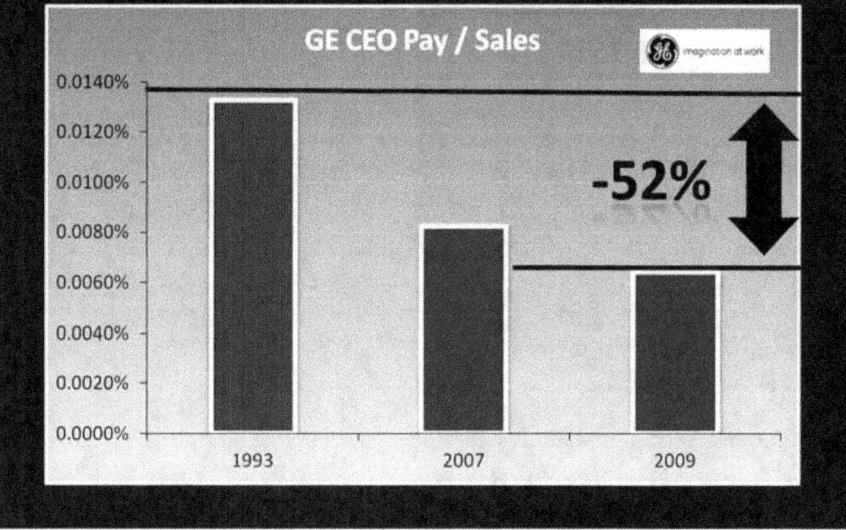

GENERAL ELECTRIC

	CEO Pay / Sales	Labor Costs / Sales
1993	0.0133%	22.7%
2007	0.0082%	23.3%
2009	0.0064%	24.2%
1993 to 2007 (Changes %)	-38%	2%
1993 to 2009 (Changes %)	-52%	6%

	Sales	CEO Pay	Labor Costs Per Employee
1993	$ 60,562,000,000	$ 8,025,534	$ 62,009
2007	$173,000,000,000	$14,209,267	$ 123,189
2009	$154,438,000,000	$ 9,885,240	$ 122,842
1993 to 2007 (Changes %)	186%	77%	99%
1993 to 2009 (Changes %)	155%	23%	98%

Illustration 112: Table shows the overall comparison between the years. The CEO/Sales ratio decreased 52%.
In dollar terms, CEO pay grew less than labor cost per employee did.

From 1993 to 2007, GE CEO's pay had shrunk by 38% while its labor, up by 2%. The average expenses of GE per employee however have jumped massively by 99%. In 2009, the ratio worsened when the CEO pay shrunk by a total of 52% compared to 1993. Those alleged high CEO pay? Not in sight at all!

On the side, we also took the liberty to calculate what is the revenue or sales attributable to each of GE's employee. We found that back in 1993, each employee was generating $272,802 a year in sales, and in 2007, a record $529,052. In our opinion, the increase in salaries for GE employees are justified, however the CEO is taking in lower pay than before, despite his good performance.

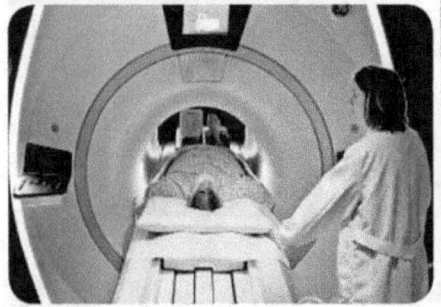

Images: GE Annual Reports

Case Study #2

Now let us analyze other famous American companies.

Let's move on to Intel, the icon of the microprocessor.

INTEL

	1990
Sales Total	$3,921,274,000
Net Profits	$650,261,000
Staffs	23,900
Sales per employee	$164,070
Marketing, general and administrative	$615,904,000
CEO Compensation	$1,000,000 (estimated)
Marketing, general and administrative minus CEO pay	$614,904,000
Costs & Expenses Per Employee	$25,770
CEO Pay/ Sales	0.0255% percent of sales
Staffs Pay/ Sales	15.68% percent of sales

Illustration 113: Summary of sales, labor and cost for INTEL in 1990

In 1990, Intel was raking in revenue of 3.92 billion dollars with only 23,900 staffs. The CEO was paid a million dollars (it was a very good pay then). The CEO pay over sales is 0.0255% while the staffs, and other related costs were 15.68% of sales. The company was very healthy and very competitive with low operating costs.

What happened to Intel in 2007?

INTEL

	2007
Sales Total	$38,334,000,000
Net Profits	
Staffs	86,300
Sales per employee	$444,195
Marketing, general and administrative	$5,401,000,000
CEO Compensation	$11,542,000
Marketing, general and administrative minus CEO pay	$5,389,458,000
Costs & Expenses Per Employee	$62,584
CEO Pay/ Sales	0.0301% percent of sales
Staffs Pay/ Sales	14.06% percent of sales

Illustration 114: Summary of sales, labor and cost for INTEL in 2007

The stalwart of the electronics industry grew its size by 10 times, to 38.3 billion dollars in sales with 86,300 staffs. The CEO was paid $11.5 million dollars. The CEO pay has increased slightly by 0.006% and the costs of labor over sales had decreased to 14.059%. But in 2009, both CEO pay and labor costs increased. The summary for Intel is shown on the next page:

Image: Intel Annual Report 2009

INTEL CEO Paul Ottelini

YOU DON'T REPRESENT US—ANSWERING OCCUPY WALL STREET

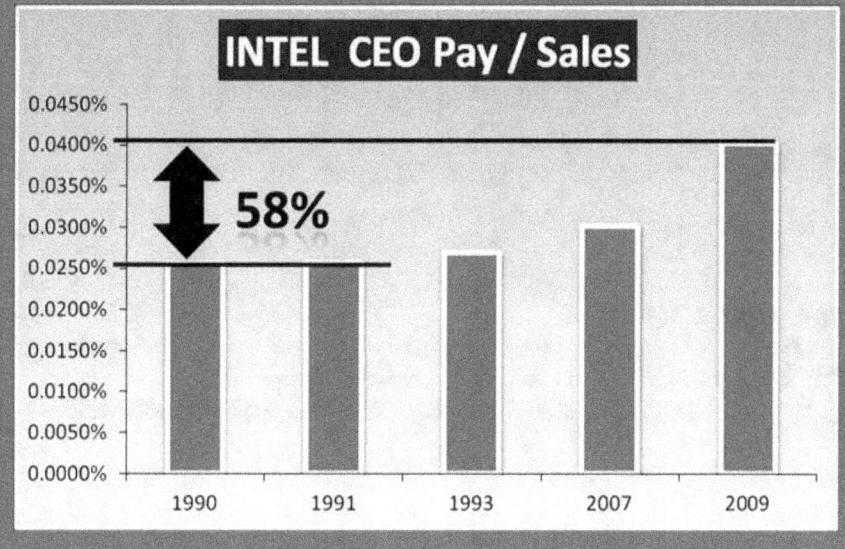

INTEL

	CEO Pay / Sales	Labor Costs / Sales
1990	0.0255%	15.7%
1991	0.0256%	16.0%
1993	0.0268%	13.3%
2007	0.0301%	14.1%
2009	0.0402%	22.6%
1990 to 2007 (Changes %)	18%	-10%
1990 to 2009 (Changes %)	58%	44%

	Sales	CEO Pay	Labor Costs Per Employee
1990	$ 3,921,274,000	$ 1,000,000	$25,770
1991	$ 4,778,616,000	$ 1,225,300	$31,100
1993	$ 8,782,000,000	$ 2,356,200	$39,593
2007	$38,334,000,000	$11,542,000	$62,584
2009	$35,100,000,000	$14,117,500	$99,386
1990 to 2007 (Changes %)	878%	1054%	143%
1990 to 2009 (Changes %)	795%	1312%	286%

Illustration 115: Table shows that CEO pay over sales rose by 58% and labor costs rose 44%. In dollar terms, the rise was big but their sales did increase nearly 800 percent. This is no where near the 350x claims by the OWS.

Intel is the only one of our case study company to show increasing CEO pay, (in terms of ratio of CEO Pay over Sales). However Intel started with very low pay for its CEO (most likely due to its CEO was the founder then), lower than the industry standard. Over the years, the CEO salary went up higher, into the band of industry's standard, especially after the founders retired. The good part is, the workers continue to enjoy good pay, as per the industry standard as well. All is well, and everyone is expecting Intel to continue to perform, despite the very tough changes in the market place.

The 35,000% more salary than the average workers' pay? Still nowhere in sight!

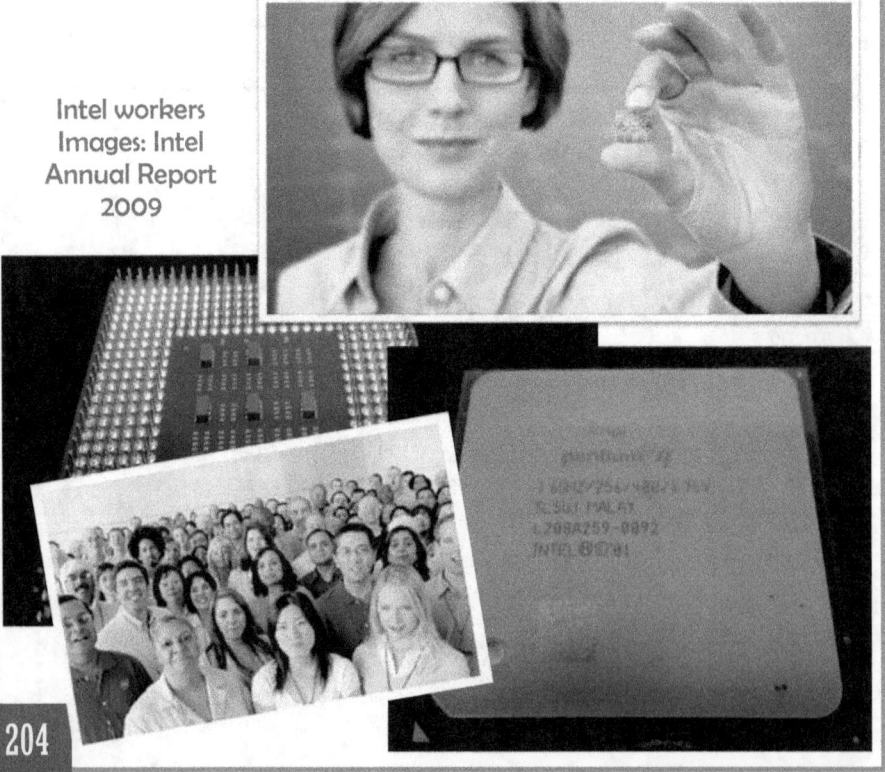

Intel workers
Images: Intel
Annual Report
2009

Case Study #3

Let's move on to another famous American icon, Nike.

NIKE

	1990
Sales Total	2,235,244,000
Net Profits	242,958,000
Staffs	9,500
Sales per employee	235,289
Selling and administrative	454,521,000
CEO Compensation	1,000,000 (estimate)
Selling and administrative - CEO pay	453,521,000
Costs & Expenses Per Employee	47,739
CEO Pay/ Sales	0.0447% percent of sales
Staffs Pay/ Sales	20.29% percent of sales

Illustration 116: Summary of sales, labor and cost for NIKE in 1990

The data is a bit sketchy because it was more than 20 years ago. We are forced to do estimation for its CEO salary based on payment records, as well as its number of staffs. In any case, we think we have it very close to the actual payout. Nike's CEO pay was 0.044% of its sales, while its employees and its other related expenses was 20.29% of all sales.

In 2007,

NIKE

	2007
Sales Total	$16,326,000,000
Net Profits	$1,492,000,000
Staffs	30,200
Sales per employee	$540,596
Selling and administrative	$5,028,000,000
CEO Compensation	$6,227,968
Selling and administrative - CEO pay	$5,021,772,032
Costs & Expenses Per Employee	$166,284
CEO Pay/ Sales	0.0381%	percent of sales
Staffs Pay/ Sales	30.76%	percent of sales

Illustration 117: Summary of sales, labor and cost for NIKE in 2007

Again, we are seeing a clear trend of declining CEO pay, while for employees, the opposite. The trend is rather significant at Nike. Below is the comparison summary for the year 1990 and 2007.

1990

CEO	1
Number of workers in 1990	9,500
Total Expenses Per Worker	$ 47,739
CEO Pay	$ 1,000,000

9,500 workers

2007

30,198 workers

CEO	1	
Number of Workers in 2007	30,200	
Total Expenses Per Worker	**$ 166,284**	**Actual**
Total Expenses Per Worker	$ 80,478	Using 1990 ratio
CEO Pay	**$ 6,227,968**	**Actual**
CEO Pay would be	$ 7,145,406	Using 1990 ratio

Images: from NIKE Annual reports/ Employee Chart from NIKE Corporate Responsibility Report

Illustration 118: NIKE's CEO pay also decline as a ratio against sales. The labor costs however have increased

In 2009, Nike's CEO pay did not change at all compared to its sales, but for employees, it went up even more!

> When the OWS (other economists) talk about CEO pay, they forget about sales and company's capital!!

> Even within the same company, it is possible to have different compensation packages due to dissimilar performance between internal divisions. Averages must be used carefully

NIKE   JUST DO IT ✓

	CEO Pay / Sales	Labor Costs / Sales
1990	0.0447%	20.3%
1994	0.0392%	25.7%
2007	0.0381%	30.8%
2009	0.0381%	32.0%
1990 to 2007 (Changes %)	-15%	52%
1990 to 2009 (Changes %)	-15%	58%

	Sales	CEO Pay	Labor Costs Per Employee
1990	$ 2,235,244,000	$ 1,000,000	$ 47,739
1994	$ 3,789,700,000	$ 1,487,411	$ 72,045
2007	$16,326,000,000	$ 6,227,968	$ 166,284
2009	$19,176,000,000	$ 7,306,694	$ 179,087
1990 to 2007 (Changes %)	630%	523%	248%
1990 to 2009 (Changes %)	758%	631%	275%

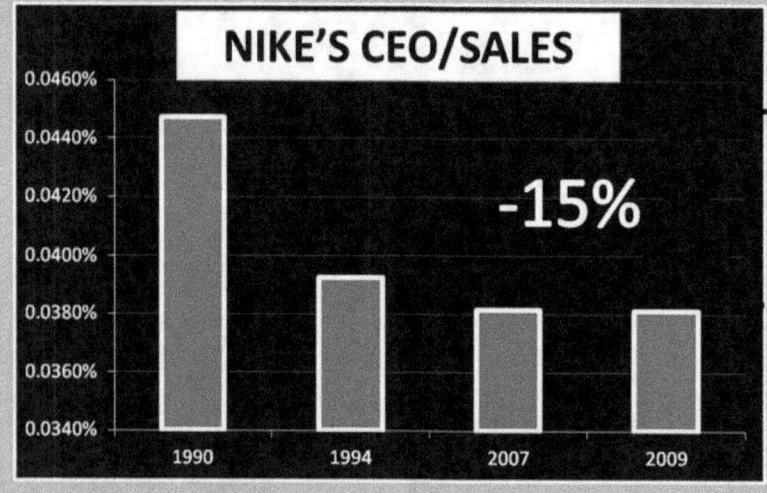

Illustration 119: Table show the overall CEO pay over sales has decreased, and that in dollar terms, the pay increase is on par with sales increase.

While the CEO pay took a tumble of 15% compared to 1990, its employees took a hike of 58%. This is a very significant increase. Our overall conclusion is, Nike has kept its CEO pay at par with its company revenue, but for employees, the costs went up very high (+275%). Essentially, the employees are taking in far more than what they used to, while the CEO is taking in slightly less, than what he used to, and in relative to its workers.

Also, take a closer look at the labor costs per employee, which grew by 275% from 1990 to 2009, while the CEO pay grew by 758%. Here, the data can easily mislead anyone and stir their feelings, and those with an agenda, they can manipulate the presentation easily. Do not be fooled. Nike's sales grew by a massive 758% over that period, and it makes sense for its CEO pay to grow the way it had.

So does the CEO's pay is getting higher while the average worker is getting less? Not so! The rich is getting richer while the poor is getting poorer? Not true at all!

If you are still not convinced, let us look at yet another American icon, Microsoft.

Case Study #4

MICROSOFT	*Microsoft*
	1994
Sales Total	$4,649,000,000
Net Profits	$1,146,000,000
Workforce	15,257
Sales per employee	$304,713
Research & Dev (include payroll, benefits, stocks grants and others)	$610,000,000
Sales & Marketing (include payroll, benefits, stocks grants and others)	$1,384,000,000
General & Admin (include payroll, benefits, stocks, and others)	$166,000,000
CEO Compensation	$457,545
All expenses - CEO pay	$2,159,542,455
Costs & Expenses Per Employee	$141,544
CEO Pay/ Sales	**0.0098%**
Staffs Pay/ Sales	**46.45%**

Illustration 120: Table shows the summary of sales, labor and costs for MICROSOFT in 1990

Microsoft's revenue was 4.65 billion dollars in 1994 with 15,257 employees. The CEO pay was a puny 0.0098% of all sales, a really small number while its employees are 'raking' in 46.45% of all sales, which is a rather high number. But since Microsoft is a predominantly 'software' company, the most important asset was indeed, its knowledge base employees.

Well by 2007, Microsoft had grown many times of its 1994 size.

MICROSOFT	Microsoft
	2007
Sales Total	$51,122,000,000
Net Profits	$14,065,000,000
Workforce	79,000
Sales per employee	$647,114
Research & Dev (include payroll, benefits, stocks grants and others)	$7,121,000,000
Sales & Marketing (include payroll, benefits, stocks grants and others)	$11,541,000,000
General & Admin (include payroll, benefits, stocks, and others)	$3,329,000,000
CEO Compensation	$1,279,821
All expenses - CEO pay	$21,989,720,179
Costs & Expenses Per Employee	$278,351
CEO Pay/ Sales	**0.0025%**
Staffs Pay/ Sales	**43.01%**

Illustration 121: Table shows the summary of sales, labor and cost for MICROSOFT in 2007

The company made sales worth 51.12 billion dollars with 79,000 employees. The CEO was paid $1.28 million, and the CEO pay over sales, shrunk significantly to only a mere 0.0025%. Microsoft's staffs made sales worth $647,000 each, and were paid $278,000 on average. The staffs pay over their sales declined slightly to 43.01%. Microsoft has indeed done quite well in managing its costs.

MICROSOFT

Microsoft

	CEO Pay / Sales	Labor Costs / Sales
1994	0.0098%	46.5%
2007	0.0025%	43.0%
2009	0.0022%	43.8%
1990 to 2007 (Changes %)	-75%	-7%
1990 to 2009 (Changes %)	-78%	-6%

	Sales	CEO Pay	Labor Costs Per Employee
1994	$ 4,649,000,000	$ 457,545	$ 141,544
2007	$51,122,000,000	$ 1,279,821	$ 278,351
2009	$58,437,000,000	$ 1,265,833	$ 275,137
1990 to 2007 (Changes %)	1000%	180%	97%
1990 to 2009 (Changes %)	1157%	177%	94%

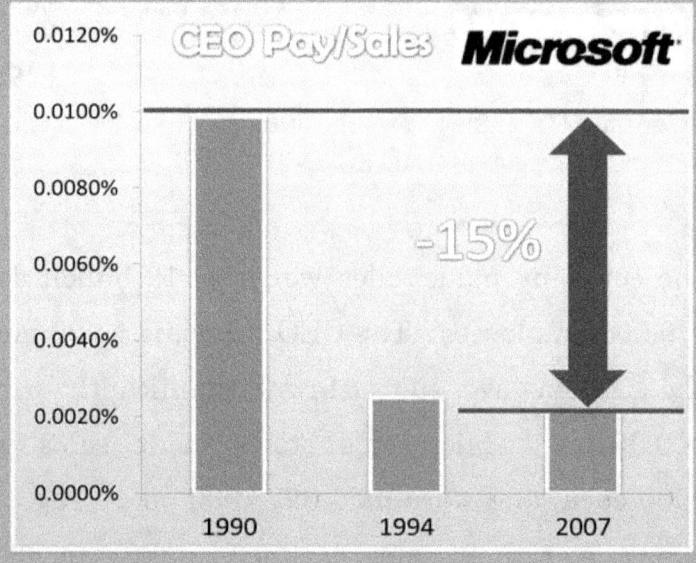

Illustration 122:
Table shows the summary of sales, labor and cost for MICROSOFT over the 3 years. This is among our best case studies on CEO pay. As sales grew by 1000%, the CEO pay only rose 180% (in non adjusted dollar terms).
In terms of CEO pay over sales, it declined by 75%. The ratio of 0.002% is the lowest in our case studies.

Overall, Microsoft's CEO pay declined by a record 78% while its employees, shot up by 94%, from 1994 to 2009. Well, we are not seeing CEO pay went up 350 times of employee wages as far as the eye can see! In fact, the opposite is happening.

With more accurate and representative data, we are able to show that CEO pay is not going through the roof, while employees are losing. It is simply not the case. Of course, there are exceptions here and there but for the most part, this is the trend we are seeing.

Major studies out there did not compare CEO pays properly, and their conclusions were thus misleading. We also have not analyzed the nature of CEO pays and its fellow employees, from capitalism point of view, such as supply and demand, value creation, education, skills and experience. Shareholders, as the rightful owners of companies, sure do know how to ensure their companies are operated properly.

Now on to the conclusions:

Conclusions

How about the famous claim that the average CEO pay is 350 times average workers' pay? If we compare the pay of each CEO to its own workers, this is rarely true. In fact, in our four case studies of American corporations, that statement is false.

As you can see on the next illustration, the actual CEOs pay is nowhere near the imaginary OWS proportion.

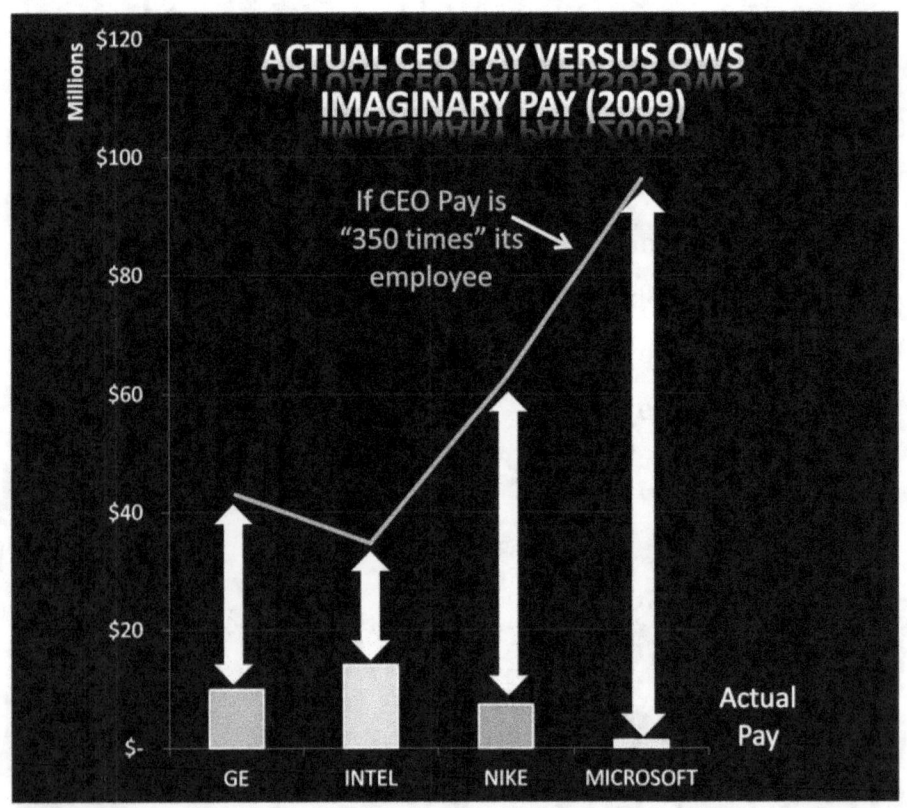

COMPANIES	If CEO Pay is "350 times" its employee in 2009 as accused	Actual Pay in 2009
INTEL	$ 34,785,088	$ 14,117,500
NIKE	$ 62,680,544	$ 7,306,694
MICROSOFT	$ 96,297,924	$ 1,265,833
GE	$ 42,994,869	$ 9,885,240

Illustration 123: If CEO pay is 350 times as claimed by OWS

Apple's late CEO, Steve Jobs, took in a salary of only ONE dollar. How should we compare him to the average worker's pay?

It is almost always the case that when the CEOs are the founders of the said companies, they tend to opt to receive lower overall salary.

As we said before, loyalty must be bought (CEOs hold all of companies' secrets) but in the case of the founders, they are always loyal to the companies they built from the ground up (it is like their offspring). Thus, that is why you even see some CEOs are paid token salaries only.

Why does a CEO deserves a High Pay?

Why should a company's CEO be paid highly in the first place? Why can't he or she be paid a lowly figure? This question can easily be answered. Company's CEO is shouldering the huge burden of managing very large amount of resources. If the CEO screws it up, billions could be lost. Heck, some people may even kill themselves over it, including the laid off employees.   This huge responsibility and the tremendous amount of stress and sacrifice expected of the CEO, requires reciprocating rewards from the company's owners. The CEO is also holding all of the company's secrets, long-term plans, winning strategies and the like. The company will be very worried if it entrust someone with only a clerk's salary, its entire confidential information that is worth billions. Just like the United States can never pay its presidents with a lowly salary for fear of him or her selling out the country to its enemies, so do corporations with huge revenue. Loyalty as it turns out can indeed be 'bought' and, will be rewarded!

Corporation's shareholders and even its employees will suffer greatly if their CEO departs and join a direct competitor. The best solution is a good pay, if the performance of the CEO is good.

Some people think CEOs set their own salaries, much like congress or parliaments all over the world. This is not so, unless the CEO is the owner of the company as well.

We urge everyone not to fake it, pretending of not knowing why a CEO, should be paid highly. These people are showing selective double standard. Don't pretend and not acknowledging it, and accuse a hardworking CEO things that are actually petty and unimportant; everyone knows actually why the CEO deserves a high pay!

When companies do well due to the vision and hard work of the CEO, (Jeff Immelt is reportedly to work at least 16 hours a day, including weekends), the public and the shareholders would benefit and get rich in the process. The workers too, since profitable (and flush) companies tend to reward its employees better by increasing wages, bonuses, medical and other benefits (stock discount, employee-matching contribution etc.). Thus, the smartest and most loyal (if the CEO is not the founder) person is the natural choice as CEO and they must be rewarded accordingly.

Capitalism will reward anyone in the economy, equal to the value they created. The Olympics however, reward on some select people, most of the time, or all of the time. Those good number 4 and 5, ignored. Capitalism reward all, in proportion to the value created, even if the person is number 5, 20 or 100.

PART 4:
CAPITALISM IS MORE EQUITABLE THAN THE OLYMPICS

SOCIETY'S 80:20 RULE

Our society favors the select few, by instinct. The reason is explained below.

The bottom 99% of the population must learn and master finance just as good as the rich could, and they will be rewarded as well. There is no doubt that this is possible. We outlined clearly how this can be done in the 259Tvs5T book series. The bottom 99% must think why the 1% exists in the first place. The widely cited Pareto rule, or simply the 80:20 rule, is easily observed in many areas of our civilization. Sports such as the Olympics, is a good example in showing how society rewards its participants efforts. It seems that society is rewarding only the top 1% or 2% of the thousands upon thousands of Olympics participants, showering them with medals and generous praises, monetary rewards, contracts and public recognition. The rest (those bottom 99%) are discarded and not recognized. This is ingrained in the society as a whole for one very good reason —those who can improve the lot of the society will be rewarded in kind. If only rewarding the winners (the 1%ers) is not fair, then why shouldn't the entire participants of the Olympics get to get gold medals, in fact, we should give gold medals to every citizen on the planet. Wouldn't that be fairer?

What is the odd of an individual to win an Olympic gold medal?
It is a tough 24 million to 1, chance.
What is the odd of being a millionaire in the United States?
It is an easy 10 to 1 chance! (of all adults)

What is the percentage of athletes in the Olympics, winning a gold medal?
3% is the answer, leaving 97% without a gold medal

Illustration 124: It is easier to be a millionaire than win a gold medal in the Olympics. The Olympics, other sports and other competitive competitions only reward the best. By far, capitalism is far fairer and rewards all its participants justly depending on effort and value put into it.

No, it is not because if everybody is rewarded then nobody will be doing their best to be the best. This is the same with the economic participants in an open capitalistic society.

Society will benefit by getting more prosperous as a whole, and the practice merely encourage these inventors to try their best by giving them handsome rewards. The balance will always be tilting on the side of society, that is, society will make more than the rewards given away. Just like when you buy a laptop from Dell setting you back by $800, the amount Dell would make from you is however puny compared to what the laptop will earn for you. The $800 investment you make will be returned to you with profits, many times over. Why would we reward someone if no actual surplus value were added? The laptop will enable you to do business and work, generating wealth in the process. The value created to the bottom 99% will be much larger than the rewards given to the rich. The reason the rich became rich in the first place, is because they gave us services, goods and the likes which the bottom 99% need. This improved the lot of the bottom 99%, far more than what the 1%ers actually make. We can prove this mathematically as well, for the end result will prove that the rich exist because they are generating something far more valuable to their customers (the bottom 99%).

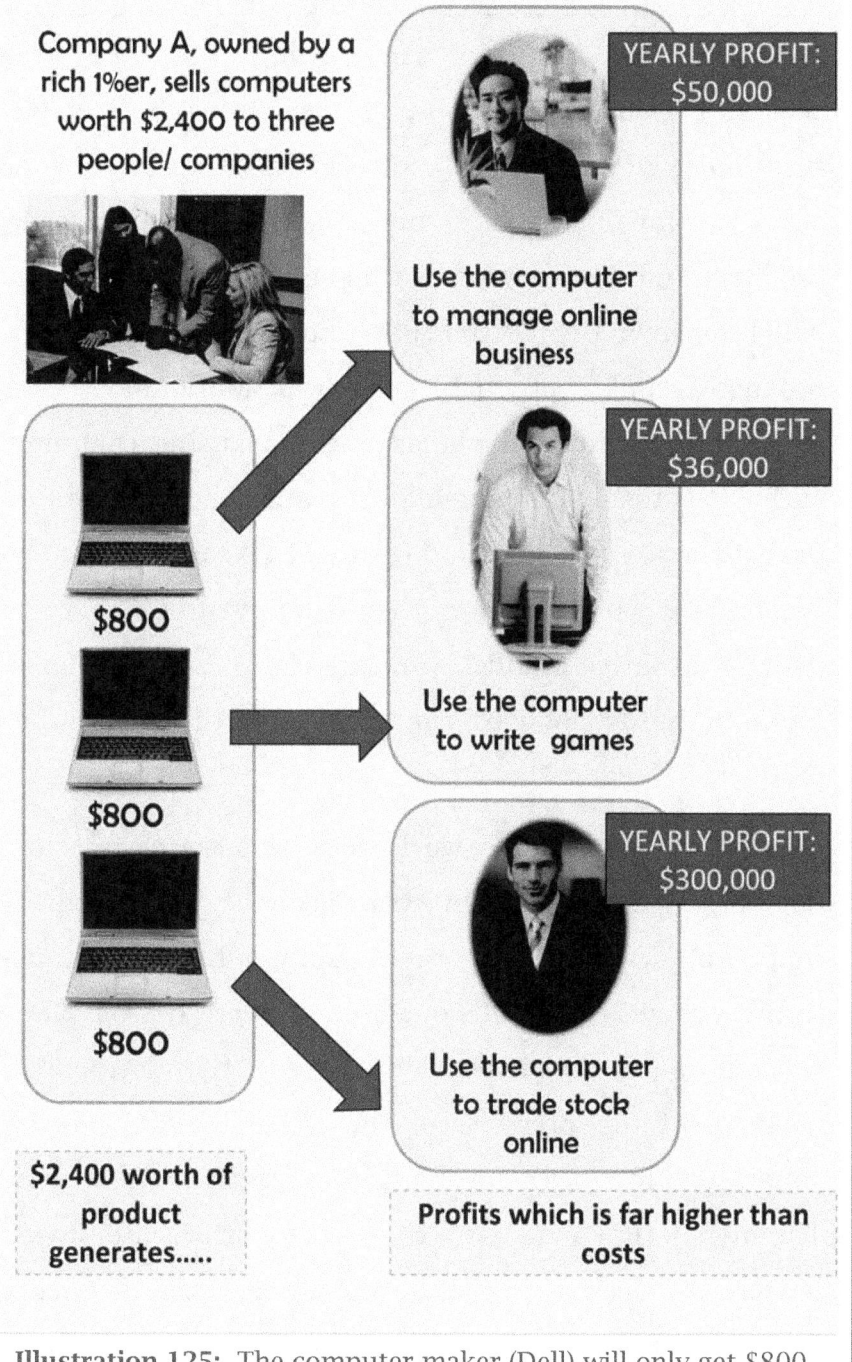

Company A, owned by a rich 1%er, sells computers worth $2,400 to three people/ companies

YEARLY PROFIT: $50,000

Use the computer to manage online business

YEARLY PROFIT: $36,000

Use the computer to write games

YEARLY PROFIT: $300,000

Use the computer to trade stock online

$800

$800

$800

$2,400 worth of product generates.....

Profits which is far higher than costs

Illustration 125: The computer maker (Dell) will only get $800 revenue (net is way less) per computer, but the $800 computer will help the buyers generate more wealth; many times over the initial investment, for many years. Thus, the founder of Dell is rewarded and became rich, because his products generate wealth and enrich his customers, far more.

Boycotting the rich, preventing the rich from becoming rich is equivalent as the entire Bottom 99% stops buying the products and services of the rich (owners of great companies making high quality and much needed products and services). Can this be accomplished? What will happen if the Bottom 99% stops buying Microsoft's products, Apple's products, food from McDonald's, stop going into Boeings' airplanes and stop using computers with Intel Inside chips, simply because their owners are part of the top 1%? The end result will be simple, the poor will end up poorer, because they will have to pay more for using alternative products and services, which costs more, and simply, do not perform as good as the world's best products.

Imagine using third world countries' software that is not properly developed and frustratingly buggy, or using that Apple wannabe corporation (Aopple Inc. for instance, selling Ipaod 5) that rolls out product directly from China without much design considerations? The Bottom 99% used all of the products of the rich, so that they can generate value for themselves, in excess of the costs paid. The money they made and the new wealth created by the Bottom 99% is very large, only a portion of it is used to pay the rich for their products. As long as the rich are contributing more to society than what they take, it is not a concern at all. Society naturally wants to reward the good products and services, from companies owned by the rich (and poor alike), and this is impossible to prevent.

They are of course, another kind of rich people who are not contributing to society, in fact they costs society wealth. These people are called 'crooks', and actually they are the same, whether these crooks are rich or not. They took in from the society by deceit, and gave little in return. This type of crooks exists because of the weaknesses of our own society coupled with our own greediness and lack of financial knowledge. Let's not be mistaken as of which type or segment of society we should really target in order to improve our economic wealth distribution.

There are "poor" crooks and there are "rich" crooks. So don't go lumping all rich people as crooks. Crooks are just crooks no matter their status. They destroy wealth instead of creating wealth.

Illustration 126: Pyramid schemes and outright lies are common in the market. These are not "good" rich people. These crooks may get rich (because a lot of people lack financial education and they feed on human greed) but they do not create value. Scam artist can be poor or rich.

THE RISK TAKERS

The rich, before they become one, are mostly risk takers. Even after they are successful, they would still take risks, in order to make society richer.

The rich cannot be faulted for being rich; they obtained it fair and square (except those crooks we mentioned earlier). This is because they are the outliers who try to innovate, to try new stuffs and to create new things, by taking big risks with their money, use their valuable time as well as risking their own future and that of their lovely dependents. Such huge risks will be compensated fairly by society, but only if the person actually successful in creating new wealth, uplifting all of society. If he fails, he will lose all and his dependents will even suffer for it. Those commenters out there who are against the rich are making false accusation that being rich is easy for those rich people and they were born into it, though the data showed that only a small percentage of them will be rich that way. Most of the time the rich have to earn it, fair and square.

How easy for anyone to reach the top? Fortune Magazine and other studies, analyzed the success rate or should we say, the failure rate of new businesses created by rich wannabes. They found that 95% of all businesses would fail within 5 years. That is a very tough odd to beat. Those who survived have what the products that society wants, and they will be rewarded. Society simply loves to reward innovators, creators and problem solvers. These people are our experimenters, the risk takers on behalf of society. If everyone is afraid to do new things, how will society progress? If everyone is so afraid to drop out from school, drop out from university to experiment and pursue something new, knowing that they can fail 95% of the time, how will the next Microsoft or Dell be created? They probably won't be created at all; China may do it in our place, which will be a great loss for America.

Remember that when you have money to be invested, financial advisers will tell you to split your investments into fixed secure asset and into high risk but less secure asset. The split is typically 80% in secure fixed income, while 20% will be in the higher risk investments. When the going is good, the high-risk asset's return will be good, making the low risk fixed income's returns to look dismal.

The 20% of your assets will look like superstar, while the other 80%, looks well, poor. You know very well that as a whole, it is necessary to have some in fixed and some in high-risk investments, in order to gain the most returns in a safe way. The reason is clear, that when the going gets tough, the 20% could be obliterated, leaving only the 80% intact. This risk is acceptable because you will only lose a small portion of your asset. Similarly, in society, a small portion of the population will have to take high risks on society's behalf. If the going gets tough, they could be obliterated (as is the case in 2007-08). Society cannot be rich if ALL of the economic participants took huge risks (as was the case just before the Great Financial Crisis). A good balance is required, and those who deserves it, be rewarded and those who fails, assisted (only for basic life requirements).

Nobody mention how the rich has protected other economic participants from the Financial Crisis of 2008. Some businesses, rather than close its doors, fund their operations using rich people's own money (their retirement nest eggs and so forth) in order to ride out the troubled time. Their income has taken a pounding since 2008 and has yet to fully recover. If the rich bail out and take their wealth out of the USA, the crisis would be far worse than it is now.

TOTAL ADJUSTED GROSS INCOME (MILLION USD)

	TOTAL	Top 1%	2-5%	6-10%	11-25%	26-50%	51-100%
1986	2,524,124	285,197	323,270	278,043	603,663	613,396	420,555
1987	2,813,728	346,635	375,586	316,000	671,168	664,480	439,859
1988	3,124,156	473,527	417,175	341,834	718,324	707,005	466,291
1989	3,298,858	468,079	450,342	368,118	767,939	750,757	493,623
1990	3,451,237	483,252	470,085	384,695	806,145	788,360	518,700
1991	3,516,142	456,603	486,747	399,852	831,563	809,238	532,139
1992	3,680,552	523,586	507,507	412,691	855,617	831,999	549,152
1993	3,775,578	520,586	527,666	426,211	883,490	854,346	563,279
1994	3,961,146	546,700	556,384	449,121	928,869	890,278	589,794
1995	4,244,607	619,610	603,113	481,790	985,307	937,722	617,065
1996	4,590,527	736,545	657,260	515,344	1,043,488	991,746	646,144
1997	5,023,457	872,826	724,281	554,294	1,116,199	1,060,392	695,465
1998	5,469,211	1,010,245	786,402	597,069	1,195,884	1,131,830	747,781
1999	5,909,329	1,152,820	858,943	641,072	1,274,473	1,198,856	783,165
2000	6,423,977	1,336,773	930,630	687,983	1,358,400	1,275,969	834,222
2001	6,241,036	1,094,296	902,196	694,097	1,380,445	1,308,252	861,750
2002	6,113,778	985,781	882,006	685,688	1,382,029	1,308,525	869,749
2003	6,287,586	1,054,567	906,109	702,794	1,414,757	1,329,624	879,735
2004	6,875,123	1,306,417	993,178	749,680	1,497,126	1,406,380	922,342
2005	7,507,958	1,591,711	1,092,223	803,076	1,582,445	1,475,369	963,134
2006	8,122,040	1,791,886	1,185,828	865,430	1,692,686	1,569,769	1,016,441
2007	8,798,500	2,008,259	1,286,283	933,297	1,817,515	1,674,859	1,078,287
2008	8,426,625	1,685,472	1,241,229	929,761	1,821,717	1,673,932	1,074,514
2009	7,825,389	1,324,572	1,157,918	897,241	1,770,140	1,620,303	1,055,215

Illustration 127: Table shows the total adjusted gross income of all groups from year 1986 to 2009. Highlighted in red is the income generated by the Top 1% just before and after the financial crisis hit.

Check the highlighted areas above. Can you see how much the income the top 1% had lost since the financial crisis back in 2008? They had lost almost 700 billion in yearly incomes, and have not recovered until today. What about the rest of the population, say, the bottom 99%?

They hardly experience a drop of such scale. The bottom 50%? What drop, there is hardly any drop at all, considering deflationary environment recorded in 2009. The rich suffered too, and suffered greatly during the crisis, and they absorbed most of the brunt, protecting the rest.

Income Bracket	2007	2009	% Change
Top 1%	$ 2,008,259	$ 1,324,572	-34%
2-5%	$ 1,286,283	$ 1,157,918	-10%
6-10%	$ 933,297	$ 897,241	-4%
11-25%	$ 1,817,515	$ 1,770,140	-3%
26-50%	$ 1,674,859	$ 1,620,303	-3%
Bottom 50%	$ 1,078,287	$ 1,055,215	-2%

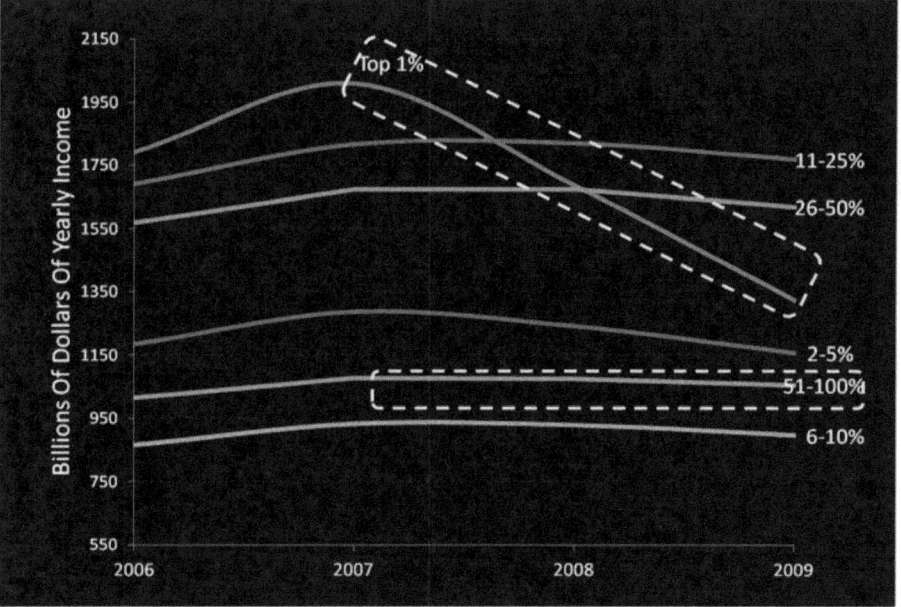

Illustration 128: Graph and table showing that the top 1% experienced a sharp decrease in their combined total income compared to the bottom 50% who remains steady, despite the recession that hit. The financial crisis hit the top 1% the most.

In 2009, exactly a thousand people on the planet, collectively lost 25 million dollars, a second, for an entire year! Wealth totaling two trillion dollars was destroyed. These people risked their wealth, time and everything they have, and when the economy went down, they lost big time!

Thailand was one of the Asian Tigers, created fifteen billionaires due to their good economic performance. In 1998, a financial crisis devalued the Thai currency, the Bath, and the billionaires dropped like dominos. By the end of the crisis, not one was left standing.

Therefore, each time recession hits, they hit the rich harder than the rest as their WEALTH is tied to their companies, which in turn tied to the economy. Of course, when the companies go down, the bottom worker would lose their jobs but the owner would have lost their lifetime work!

Forbes.com has a nice site where they track the rise and fall of the rich in real time. Go to http://www.forbes.com/real-time-billionaires/ and you will be astounded to see how their day-to-day (or minute-to-minute) wealth is tied to the economy. For the bottom worker, as long as the company exists (it does not matter if it is doing well or not, as long as the owner refuse to give up, the workers would have their jobs), and would not experience daily increases or decreases of hourly wages. Imagine your hourly wage is tied to the company performance or even worst– the stock price! You won't have any piece of mind.

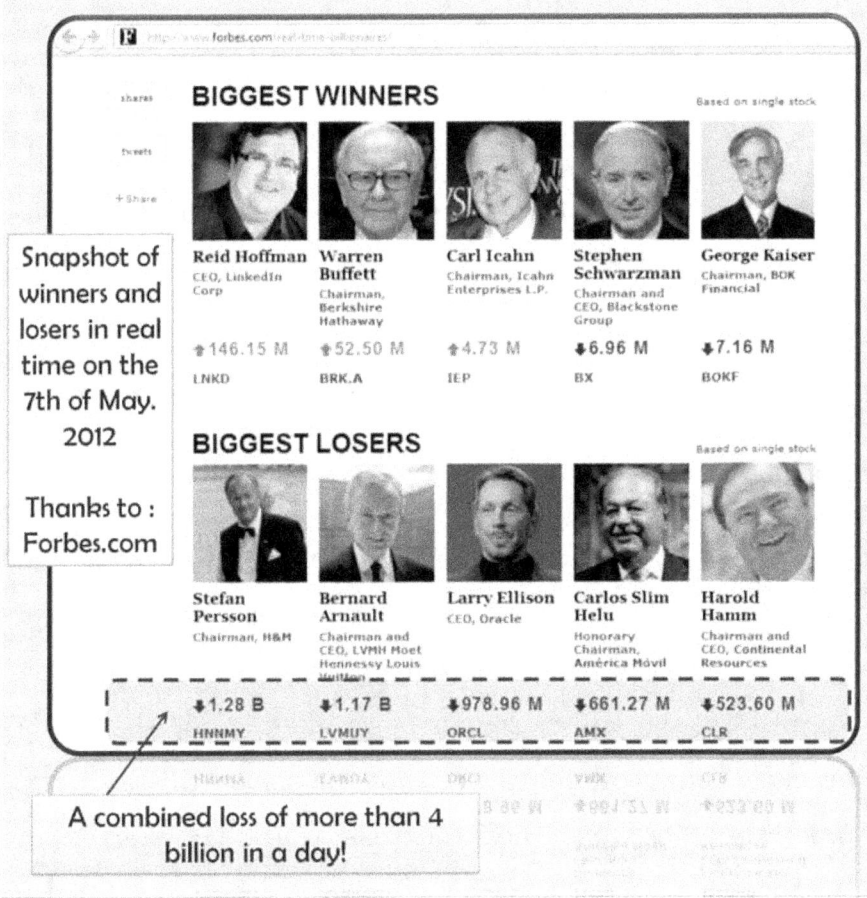

Illustration 129: A snapshot of the billionaires gains and losses in a single day (based on single stock owned). Updated in almost real time.
A day's loss is far more than what they gain.
Total loss (today) is more than 4 billion versus gains of about 200million!

Oprah Winfrey who was once a poor; living in the same bracket as many other poor; later became a billionaire, and now is listed at the top most brackets. However, she should be listed as a poor who had made it, within her own original bracket.

The poor is not getting poorer, they went on to become rich, and very rich too.

Steve Jobs was from a working background as well. So is Larry Ellison, the Oracle. They moved on to become billionaires.

Suze Orman was a poor waitress, living inside her car for a time. She went on to become a successful multimillionaire (and a good financial advisor). She went from the bottom of all brackets, to the top most. Is she counted inside's the poor's bracket? No. And why not? Why is it that the moment she jumped up, she will no longer be counted inside the poor's bracket? This will guarantee that the poor, will stay 'poor' indefinitely because their 'successes' are transferred to the top.

Well, how many more people from the bottom of the bottom, left their bracket and moved to the top? There are so many (millions in fact), and their removal from the bottom list, had ensured no improvement could be seen at the bottom, because their immense fortunes were carried to the top, further tilting the distortion between the brackets. That is why the 1% vs. 99% is a useless statistic to pursue, created by ill-informed people who misled others unknowingly.

Currently, according to Forbes Magazine, there are 946 billionaires (their number actually vary quite severely – some can lose billions in a day) and nearly two thirds were self-made, often coming from the poor and the not so well to do. The common thing they have is high-risk tolerance (guts), hard work and innovation (they make something that the majority of the public need or want).

Tens of millions of workers used to make the minimum wage but managed to jump to a higher bracket due to perseverance, by upgrading themselves with knowledge. Many have pride in their work, no matter how small the pay is. People always move towards bettering their lives and only become successful if they are hardworking, smart, prudent and do not waste resources on stupid and non-important things.

We would like to part this section with one sentence:

"It doesn't take a million or even a billion to have a happy and productive life."

Do Unto Others As You Would
Have Them Do Unto You.............

......And Don't Do Unto Others
Lest They Do The Same Unto You

PART 5:
HISTORY REPEATS ITSELF

OCCUPY AMERICA NOW

The Americans are the top 4% of the world. The bottom 96% of the world doesn't think that is fair. Occupy America Now movement the OWS way!

To make the OWS and its supporters alike feel even guiltier, we will make a comparison of America, to the whole world.   As the richest country on the planet, America is controlling more than its 'fair share' of the world's resources and incomes. Well, according to OWS & Co, this is unfair and this issue should be 'occupied'—perhaps forcefully.

America, with a population of only 300 million out of the 7 billion in the world (4.3% of world's population), is controlling a full 30% of the world's wealth, and 28% of its yearly income (data obtained from the World Bank, Credit Suisse and the Fed). To show how unfair averaging and making percentages out of a set of data is, we calculated that on average, each American owns wealth totaling

$230,000, whereas the rest of the world, only $24,000 for each one of them. This already includes the rich European and Japanese within the rest. If we take out all the G7 countries, the number disparity will astonish you (have fun doing the numbers and post your analysis to us!). These non-Americans are far less wealthy than the typical Americans by a factor of 10. That's 1,000% difference folks. Perhaps, the world will launch its own OWS against America itself. After all, there are more than a billion people on the planet, who are making less than one dollar a day. These people should be occupying America to claim fairness ala OWS style. It will be named;

OCCUPY AMERICA NOW.

What if the Occupy America Now movement come into play due to 'jealousy' of Americans at the top of the world? Now this OAN will be an additional enemy out there for America to counter and tame.

Illustrations on the next pages are the Occupy America Now (OAN) movements propaganda posters.

Americans are a mere 4% of the world's population

BUT ...

MONOPOLIZES 30% OF THE WORLD'S WEALTH AND 28% OF THE WORLD'S YEARLY INCOME

SPENDS THE EQUIVALENT TO THE ENTIRE WORLD'S MILITARY EXPENDITURES COMBINED, FOR ITS MILITARY, EVERY YEAR! IT IS A GARGANTUAN AMOUNT!

CONTROLS PER CAPITA WEALTH OF $230,000 FOR EACH MAN, WOMAN AND CHILD

The rest 96% of world's population only control $24,000 each, while the Bottom 20% control a negligible $365

GOD BLE
AMERICA

POSTER FROM OCCUPY AMERICA NOW (OAN) BRAINCHILD OF OWS

Occupy America Now.. United Against Injustice !!

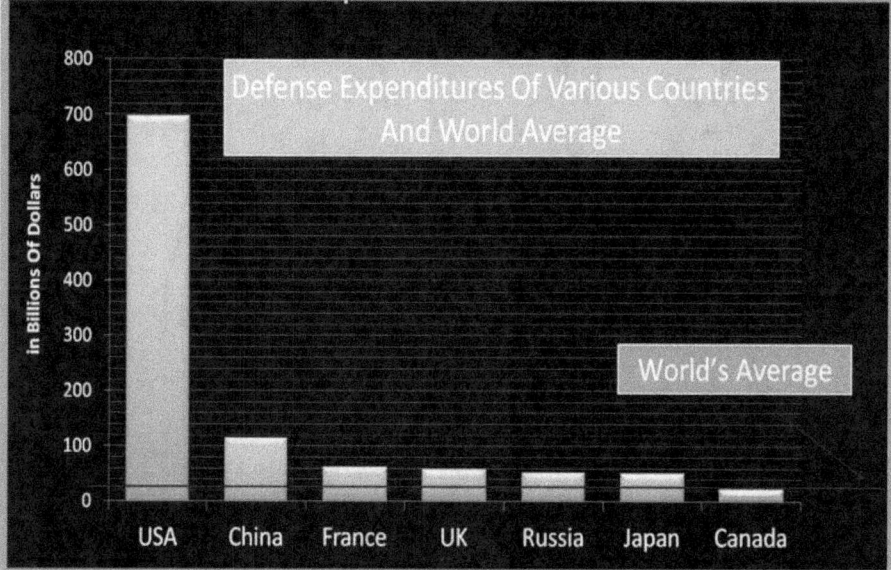

Defense Expenditures Of Various Countries And World Average

World's Average

in Billions Of Dollars

800
700
600
500
400
300
200
100
0

USA   China   France   UK   Russia   Japan   Canada

USA is building its armies for war against other countries!!

Occupy America Now.. Before it is too late

Illustration 131

POSTER FROM OCCUPY AMERICA NOW (OAN)
BRAINCHILD OF OWS

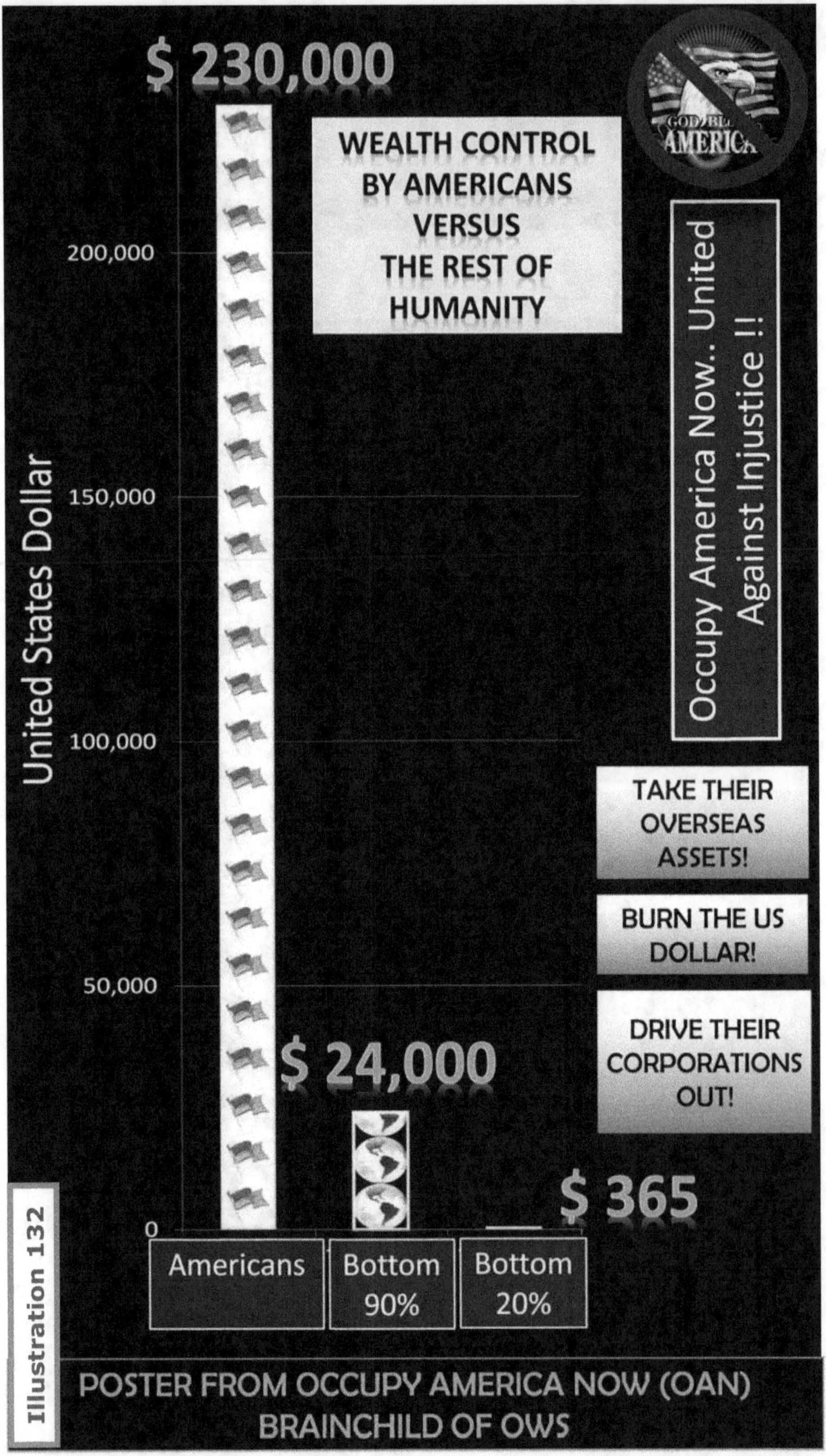

Illustration 132

POSTER FROM OCCUPY AMERICA NOW (OAN)
BRAINCHILD OF OWS

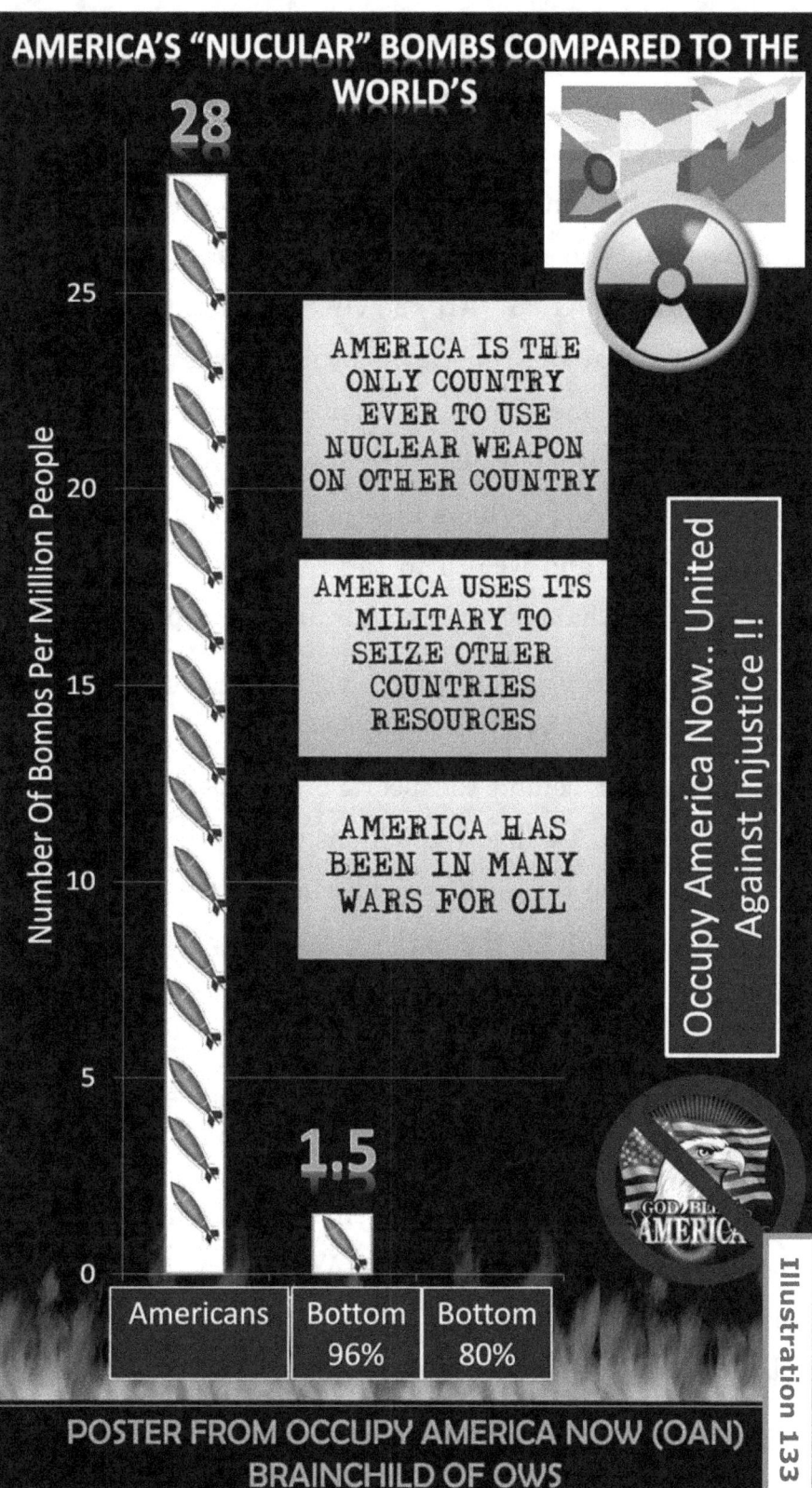

Illustration 133

So how does it feel, all Americans, including the OWS, are now called unfair themselves for monopolizing the world's wealth and resources? Being accused of taking the wealth of the poor, leaving behind a huge gap between the poor and the rich? Are the OWS going to tell the non-Americans that we, Americans own this vast wealth fair and square, and hope the non-Americans to simply accept? We wonder how OWS would respond to the demands of OAN; perhaps they might agree to give away their incomes and wealth to the rest of the world? Isn't the OWS the champion of the poor and the oppressed?

OWS dares to accuse the Top 1%ers, however the fact of the matter is, OWS is included in the Top 4% of the world, leaving behind the poor 96% of the world in the dust. The Top 1% invested billions of dollars, all over the world to enrich the entire world whereas the OWS would like to keep it all for themselves, taking by force from the Top 1%. Didn't OWS state that outsourcing jobs are not good and enriched only the corporations? They want corporations to close their overseas ventures and only invest and hire in America, and pay them high salaries.

This OWS is just one-step short of becoming evil, for not wanting to help humanity. Who is poorer, an OWS earning $25,000 a year, or one who earn only a dollar a day?

OWS AND NAZI—WHAT THEY HAVE IN COMMON?

Find out what both have in common. Is the Nazi being reborn?

We would like to highlight and bring to attention of our readers how OWS thinking and perception of the economy is dangerously close to the thinking of Nazi Germany and Hitler, back in the 1920s. Jews, who apparently were about 1% of Germany's populace, closely resembles the "Top 1%" of America's population because the Jews were then controlling a significant level of Germany's wealth. They were in the Top 1% then. The bottom 99% who were obviously mostly Germans, were incited by the Nazis to expunge all Jews from Germany. The end result was a great world war, plus widespread killings of Jews in Germany and the surrounding countries. Many Jews, fled to the United States to escape the Nazis, in search for better lives. Many of them as it turns out, went on and generated trillions of dollars of new wealth, for who else but America. Migrant Jews such as Andrew Groove (Intel's founder), billionaire George Soros (from Hungary), plus many other today's prominent and rich Jews, who mostly fled Europe without much money, have contributed tremendously to America.

Other genius and prominent scientists such as Albert  Einstein, with several others such as Oppenheimer, together assisted the United States with the "Manhattan Project" to harness the power inside atoms and thus ensuring America's victory in WW2.

Moreover, of course, many more smart and creative Jews have no doubt, helped America tremendously. If these people remained in their home country and go on to discover and invent all the things they had done, what would become of America today?

This is only one example. Prosecution of a minority group due to them being a minority is never a good thing. It does not matter on what grounds the public are doing it. When the blacks in America were prosecuted because they are black, it was done on the "good of the white majority" premise.

Money is also one aspect of it. Can the OWS show any proof that these 1%ers took the Bottom 99%'s money by force? Did any of them point guns so that the 99% consume their products or engage their services? Did all the people who flock to Tweeters, Facebook, Yahoo, Amazon or other internet services did it due to force? They gave something that many people perceived as valuable and they were rewarded. Nobody is forcing anybody to use his or her product and services. In the recent run up of the previous real estate bubble, nobody point big guns to the masses when the majority of them started buying houses they cannot afford. The housing market would not have crash if the masses did not participate in the speculative buying of properties during the bubble. As we have explained in Book 2, when everybody you know recognize nothing about what they are buying and start quoting scam lines- which is "up-up and away", then well, you should get far-far-and far away from that crazy situation.

The point is, the rich got their money fair and square. Taking their money when they reach certain income level is one type of a prosecution and overly high taxes is also another type of prosecution.

NOBODY SHOULD ENDURE DISCRIMINATION. NOT DUE TO RELIGION, RACE OR INCOME.. DRIVING FACTOR OF DISCRIMINATION IS JEALOUSY OF OTHER PEOPLE... EVEN ON WHAT THEY HAVE OR THEY HAVE NOT

Today, Occupy Wall Streeters are blaming the Top 1% for the ills of the country, echoing the very thing the Nazis did. Even if there is no direct persecution of the Top 1% occurring just yet, implementing the many demands of the OWS can and will result in many of the nation's top and most capable people, to leave the country for good. The next Microsoft, the next Intel or the next Warner Brothers will probably be made in China, or some other countries. People with brains need to be welcomed, not ridiculed and "persecuted" for their money (high tax). It will be a great loss for America if these people leave, and these losses will no doubt affect the bottom 99% hard.

Illustration on the next page is a truncated version of the Latest Y! news on the rich giving up their American citizenship due to America's "predicted" heavy tax burden.

YAHOO! FINANCE
Facebook Co-Founder Saverin Gives Up U.S. Citizenship Before IPO

By Danielle Kucera, Sanat Vallikappen and Christine Harper
Bloomberg – 13 hours ago

Eduardo Saverin, the billionaire co- founder of Facebook Inc. (FB), renounced his U.S. citizenship before an initial public offering that values the social network at as much as $96 billion, a move that may reduce his tax bill.

Facebook plans to raise as much as $11.8 billion through the IPO, the biggest in history for an Internet company. Saverin's stake is about 4 percent, according to the website Who Owns Facebook. At the high end of the IPO valuation, that would be worth about $3.84 billion.

[truncated...] Saverin, 30, joins a growing number of people giving up U.S. citizenship, a move that can trim their tax liabilities in that country.

[truncated....] "Eduardo recently found it more practical to become a resident of Singapore since he plans to live there for an indefinite period of time," said Tom Goodman, a spokesman for Saverin, in an e-mailed statement.

Singapore doesn't have a capital gains tax. It does tax income earned in that nation, as well as "certain foreign- sourced income," according to a government website on tax policies there.

[truncated....] Renouncing citizenship is an option chosen by increasing numbers of Americans. A record 1,780 gave up their U.S. passports last year compared with 235 in 2008, according to government records.

[truncated....] Income-tax rates for top U.S. earners will rise to 39.6 percent from 35 percent next year, and rates on capital gains and dividends also are scheduled to rise ..

"It's a loss for the U.S. to have many well-educated people who actually have a great deal of affection for America make that choice," said Richard Weisman... -truncated-

To contact the reporters on this story: Danielle Kucera in San Francisco at dkucera6@bloomberg.net Sanat Vallikappen in Singapore at vallikappen@bloomberg.net Christine Harper in New York at charper@bloomberg.net

Illustration 134

Such widespread condemnation and persecution of the top 1% occurred several times in our history. The rather recent one is Zimbabwe, a corrupt government led by a dictator named Mugabe, who confiscated fertile lands that are managed and worked on by rich experienced Zims, and gave it away to 'poor' Zims who have little experience in managing such farmlands, or perhaps not even interested to be farmers, and in the end, food production dropped tremendously. This is in spite of the abundance of lands available to all. The country is basically ruined; the rich mostly had fled the country where they were born, to other countries, in the hope of creating new riches.

> **We are no longer going to ask for the land, but we are going to take it without negotiating.**
>
> **Robert Mugabe**

Quote from: www.brainyquote.com

Confiscating the wealth of the rich will not solve the problem of the poor at all; it will create a disaster of mega proportion. You reap what you sow. We found that one of the stated goals of OWS is to have a revolution to topple the government, and implement their way of thinking, and to perhaps, confiscates and redistributes all wealth in the country.

No doubt, the country will be poorer, by a lot, for a very long time.

We should not be jealous of others. The rich in America is one of the most generous groups of people with their money. Ask for their assistance, and ask them to help you change your life. The rich is already paying a huge tax burden in order to assist the country and the bottom 20%, blaming them for something they did not do is grossly unfair. They donated billions of dollars every year to help others, it is a proof beyond doubt that this group meant well.

God created humans capable of many different skills and abilities, we need to use it to the best, generating and making the most wealth we can, for we will be rewarded whether in this life, or the next.

DON'T BE JEALOUS OF OTHERS

Forbes.com

Home Page for the World's Business Leaders

U.S.   EUROPE   ASIA

Home   Business   **Investing**   Technology   Entrepreneurs

The Forbes 400
Billion-Dollar Donors
David Whelan, 10.01.09, 12:40 PM EDT
Forbes Magazine dated October 19, 2009

The most exclusive subset of this country's wealthy may be this one: those living philanthropists who have given away $1 billion or more. That elite group includes only 8 members of The Forbes 400. Joining them are one couple, bankers Herbert and Marion Sandler, and mutual fund entrepreneur James Stowers, who have fallen off the list because they've given away so much of their wealth. "I'm surprised there aren't more," says Herbert Sandler. "It's a shame there aren't a lot more."

	PHILANTHROPY ($BIL)	FOCUS
Bill Gates	$28	Eradicating worldwide disease and poverty
George Soros	7.2	Promoting democracy, fighting discrimination
Gordon Moore	6.8	Environmental causes, nursing education
Warren Buffett	6.7	Supporting the Gates Foundation
Eli Broad	2	Improving education, genomics research
James Stowers	1.9	Medical research
The Sandlers	1.5	Investigative journalism, civil liberties
Michael Bloomberg	1.5	Public health
Ted Turner	1.3	The United Nations, nuclear nonproliferation
Michael Dell	1.2	Children's health and education

Note: Gifts are not adjusted for inflation but counted at the time of transfer to a nonprofit institution. Sources: Forbes research; Chronicle of Philanthropy.

DONATE A BILLION OR MORE CLUB

Illustration 135: This is a list of billionaires who gave at least a billion dollars away during their lifetime. Some fallen off the billionaire club because they gave so much... Greedy rich? Far from it!

CAN WE TAKE THE WEALTH OF THE TOP 1%?

Think it is easy to just take the rich's possessions?

Find out what will happen if the public simply expropriate the wealth of the rich

What will happen if the wealth of the Top 1% is taken by force and then distributed to the rest of the population?

Let say you take $1,000,000,000 from a billionaire and give the money to all Americans. Each will get, only $3.2 once in a lifetime.

By confiscating that money from the rich billionaire however, he have no choice but to close his factory and move to China (or go fishing to live). The end result, a few thousand employees would lose their jobs!

Let's calculate. A billion in cash can make a person commands assets in excess of 10 billion dollars, with around 20,000 employees. These employees probably make 25 dollars an hour each, so the monetary losses to the bottom 99% would be, 1.1 billion dollars, A YEAR. That is exclusive of other effects of mass unemployment.

Enjoy your $3.20!

Illustration 136: This is the consequences of taking someone else's money by force

From this one example, you can see that by confiscating the assets of the rich, nobody wins and the takers would end up losing more than what they thought they would gain from the rich billionaire when they happily confiscated his money. The $3.2 in each of the population hand is useless, as nobody will have any equity to build new plant and nobody can pool enough capital to be redeployed, for fear of, well, the rebirth of a new breed of rich top 1%ers.

As a result, everybody will end up poorer. Wealth and assets, in the wrong hands, will bring no value to anyone. In the end, that wealth will be destroyed.

What if instead of taking by force, we tax more?

Excessive taxes also would stifle innovation, as few would do work above and beyond without any compensation. Free money by government (aid) will not push people to work harder.

Further, when the Top 1%ers are taxed more, they will suffer shortage of money to run their businesses. They will make less than before and when this occur, they will start charging their customers, higher costs for their much needed products and services. Who are their customers? None other than the majority, which includes the poor. Their gullible minds think they can simply take away others' possessions without consequences, but we hope they think hard! What goes around comes around. In the end, they (the Bottom 99%) will end up paying for the high taxes they themselves forced the government to levy on the Top 1%ers.

Simulated Impact of normal taxes

A person in the Top 1% owns a factory:

Factory Build Costs	50,000,000
Revenue	10,000,000
Labor Resources	-2,400,000
Raw Material Resources	-3,500,000
Capital/Loan Resources	-2,600,000
Profit	1,500,000
Tax (at 25%)	375,000
After Tax Profit	1,125,000
Profit Over Assets	2.3%

Saves money for wealth creation ventures

Minimum profit accepted for investing in this risky ventures

Illustration 137: Table shows the simulated impact of a normal tax of 25% on a factory own by a rich person residing in the Top 1% line.

Sales is good. Tax is low. Profit is good. Business can go on.....

Simulated Impact of high taxes	
A person in the Top 1% owns a factory:	
Factory Build Costs	50,000,000
Revenue	10,000,000
Labor Resources	-2,400,000
Raw Material Resources	-3,500,000
Capital/Loan Resources	-2,600,000
Profit	1,500,000
Tax (85%)	1,275,000
After Tax Profit	225,000
Profit Over Assets	0.5%

Saves money for wealth creation ventures

Minimum profit NOT ACCEPTABLE for investing in this risky ventures

Illustration 138: Table shows the simulated impact of when high tax of 85% is imposed. Note that the bottom line of the factory has been eroded and minimum profit for risky ventures has dropped to unacceptable level.

Tax is too high. Profit is too low. I have to close my business if this continues...

Increase price to get more revenues, or cut cost by firing some workers or get cheaper materials thus decreasing quality of products

Simulated Impact of high taxes when the owner fights back

A person in the Top 1% owns a factory:

Factory Build Costs	50,000,000
Revenue	25,000,000
Labor Resources	-6,000,000
Raw Material Resources	-8,750,000
Capital/Loan Resources	-2,600,000
Profit	7,650,000
Tax (85%)	6,502,500
After Tax Profit	1,147,500
Profit Over Assets	2.3%

Saves money for wealth creation ventures

Minimum profit accepted for investing in this risky ventures achieved (again)

Illustration 139: Table shows how the owner reacts to this high taxes.

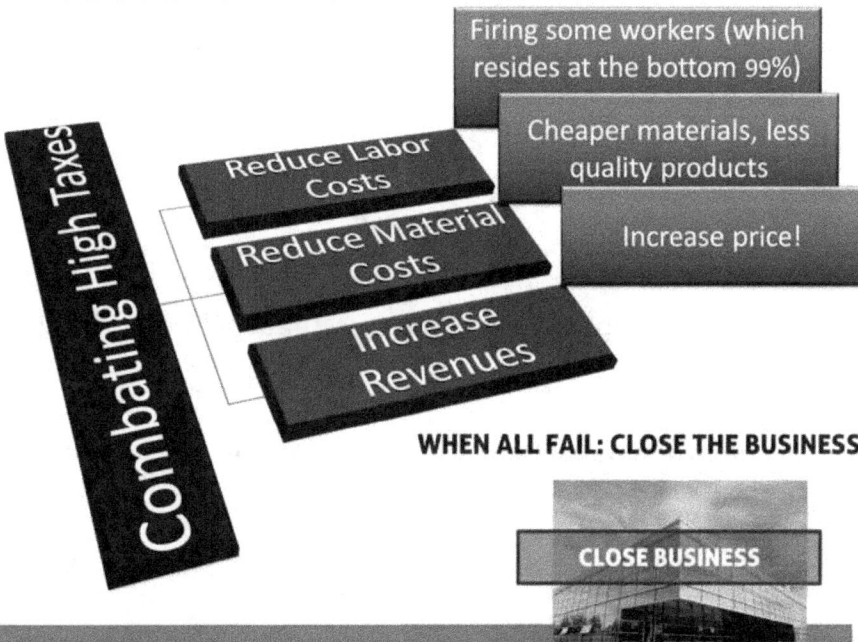

So who pay for the higher revenue? The bottom 99% do. So think increasing taxes on the rich will only make the rich suffer? The poor will suffer more, because they are at the bottom.

If they can't raise revenue (because nobody can afford to buy their products) they'll close the factory because they are not running a non profit organization.
So who suffer? The workers who resides on the bottom 99%.

The poor will suffer more, because they are at the bottom.

Illustration 140: Normal reactions by a company when faced with lower revenues due to taxes or other effects.

The economic system is very fair; it was designed as such. **Those who think they can profit from it, by forcing others to pay for their misdeeds, by forcing others to bear the costs, will end up paying for it one way or another.** The system is very honest and fair, we just hope everyone realize that if they play it fair and honest, they will be rewarded accordingly.

The following table is our version of how the economy would reward its participants. It is divided into several levels, just like playing a computer game— the higher your level, the more you can command.

Please note that in order for the economy to reward its participants fairly, the system must not be interfered overtly by the government especially the critical reward and punishment mechanism which would have a direct impact on resource allocation.

At the bottom most, it is Level 0, filled with those who are not exhibiting the necessary human traits, that is highly demanded by the economy. These people will be poor, destitute, and in absolute poverty because nobody trust them, they cannot even trust themselves. They are lazy and many times, they cheat and steal.

Wealth Management By Capitalism

Level	Skills	Type	Status
Level 13	Can you take risks?	Intuition	Billionaire
Level 12	Can you manage people, resources?	Advance Education & Human combined	Multi Millionaire
Level 11	Can you create?	Advance Education & Human combined	Multi Millionaire
Level 10	Can you innovate?	Advance Education & Human combined	Multi Millionaire
Level 9	Are you extra dependable, can be counted upon?	Advance Human	Millionaire
Level 8	Can you overcome your own limitations?	Advance Human	Millionaire
Level 7	Do you learn from mistakes & invest in yourself?	Advance Human	Upper Income
Level 6	Do you give up easily?	Advance Human	Middle Income
Level 5	Are you patient?	Advance Human	Middle Income
Level 4	Can you count?	Basic Education	Decent Income
Level 3	Can you read?	Basic Education	Decent income
Level 2	Are you hardworking?	Basic Human	Low income
Level 1	Are you trustworthy, honest?	Basic Human	Low income
Level 0			Poor, destitute

Illustration 141: Table showing wealth management by capitalism

The moment a person can exhibit one basic trait required by the economy, which is trust and honesty; this person will be able to get a job, and work for a living. The person will be getting low incomes, because he or she does not have any other trait needed, such as hardworking. Upon exhibiting the hardworking trait, the person will earn more money, but will still be in the low-income bracket. Next, in Level 3 and 4, some basic education is needed. Most importantly, the person is able to read and write, and then has good acceptable math skills. His or her income level will increase somewhat (decent income), but not enough to be lifted out into the middle-income bracket.

The next level is Level 5 and patience is a virtue here. One must have good patience, on top of working hard and staying honest. The income level will finally entering the territory of the middle class. As the person progresses, he or she will need to exhibit plenty of Advance Human traits so desired by the economy, and the reward will be a middle class job with good acceptable incomes. Most people will stop here and be content with what they have.

However, the economy requires more in order to advance the entire society. The economy demands that the next person advancing to the next level to overcome his or her limitations, to start thinking, to learn from mistakes and can be depended upon. Here, the person will be rewarded with an upper middle class income level, and given enough time, the person will be a millionaire.

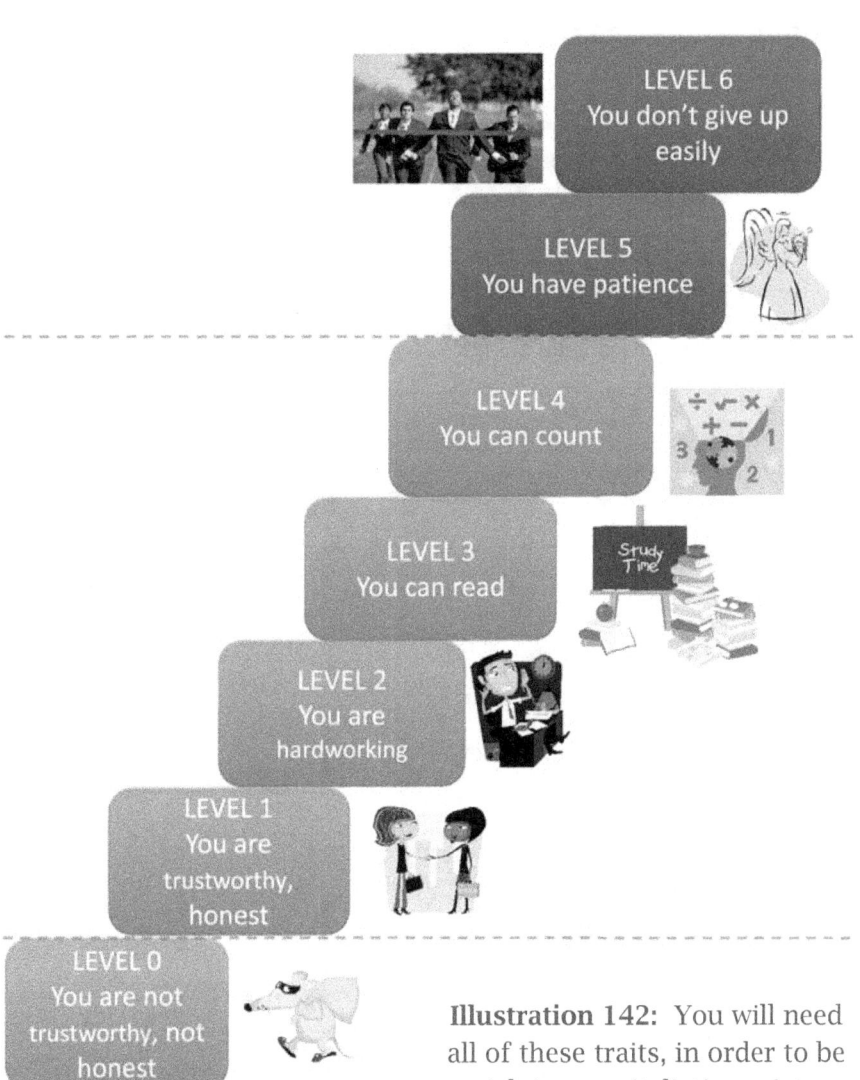

Illustration 142: You will need all of these traits, in order to be rich in a capitalistic society based on values

In order to go higher, the person will need to tie the knot between Advance Human traits, and Advance Education. The combination of these will enable the person to earn multi million dollars, a trait so rare, the economy yearn for it day and night, without stopping. Those who can combine the two will be amply rewarded.

LEVEL 13
You can take risks

LEVEL 12
You can manage people, resources

LEVEL 11
You can create new things

LEVEL 10
You are an innovator

LEVEL 9
You are most dependable, can be counted upon

LEVEL 8
You overcome your own limitations

Illustration 143:
Not easy to be the world's billionaire (Level 13), only a thousand people of 7 billion people are called as such

LEVEL 7
You learn from mistakes, study everyday

Finally, one ultimate level is required, if the person wants to reach the pinnacle of wealth creation, and thus obtaining the highest of all incomes. He or she must have the guts to take risks, in order to improve society. That person must risk everything that he or she has accumulated. The person also must sacrifice tremendous amount of personal time, in order to reach this final level. Here, the reward is unlimited— it is the Billionaire level. Not just the person will need all the traits from Level 1 through 12, he or she must now risk everything and combined them with an amazing power of intuition. This person will be influencing the lives of millions of people, upgrading their life substantially. Whole society will benefit, and the human race, will advance one-step further.

All of us should target the highest level we could, for our dedication would touch and improve the lives of millions of other people around the world. It will be a source of pride and we can indeed, leave the world in peace, knowing we have contributed.

There is of course, another set of traits and skills, which can take a person, through a different channel in life. We do not want to waste much time thinking about it, but just for the fun of it, here it is!

Wealth Management By $HORT CUTTER$ (LAZY BUM)			
Level	Skills	Type	Status
Level 13			
Level 12			
Level 11			
Level 10			
Level 9		Advance Suck-Up	Extra Rich
Level 8	Can you lie and say others did it?	Advance Suck-Up	Extra Rich
Level 7	Can you organize more of your kind?	Advance Kisser	Rich
Level 6	Can you blame others and then take what's theirs?	Advance Kisser	Rich
Level 5	Can you blame others?	Advance Kisser	Rich
Level 4	Can you count?	Basic Education	Decent Job
Level 3	Can you read?	Basic Education	Decent Job
Level 2	Are you hardworking?	Follower	Food & Lodge
Level 1	Are you trustworthy, honest?	Follower	Food & Lodge
Level 0	You are alive	Follower	Food & lodge

Illustration 144: Table showing wealth by deceit, based on unfairness and shortcuts.
Use your imagination to fill up the rest!

After reading and thinking about what we had put down in this book, you will realize that it is not a given and automatic in going up the level of incomes. A person cannot be earning a middle class income, accumulating wealth of middle incomes proportion, if the person is not yet qualified. The poor will stay poor indefinitely, if they never upgrade themselves as described. The economy is very fair indeed. Therefore, the conclusion is very simple. We spell it out for you. When they are more rich people in the economy, that means the population are moving up the Levels, en masse. They are getting better, as human beings. If however more are getting poorer in the economy, then the opposite is happening. The population is getting lazier, more stupid by the day, en masse too. This is not similar to a temporary economic correction, where millions of people are out of work, waiting to be reallocated to where the economy needs them most. When millions and millions of people are out of work due to they are becoming lazier and more stupid, the economic data will show exactly that.

Do not blame China or other country for it. So take note, and always work and study hard!

Don't give up!

OCCUPY WALL STREET ARE NOT THE LEGITIMATE REPRESENTATIVE OF THE BOTTOM 99%

OWS are claiming to represent the masses. However they are not the masses, or the majority. OWS has no right to claim to be representing the masses, because not all in the 99% are angry about the economic system.

Read and find out more!

OWS are claiming to represent the masses. However, they are not the masses, or the majority. OWS has no right to claim to be representing the masses, because the 99% are not angry at the economic system. There are parts of the population who are not active economic participants and many of them chose to be that way.

Earlier, we talked about someone who flips burgers for a living. If after 10 years he or she is still doing the exact same thing, the person has not participated in capturing the new opportunities given away by the economy. Education plays the most important role here.

In order to upgrade oneself, better skill and knowledge is necessary. One cannot blame the economy, the government or worse, the Top 1%, for one's ill fortune of continued burger flipping, if there is no self-improvement.

The economy provides ample opportunities, assistance and many more, to allow workers to upgrade their knowledge and skills. There is just no excuse. There are millions of job vacancies currently in the United States, but millions of people are still unemployed because of clear skills mismatch. The economy requires something else, but the workers are slow in shifting. The government must assist people to meet and fill the vacancies quicker. Those who refused to change and adapt, is bound to be languishing behind at their previous income or worse, lower, due to stiff competition.

There are however millions of people, in fact almost a hundred million who participated in the economy and benefit immensely from it. We called these people, the economic participants. Economic participants participated willingly and fairly, and of utmost importance, honestly. There are of course those who languished behind, refusing to participate. They keep asking assistance from the government, and keep blaming others for their malaise. We want these people to stop blaming other people, and start upgrading themselves.

Education is paramount, and one need not go to school in order to improve. Learning can be done on the job, around the clock, anywhere and wherever time permits. Read a book; think on self-improvement, rather than endless partying and other useless endeavor for little economic returns.

What are 10,000 demonstrators compare to hundreds of millions of adults in America? It is much less than a percent. What about when you have a million on the streets? It is still less than a percent.

Simply claiming your group represents the majority does not make your group as the majority. Who in America have the most legitimate claim of being representing the majority? Is it the President? During elections, the would be president typically obtained only 50+% of the votes, and he claimed to have the majority. Few groups in America can actually make a claim as big as the President. OWS is simply not one of them.

Public places are for the public. If you have a right to that place, then somebody with a different opinion than you also have the same right and as such occupying that place would then infringe on the other person's right. Rent a stadium or on the lawn of your own properties, convene, and rant all you want. Then you certainly have the right to be there without encroaching on other people's right. Only then could you claim justice. Until then you are not just and you are not honorable.

Illustration 145: What is 10,000 people on the streets or even 1 million on the streets compares to the US population? It is still less than the Top 1% group. Stop deluding yourself.

THE BOTTOM CLAIMS OF NO SAY IN THE GOVERNMENT

Is it even possible to have the majority, yet have no say in the government? Well, find out!

The headless Occupy Wall Streeters claimed that they have little representation in the government. They also claimed that everything is controlled by the Top 1%, leaving them marginalized. They claimed that politicians worked for the rich only, and many other claims of amazing proportion.

Clearly in a democracy, the majority will select their chosen candidates. We cannot imagine how 99% of the population, cannot select their own chosen candidates, since they are in the majority. Therefore their claims are truly baseless. But if their claims are true, it will show that the claim of corruption and greed of the top, bribing votes from the bottom 99%, is a statement that shoots their own foot. It will show that the Bottom 99% group is also corrupt and greedy, for they sell their votes to the highest bidder.

Don't blame others for the things you do not like in the country. The Bottom 99% group is the people, and they have the majority needed to bulldoze through anything they want. Therefore claiming others of controlling the nation is a big BS on their part. We read carefully their writings in their websites, and they claim that the rich are controlling everything (not true) and they want to take it back by instigating a revolution. What kind of revolution, we do not know, but taking back of what's theirs, is so easy, no revolution is even necessary, for they have the majority in Congress, and have the power to directly elect one of their own, to be the president.

Therefore, it is clear that OWS claim of representing 99% of the population is not true because they cannot even select their own president. They are not. We don't know how much they represent, but it seems to be not the majority of the population.

1% = 1% VOTE
99% = 99% VOTE

Illustration 146: The 1% group only has 1% of the vote and the 99% have 99% of the voting power. It is a simple math. If OWS represent majority, thus the government is their elected government. If doesn't matter how much money the rich people contribute to the senators/presidential campaigns, they can only still cast one vote. If you know your candidate is corrupt, then vote for somebody else. Else, when the majority has spoken and you are not happy, think before you leap because you are not the majority.

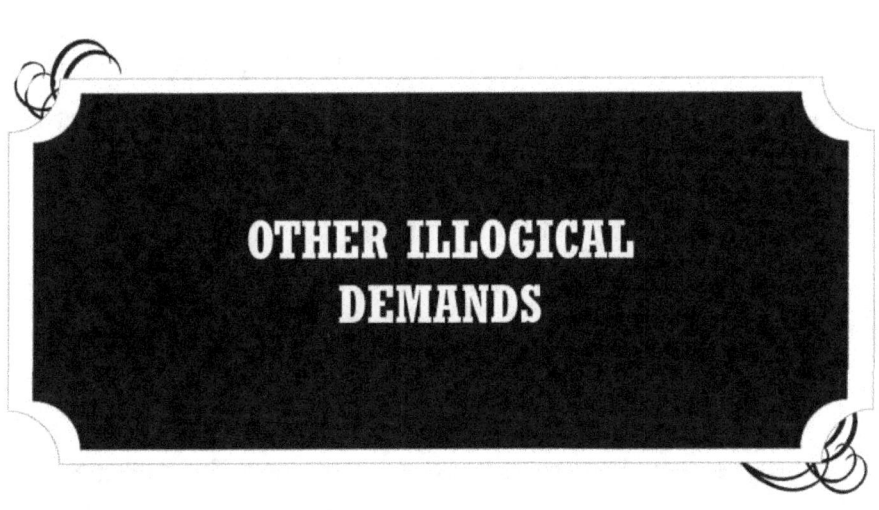

OTHER ILLOGICAL DEMANDS

Let us have a bit more fun by looking at some of the illogical demands of the headless OWS. We collected these from various sites claiming to represent and support the OWS 'cause', whatever that is.

PROPOSED LIST OF DEMANDS FOR OCCUPY WALL STREET MOVEMENT

Demand one: Restoration of the living wage. This demand can only be met by ending "Freetrade" by re-imposing trade tariffs on all imported goods entering the American market to level the playing field for domestic family farming and domestic manufacturing as most nations that are dumping cheap products onto the American market have radical wage and environmental regulation advantages. Another policy that must be instituted is raise the minimum wage to twenty dollars an hr.

Demand two: Institute a universal single payer healthcare system. To do this all private insurers must be banned from the healthcare market as their only effect on the health of patients is to take money away from doctors, nurses and hospitals preventing them from doing their jobs and hand that money to wall st. investors.

Demand three: Guaranteed living wage income regardless of employment.

Demand four: Free college education.

Demand five: Begin a fast track process to bring the fossil fuel economy to an end while at the same bringing the alternative energy economy up to energy demand.

Demand six: One trillion dollars in infrastructure (Water, Sewer, Rail, Roads and Bridges and Electrical Grid) spending now.

Demand seven: One trillion dollars in ecological restoration planting forests, reestablishing wetlands and the natural flow of river systems and decommissioning of all of America's nuclear power plants.

Demand eight: Racial and gender equal rights amendment.

Demand nine: Open borders migration. anyone can travel anywhere to work and live.

Demand ten: Bring American elections up to international standards of a paper ballot precinct counted and recounted in front of an independent and party observers system.

Demand eleven: Immediate across the board debt forgiveness for all. Debt forgiveness of sovereign debt, commercial loans, home mortgages, home equity loans, credit card debt, student loans and personal loans now! All debt must be stricken from the "Books." World Bank Loans to all Nations, Bank to Bank Debt and all Bonds and Margin Call Debt in the stock market including all Derivatives or Credit Default Swaps, all 65 trillion dollars of them must also be stricken from the "Books." And I don't mean debt that is in default, I mean all debt on the entire planet period.

Demand twelve: Outlaw all credit reporting agencies.

http://www.conservativedailynews.com/2011/10/occupy-wall-street-releases-totally-reasonable-demands

Illustration 147: The list of demands of the OWS Movement #1 (there are many lists as OWS is a "headless" movement)

And from the Socialists, their party published the following in their website:

SOCIALIST OWS MOVEMENT

The rights of the working class

The Socialist Equality Party proposes that the working class adopt the concept that there exist social rights that are essential to life in a complex modern society and, therefore, inalienable and non-negotiable.

These rights include:

- The right to a job and a livable income

- The right to high-quality public education and health care, free of charge

- The right to housing and utilities

- The right to a secure retirement

- The right to a healthy environment and access to culture

The rights of the working class must be counterposed to the rights of the corporations, which are unconditionally defended by the two-party system the "right" of corporations to destroy jobs and slash wages; the "right" of the banks to kick people out of their homes; the "right" of the political system to destroy social programs upon which millions of people depend.

For the expropriation of the banks and major corporations!

In its very name, the Occupy Wall Street movement expresses a basic understanding that all of the needs of the working class come into conflict with the dictatorship of the banks and financial institutions over economic and political life. These corporations control vast resources, the product of the collective labor of billions of people the world over.

To break the stranglehold of the corporate and financial elite over society and politics, the banks and major corporations must be placed under public ownership and operated under the democratic control of the working class. This will make available the resources for a multi-trillion-dollar public works program to ensure full employment, eliminate poverty and meet social needs in the US and internationally.

For social equality! Make the capitalists pay for the crisis!

The apologists for capitalism claim that inequality is not related to the economic crisis, as if the withdrawal of trillions of dollars from productive use has no economic impact. The insatiable drive of the financial aristocracy for more and more money has fueled one speculative binge after another and bankrupted the country. The same CEOs who say they have no money to pay decent wages and who carry out job cuts manage to pay themselves and their top executives millions or even tens of millions of dollars every year.

Working people must reject with contempt the claim that "there is no money" to meet basic social needs. Immediate measures must be taken to establish social equality, including reintroducing a progressive income tax and a 90 percent tax on all incomes over $500,000 the tax rate that existed in 1950 along with a wealth tax on multimillionaires and billionaires.

http://wsws.org/articles/2011/oct2011/pers-o15.shtml

Illustration 148: The demands of the OWS Movement #2 (World Socialist Web Site)

We also wonder why the real organizer of OWS never wants to reveal what their actual demands are. Perhaps they are afraid very few people will support them when those people realized they are being duped into joining a movement to further some stupid and lazy people's agenda who only wanted to collect free and easy money from other people. It will be impossible for the organizers to rally a multitude of people with different agenda between them, unless the rally is about something vague and universally hated, such as the Top 1%, Wall Street, the banks etc.

Their demands are so easy to counter; almost anyone with a good brain can answer them. What we have done in this book is to answer the more difficult accusations they raised. They asked for universal and guaranteed living wage regardless of employment. What that mean is, anyone can do anything they want, when they want, and be paid an income, guaranteed. This is clearly impossible. We thought the communists had tried them, first in Soviet Russia (which collapsed), in China (which embraced capitalism a few years ago to escape from terrible inefficiencies of communism), and of course the pariah state of N. Korea (which is in terrible shape, many of their population is under poverty and die of hunger). Who would want to work if there is no reward?

North Korea is forcing their farmers at gunpoint, to ensure they planted crops and take care of these crops. Yet many still die of hunger.

They demanded free college education. Who will pay for the hundreds of billions of education costs? Didn't these OWS people hardly pay any tax at all? In addition, if they had already removed the Top 1%, all of the rich people, who would be paying taxes now? Martians? Klingons?

They demanded 'someone' to spend ONE trillion dollars for public works projects, NOW. Additionally, they demanded another trillion more, for the environment, and decommissioning of nuclear plants. If you ask anyone on the street, anywhere in the USA, almost everyone will have such noble intentions. We ourselves would also prefer to spend many trillions for such noble causes. The problem is, where are we going to get the money? Who will be paying for all of these, which we want to enjoy? Can the government just create two trillion dollars out of thin air? If they can, they would have. In fact, we have explain thoroughly in **Book 2** of the **259T VS 5T SERIES** that the paper money we have now is not created out of thin air and thus required the backing of the wealth of the entire country.

It has been tried in the communists' countries (or

socialist); it was a total flop, even when they forced people at gunpoint. Show us one great socialist country that exist on this planet or even Mars, that you are jumping happily to go to.

We think these people; have no clue how large a TRILLION dollars really is. They shout like wanton children everywhere else, but forgot to do their homework. You can demand anything, especially if you knew that someone else is paying for it, not you. But these headless OWS have no inkling as to the workings of the economy, because the one who will be paying is none other than they themselves. Wasting money unnecessarily is a recipe to ensure they will stay poor, indefinitely.

They also want all debts to be eliminated. In fact all debts in the whole world. This is just pure fantasy on their part. It has been tried in many countries (don't they ever read history books?), and the results were almost always, disastrous. Will these people ever learn not to take on debt, and more debt, if they cannot afford it? Not if every time they get into trouble, someone bail them out. Do these banks forced people to take on debts? At gunpoint? Not that we know of. These debt hungry people are the one who obtained the debts on their own, voluntarily, and they intend of not paying it back. They are not respectable people. They then gamble and speculated with the borrowed money, and bought tons of junks with it. Now they don't want to pay a cent on the debt? And try to duck the issue and say everyone should be forgiven for his or her debts? Grow up and learn!

These Occupiers think that the rich are not being made to pay for the recent financial crisis. Our data showed they are paying dearly for it. There is no doubt. Stop portraying the untruths, and show the true, actual data. We found that when these so called Top 1%ers has no more money for their businesses, they will have to lay off their workers, who unfortunately made up of the OWS themselves and their friends and just about everyone else.

We have suggestion for this "universal wage", dear OWS. Go to North Korea, or Zimbabwe, and experience the universal justice and universal living wage they so demanded. There is hardly a Top 1% there except the dictators friends, but everyone else are on even footing. Government controls everything, including what you can eat, and everyone will be able to eat the same thing.

We found that the Europeans were highly cited by the Occupiers and their supporters. They mentioned Europe have successful socialists programs, which America should emulate. We wrote in our **259 TRILLION VS 5 TRILLION** book series about this, so let us write it once again; ALL programs must be paid for. Giving out free things, will result in inefficiencies. The Europeans are now suffering from decades of stagnation, with high unemployment. The OWS made big noise when unemployment went up to 10% in the US, but try imagining unemployment of 24% as in Spain, with 50% unemployment of new job seekers. Blanket assistance for everything in the economy by the government, if given without much thought, will begets laziness and the feeling of entitlements, one of which, the OWS have a truck load of.

Nope. Nobody is entitled to any wealth, if he or she does not deserve it. If it is given to them regardless, they will squander it. The Europeans resorted to easy borrowings, and now look at them, they are suffering and there is no way out for them. Do not follow them blindly.

The Occupy Wall Streeters and their friends want big government. They want government to take over corporations, businesses and run it for the public. Everyone knows government is not efficient. Government is like a big elephant, they cannot even run their own departments easily and efficiently, let alone managing public companies. There is no way government can beat businesses in their own game.

We also want the Occupiers and their friends, to create their own banks and start giving out loans to their lovely friends. Loans of zero interest and with the expectation of never being paid back should be instilled. Would they dare give out such loans? By the way, there is no more money from the rich to take, if you all drove them out from the country already. Then we know what they will eventually do, they will invade that other country where the rich resides, and take everything they have, once again. Just look at North Korea. They wanted to invade the South, for ages, but luckily, the South is stronger and more equipped than they are. So what do the "equal rights movements- the communists– the socialists- and the Occupiers of the world" have to show for the many years that they have been doing this socialist thing? Do the OWS think that they can do better? How do you force people to work when they can get money by not working and just simply breathing? Nobody also wants to be rich (or work harder) as they will be taxed 90% (as per the World Socialist Web Site demands), the rich would run en masse to other countries (how many North Korean die trying to cross the border?). So who would pay for all these?

Contrary to the belief of their deluded minds, banks do not control money, or the money supply, even if they can do it. They have no reason to do it. Only the central bank can do that. Bright central bankers know they cannot simply print money if there is no justification for it. Banks are in the business for profits just like any other business as we have explained in our previous books. They can go bust and in fact, many banks indeed go bust just like any other businesses. The facts that the government bails them out rather than let them learn their lessons to be prudent with resources and other people's money; do not mean that they control the world. The one that put the government in power are the majorities and the one that gave money to the banks are therefore the majorities as well. Do not be deluded to think that government that spends and not taxing their populations could be doing it forever without any repercussion.

The demands of the Occupiers, and the people like them, will drain the resources of the planet and waste it. We think that when resources of the planet are no longer a limiting factor (for example, we found another planet to scrounge on or we have replicator technologies or Stargates to get resources from other planets), only then the demands of the OWS can be met (but with big wastage of course). Until then, capitalism is necessary, in order to ensure resources are managed wisely and directed to where they are most needed.

QUICK REVIEW

As usual, we summarize our book in simple notes.

Thank you.

Giving free money is not justice. It will degrade society, destroys wealth.
Teach how to make money ...
..and create value and wealth required by society

Capitalism is the most fair of any system we analyzed out there...

Justice, Equitability, Trust,
Honesty --
Are the pillars of capitalism.

Taking money from the rich will ultimately make the poor, poorer and..........
Our analysis confirmed the benefits of education and good human traits; it will make you rich, nothing else matters.

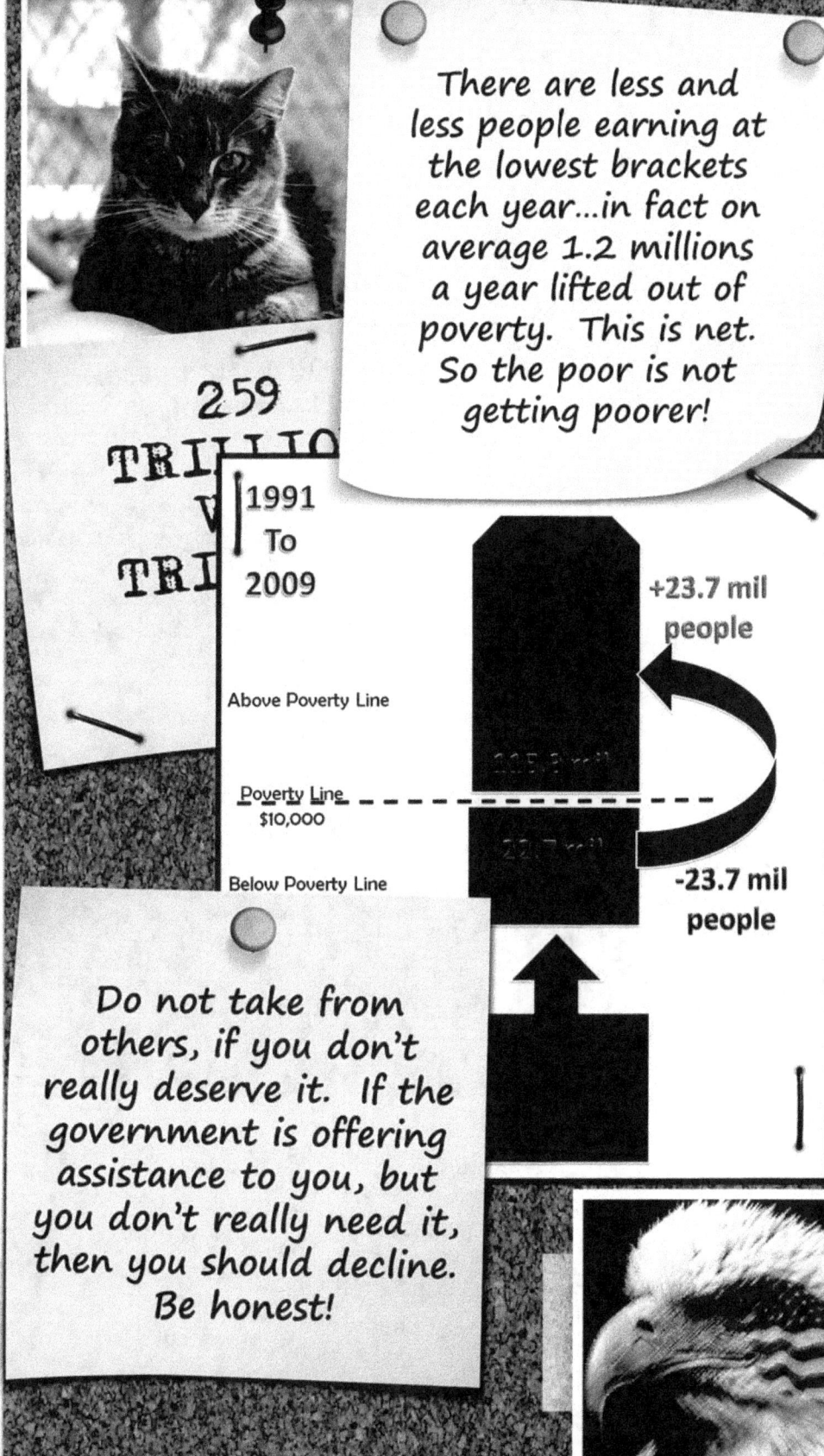

Society will always reward those who perform. The more risk is taken, the more the reward

Existing comparison methods are erroneous. Remember the students in the class example and the new CEO from the bottom most examples?

Occupy Wall Streeters do not represent the majority, in fact, they are the minority

The moment the poor make themselves rich, they are then immediately counted as the rich. But wait a sec, they ARE the poor who had made it in life, they should be counted in their original bracket. Economists do not have a clue on their own data and has misled all of us

How do you express gratitude? Can we say thanks to the government? Have we ever say thanks to the taxpayers?

The   rich is already paying the most taxes, accusing them of not paying their dues is preposterous!

—

CEO Pay is not ≠ 350 times the average worker's pay

The rich suffered just as much as the poor, if not more. Many went bankrupt, some even committed suicide

—

To alleviate our weaknesses in capitalism, better education is needed amongst the participants. Crooks and cheats live within the Top-1% as well as the Bottom-99%. Prosecute them instead, not the honest Top-1%ers.

We need to promote more trust and honor in our society by following an honor code.

The freer the economy, the better it is for all participants

Imposing high taxes on the rich, will ultimately caused the poor to bear the burden of high prices

Contrary to what you may have heard, it is way better to live in today's world, than at anytime in the past

Visit http://259trillionvs5trillion.com For more exciting revelations

END THOUGHTS

DON'T GIVE UP!

We are not celebrating the rich but what we actually celebrate is the creation of new wealth. This will upgrade the society as a whole and will benefit everyone, including the poor. We are happy to disclose, that we are not sitting at the so-called top 1% of the population and has nothing for them or against them. We only want to show the truth and display the data as honest as we can, without any prejudice, biasness, preconception and the like.

People can be measured from their initial incomes, until they die, in their own original respective bracket. Or better still, the same person is tracked until he or she dies. This will truly give us, an accurate data on how the poor performs. Simply using IRS or BLS data without clear understanding of its implications on the conclusions obtained is dangerous. America should not beat itself up over wrongly diagnosed problem! How do you solve a problem, if it is not even there? Nobody seems to know what to do, the solution is clear however.

We also must highlight yet again, the use of inflation corrected numbers must be viewed with a pinch of salt, or several. We wrote our opinion on comparing economic conditions of many decades apart in the **259TVS5T** series, and provided the best solution for comparison.

The OWS and the economists that used data from the IRS to measure income disparities have many flaws and we have pointed them out several times in this book. One could grab anything and proclaim anything they want and people who are already frustrated are prone to accept anything that confirm their belief of the evil rich people and would gobble the data up to support their accusations towards others. We already did a study on income using BLS data for our "**The 'Disappearing' Middle Class**" topic in **Book 3** (different than using IRS data, but with the same conclusions). Please take a look at that data as well.

When a person talks about hardship, he or she should look back at what the previous generations have endured and then look at today's events optimistically. One thing that we are sad is that human beings like to blame other people for their problems and would then direct their anger towards that perceived target. Many problems are brought upon by their own error, mistakes, greed or stupidity. Sit and think on how to improve yourself first and take part in free capitalism, which we have shown to be more equitable than the Olympics and just about anything else out there. In capitalism, all participants will be rewarded, not just the top three winners. The amount of rewards varies depending on what were put in in terms of value. Before capitalism, capital is not mobilized fully and properly. Economic participants have little initiative to try to achieve more, for there was little reward to be had.

Free government assistance is not a birthright. Everyone must chip in and help each other, and only ask for assistance if you really need one. In a democratic society, everyone must pay taxes, so that the taxpayers will check on their government's expenses to ensure no wastage and abuse.

We do think that the new generation tend to whine a lot and do not work hard enough. When the going gets tough, they protest first, rather than work harder. They seem of wanting it easy, not acquiring the necessary skills and knowledge to enable them to move up. They only need to ask their parents about it, and for once, spend more time listening and thinking.

Don't Give Up

Sharif Rahman & Amy Norwood Maine

May 2012

AUTHORS BIOGRAPHIES

Sharif Rahman is an experienced chemical engineer graduated from Vanderbilt University with a good set of problem solving skills. He likes to jump into complicated problems and will get to the bottom of it and lay it bare for others to see in a different angle. Using his engineering knacks and other hidden 'talents', he then presented the solution in a simple way. His motto is simple, which is "Make things 'as simple as possible'". He is currently busy working full time in a power and water company as a senior manager and uses his weekends to write.

He is married to his VU sweetheart and has four kids. Together they analyzed the world in ways that few people can imagine!

FROM THE DESK OF THE AUTHOR

Amy Norwood Maine graduated magna cum laude from Vanderbilt University, where she spent part of her teenage years obtaining her engineering degree. Her mathematical skills and her reading abilities will amaze anyone around her. Don't simply believe those old economists with thick moustaches, is her mantra. Many of them are too busy to really think through what they wrote, and they only wanted publicity and most important of all, they like to scare their readers.

Amy Norwood lent her valuable expertise to ensure this book will amaze the readers and offer a different and more down to earth understanding of our forefathers economic designs.

This book was a culmination of in depth study of the rich and the poor. Great misunderstanding resulting in "class war" is now happening all over the world for reasons of none other than the failure of economists to portray their data accurately.

Look at our data and be thrilled, you won't be disappointed. We pinpoint where the confusion lies and what can be done about it.

You will be happy to read this wonderful book and understand that you deserve what you had worked for, fair and square, regardless of your economic standing.

www.ingramcontent.com/pod-product-compliance
Lightning Source LLC
Chambersburg PA
CBHW072351290526
45794CB00001B/51